A SHEARWATER BOOK

WHERE THE DRAGON
MEETS THE ANGRY RIVER

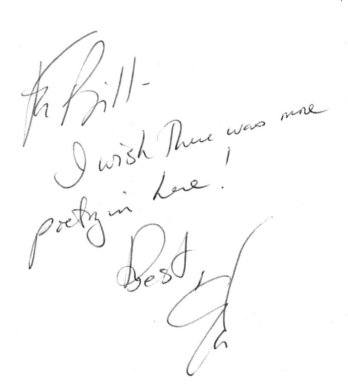

To Bill—
I wish there was more
poetry in here!
Best

Where the Dragon Meets the Angry River

Nature and Power in the People's Republic of China

R. Edward Grumbine

ISLANDPRESS / Shearwater Books

Washington | Covelo | London

A Shearwater Book
Published by Island Press

Copyright © 2010 R. Edward Grumbine

Library of Congress Cataloging-in-Publication Data
Grumbine, R. Edward.
Where the dragon meets the Angry River : nature and power in the People's Republic of China / R. Edward Grumbine.
p. cm.
Includes bibliographical references and index.
ISBN-13: 978-1-59726-551-5 (cloth : alk. paper)
ISBN-10: 1-59726-551-9 (cloth : alk. paper)
1. River engineering—China—Nujiang Lisuzu Zizhizhou.
2. Water resources development—Environmental aspects—China—Yunnan Sheng. 3. Yunnan Sheng (China)—Economic conditions.
4. Yunnan Sheng (China)—Social conditions. I. Title.
TC502.N85G89 2010   333.720951'35—dc22
2009045718

British Cataloguing-in-Publication data available.

Printed on recycled, acid-free paper ♻

Design by David Bullen Design

Manufactured in the United States of America

10   9   8   7   6   5   4   3   2   1

Keywords: Yunnan, Nujiang, Three Parallel Rivers World Heritage Site, Kunming, Beijing, dam moratorium, hydropower, energy, development, conservation

To the ancient Chinese masters
of philosophy, poetry, and painting;
and to the mountains, rivers, and
wildlands of the Middle Kingdom
that so inspired them.

Contents

WHERE THE DRAGON
MEETS THE ANGRY RIVER

Introduction

*I*MAGINE A RIVER in southwestern China that has remained undammed for a thousand years, cutting through the world's highest mountains to escape to the distant sea eighteen hundred miles away. Those mountains are the Himalaya, and that waterway is the Nujiang, in Mandarin Chinese, translated as Angry River. The Nu tumbles off the Tibetan Plateau and rages due south through China's Yunnan Province, carving a trench deeper than any canyon in North America before sinking into the hills of Myanmar, Thailand, and, finally, the Indian Ocean. The Nu remains the longest undammed river in mainland Southeast Asia.

China, about the same size as the United States, has already built more dams than any country in the world. The Nu holds the promise of adding even more megawatts to the nation's power grid. By 2003, thirteen dams were planned to tame the Angry River.

Then something unprecedented happened in the People's Republic of China (PRC). An international grassroots outcry swayed China's one-party state to declare a dam-building moratorium on the Nu. People rally, resist, and stop development schemes as a matter of course in the United States; not so in China. The Nujiang moratorium made history as the first time Chinese citizens were successful in pushing the government to change national environmental policy.

But what is "success"? A moratorium is not a ban, and though the Nu remains free for now, China's demand for power continues to surge as the world's largest human population grows toward developed-world status. It is said that the original proposed thirteen dams have been reduced to four. But the Nu will be transformed into a tamed version of "Angry" even at the lower figure.

It is not the only Chinese river to be tamed. The Nu is joined in Yunnan by two larger and longer rivers, the Lancangjiang (Mekong) and the Jinshajiang (upper Yangzi).[1] Each begins life high on the Tibetan Plateau and cuts deep, parallel canyons through the eastern edge of the Himalaya before flowing their separate ways. Unlike the Nu, there are already a few dams on the Lancang and Jinsha—and many more are on the way. The combined hydropower potential of these three parallel rivers is staggering: if all proposed dams were built, they would generate almost as much hydropower as is produced today in the United States. Still, this latent capacity is overwhelmed by China's insatiable demand for electricity as the country adds the equivalent of France's entire power production every single year.

The three rivers share more than potential megawatts. They all run through the heart of the Three Parallel Rivers World Heritage Site, a UN-designated protected area more than twice as big as Yellowstone. Most of China was transformed by human hands millennia ago; not so Yunnan. The province is about 4 percent of the United States' size but is home to more flowering plants and some groups of animals than all of North America. Orchids and snow leopards, Indian cobras and endangered black-necked cranes, fifteen species of primates, bears, bamboo, and wolves—Yunnan is a biological paradise, one of the richest landscapes on Earth.

Three Parallel Rivers represents a huge investment in conservation, but then, on paper (and little-known to Americans), China has set aside more land from development than the United States has. The question is, are China's reserves really protected, or are they merely "paper parks" lacking adequate enforcement on the ground?

As a professor (and student) of environmental policy, I came to

Yunnan to see if the PRC—notorious in the West for unbridled development at any cost—might actually conserve one of the most remarkable places on Earth. But what I found led me to larger and thornier questions. What does landscape "protection" mean to local peoples who get their living from the land? How do you balance conservation and development when villagers are desperate for a path out of poverty? Is globalization, community-based conservation, or some combination of the two the answer to sustaining both people and the planet?

One thing I learned immediately was how different conservation is in China compared to in the United States and other wealthy countries. Despite the PRC's meteoric economic rise, per capita earnings remain less than those in Albania and El Salvador, countries not often considered role models for wealth. In much of rural China, some measures of poverty match or exceed those of sub-Saharan Africa. There are hundreds of millions of Chinese without safe drinking water and the simple waste sanitation that Americans take for granted. Because of these facts and others, conservation without concomitant economic development is simply not an option in the PRC.

Another discovery I made on my first day in the Nujiang valley was the tremendous cultural diversity at stake in Yunnan. Twenty-six of the PRC's fifty-six officially recognized ethnic nationalities live in the province. Within hours of my initial village visit, I met ethnic Nu farmers, Lisu hunters, and Tibetan trekking guides on their home territory. Many of these people didn't speak Mandarin, let alone English. Most of them were subsistence farmer/grazers making less money in a year than I do in a week. Like minority peoples worldwide, many villagers in Yunnan lack a voice in decisions affecting their livelihoods. The dams will trigger a tidal wave of change: hordes of tourists, fewer farmlands, more out-migration for urban jobs, less dependence on traditional ways of life.

National development plans and policies aren't solely at fault. China, like many countries, borrows heavily from wealthy world models of conservation, and international organizations (The Nature Conservancy, World Wide Fund for Nature, Conservation International) play a high-profile role in creating plans for both protected areas and sustainable development. But is what works in California, New England, or the Netherlands appropriate for Yunnan? As I met the staffs of international nongovernmental organizations (NGOs) in China, I began to realize that, while most foreigners were experts in conservation, they were much less savvy about Chinese cultural conditions. As an academic not affiliated with any group, I had the freedom to try to understand China on its own terms.

This is, of course, easier said than done. Serious students of China describe the PRC as less a sovereign state and more a "civilization pretending to be a nation." In myriad ways, China challenges the imagination; the country is vast, magnificent, and deep—and opaque to most of the rest of the world. In fundamental areas, Americans and Chinese lack common ground; China's history, stretching back for thousands of years, is infinitely deeper, the culture more cohesive, the government unitary as well as nondemocratic. The Chinese (including the ethnic nationalities) don't split the world into the "nature" and "culture" categories that we employ without a second thought. There is no "wilderness" akin to American ideals in classical Chinese philosophy or contemporary conservation planning and practice.

Chinese and Americans do share an intense national pride as well as an uncommon entrepreneurial zeal. Despite worldwide recession, in China you hear bankers and farmers, hydropower executives and conservationists everywhere speaking of economic integration, of globalization. I think that the latter term is inaccurate at best; I would prefer to substitute *interconnected* for *globalized*. After all, money may be exchanged between human economies the world over, but only natural forces like the water or carbon cycles are truly global phenomena. From this broader view, dams, transnational highways, rubber monocultures, and even a few protected areas may lose a bit of their luster.

The Nujiang and its neighboring rivers, Yunnan Province, and

China itself have all conspired to stretch, shape, and recalibrate my views on conservation and development. I grew up expecting that saving the planet's wild ecosystems was necessary *and* sufficient; the world was vast, development was limited in scope, and conservation was about getting the balance right. In my quest to create better protected area policies in the United States, however, I forgot about the people of China, India, and the 88 percent of the world's humans who are still awaiting access to electricity, potable drinking water, and basic education and health care. Then I went to Yunnan. Meeting little girls whose families can't afford to send them to school and workers who are melting scrap metal wearing rubber flip-flops does a lot to widen your perspective.

That's not to say nature doesn't matter. People remain utterly dependent now and forever on what the Chinese term *Wu xing*, the "Five Elements": energy, land, wood, water, and metal, what a scientist would call biodiversity or an economist might describe as ecosystem services. Whatever label one chooses, China teaches that the wall many of us have erected between wild and tamed lands, conservation and development, people and nature, is an illusion. As long as this barrier remains in place in our hearts and minds, there won't be enough habitat for Yunnan's wild tigers and elephants, space for the province's tropical rain forests, or a climate with temperatures cool enough to maintain China's Himalayan glaciers that feed precious water to hundreds of millions of humans downstream.

This book is an exploration of these complex, sometimes frustrating issues. In an effort to untangle them, I followed the flow of the three parallel rivers, the Nu, the Lancang, and the Jinsha. I explored tiny hamlets in backcountry Yunnan and the teeming streets of the regional capital. I ate meals of dofu and chilis cooked over an open fire inside a wooden house built by hand out of trees from the nearby watershed. I trekked through centuries-old forests and drove along new roads linking previously secluded villages to global supply chains. Most importantly, I talked with people who are witnessing their whole world changing in the blink of an eye.

No matter where I went, one lesson stayed with me—no conservation plan can be successful without community input. This is a tremendous source of conflict in China and many other countries with a history of top-down government decision making.

Yet even as I recognized the importance of local control, I also witnessed the power of international forces. Following the Lancang downstream out of China into Southeast Asia, I saw how the PRC is reclaiming its historical role as the economic and geopolitical heavyweight all across this region. China's influence is spreading out, but regional and global economic trends are also pushing in—creating wired power grids out of free-flowing rivers, rubber entrepreneurs out of impoverished Laotian and Myanmar hill tribes, and the last skeletal fragments of tiger and elephant habitat out of what was until recently intact tropical forest.

Whether globalization is the answer to closing the gap between Yunnan and the rest of China or functions as the main driver of disparities between the developed and less-developed worlds is a huge question. The PRC would like to believe that Earth's environmental resources haven't changed much since the last time China held economic center stage over two hundred years ago. Many in China think that emulating the fossil fuel–based lifestyle of the West is the quickest and least expensive route to reestablishing national power. For their part, the United States and its wealthy world allies are not ready to forsake the benefits that have accrued to those who industrialized first. But can the planet provide enough for villagers in China along with all the other poor people in Asia, Latin America, and Africa who want to live as average Americans and Europeans already do?

There are many who believe that China is the main problem. I see the PRC as the dealer in a high-stakes game of chance who is finally announcing to the world: "Show your hand." China is but the critical player tipping us toward a sustainable future or some darker destiny.

There remains precious little time to act. In early 2007, I published a paper about China's ecological impact and forecast that the next U.S. president would likely have a two-term window to help create a sustainable international carbon emissions policy. In a few brief years, however, that opportunity has shrunk down to one term—if we are lucky.

Maybe not so much has changed. Twenty-two hundred years ago, Qin Huang, the first Chinese emperor, embraced Long, the dragon, as his symbol of power and authority. Chinese emperors' main role throughout history has always been to mediate between Heaven and Earth. At times, the Son of Heaven was successful in this task and rains replenished the fields. In other periods, lengthy droughts left millions without food despite the emperor's best efforts.

For a century now, China hasn't had an emperor, though today's Communist Party leaders continue to invoke the dragon as they act to expand the international influence of the PRC. After all, Long is no mythic beast fit only for saints to slay; to every Chinese, dragons symbolize great good fortune. Chinese dragons are certainly auspicious; it is less clear what the wild Nujiang means to the Chinese people. When an untamed river encounters a dragon, what happens next?

Far back before the first millennium, Chinese sages understood that water was life and that to grasp the Dao, the primal source, one had to "imagine rivers and the sea." For Daoists, the power of water is predominant: "against the hard and strong / nothing excels it." If China's modern emperors (and other world leaders) would heed the ancient wisdom that a great state is like a watershed, there will be no conflict between rivers and dragons. After all, the Nu appears to be angry only because it is compelled by geology to flow with great haste toward the sea, and Long can only bring good fortune when the people and their leaders act within their means.

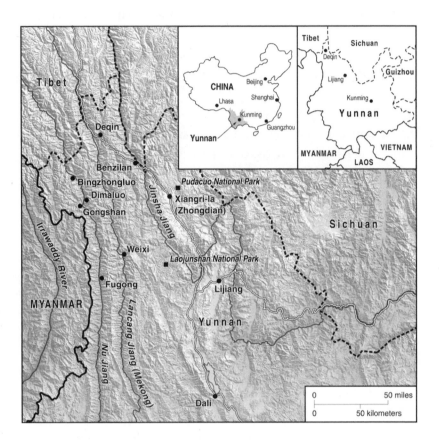

Chapter 1

The Highest Good

The highest good is like water.
Water gives life to the ten thousand things and does not strive.
It flows in places men reject and so is like the Dao.
LAO-TZU, sixth century BCE
(translation by G. Feng and J. English)

*T*HERE ARE FEW PLACES left in the twenty-first-century world where conversation can be numbed into silence by the power of raging water. The Nujiang (Angry River) in Yunnan Province, PRC, at the tail end of the summer monsoon, is one of them. And barely an hour into our upstream journey, I was also losing my ability to count—I simply could not keep track of the number of roaring rapids we were passing. Nor could I comprehend fully their size—some of the standing waves looked like they could swallow our bus. The river mesmerized, pulled at my power to think clearly, as if it wanted to replace my normal consciousness with something wilder.

Maybe it was the all-night ride on a Chinese sleeper bus (narrow bunks, no seats) or waking to a world of dense, humid air, banana trees, and terraced rice paddies. Perhaps it was that I understood none of the nine languages spoken in this region, or that the Myanmar border, replete with rumors of smuggled timber, drugs, and people, defined the mountains immediately to the west. All I knew was that it was difficult to count and speak and impossible to take my eyes off the Nujiang.

Riding in a minibus a few yards from the Nu was a far cry from reading about the Angry River in the *New York Times*. In 2004, comfortably nestled in an armchair at home, in the pine woods of central Arizona, I had come across an article about the PRC's decision to halt hydropower construction on the last undammed river in China. The plan had been to build thirteen dams along the Nu to generate electric power and enormous profits; local tax revenues would skyrocket if all the dams were built. It was unclear exactly where the power would go and how much money might trickle down to valley residents, although it was abundantly clear that the wild Nujiang would become a series of slack-water reservoirs. Against all odds, however, Beijing appeared to be giving in to pressure from both Chinese citizens and international NGOs, overruling local government officials to slow construction down.

If the dams were built, it wasn't just the Angry River that would be tamed. The Nu flows through the Three Parallel Rivers World Heritage Site, a protected area twice the size of Yellowstone National Park containing some of the world's greatest concentrations of unique plants and animals, from apes and brown bears to more rhododendrons and bamboo that any place on the planet.[1] Such a designation, however, does not confer complete protection; it was known that eight of the thirteen Nu dams would be built near or within the boundaries of Three Parallel Rivers. But no one knew what negative consequences might be in store for the Nujiang's biodiversity—the government refused to release the results from environmental impact studies.

Maybe most disturbing, thousands of local people would be displaced. Beijing was debating how to relocate the fifty thousand ethnic nationality residents who would be flooded out of their homes by the dams, not an easy task in this part of Yunnan where poverty, life expectancies, and literacy rates are lower than they were in the United

States sixty years ago.[2] I knew that the central government was committed to raising living standards in western China up to the level of the wealthy eastern coast. But did that mean that wild Yunnan's future was to become as densely populated and polluted as the rest of the PRC?

For me, this question held more than academic interest. I had been fascinated by Chinese philosophy, classical poetry, and history since high school. And as an environmental studies professor and researcher, I was well aware of China's ever-growing ecological footprint. I had read countless academic papers about Yunnan and the country at large, but the *Times* article was truly revolutionary. This was the first time Beijing was actually considering changing a major environmental policy due to public pressure. Yunnan could conceivably set a new precedent for development in China. And as unlikely as it seemed, this poorly known province might even serve as a model for the rest of the world.

Having worked for twenty-five years on biodiversity protection in the United States, I saw that the PRC had an opportunity to move away from its modernize-at-all-costs mentality toward leadership in sustainability. But if China, with its 1.3 billion people, could not diverge from business as usual, then what did that mean for the future? If the huge population of the PRC adopted American consumer habits, was there enough Earth to go around? Given all that was at stake, I was driven to visit the Nu and see for myself.

So in September 2005, I packed my bags, ready to trade in dryland Arizona for the steamy subtropics and Himalayan snowfields of Yunnan. I had a month before my students returned to Prescott College for classes and a challenging itinerary. I would travel up the Nujiang, a place for which I could find no English-language guidebook, all the way to Dimaluo, a small village where the road system ended and backcountry trails began. For company, I had convinced my friend Albie, an agroecology researcher at the University of California, Santa Cruz, to join me. Like me, Albie preferred field travel to armchair research.

———

To get to wild China, you first must travel through some of the largest, most fast-paced cities on Earth. After Beijing, Yunnan's capital city, Kunming, seemed slow, but with three million residents, endless high-rises, and digital billboards twenty stories high, it was thoroughly modern. On my first full day in Yunnan, I stood in a glass skyscraper gazing down at six huge cranes moving bundles of steel at as many nearby construction sites. I had come to Kunming to visit the offices of The Nature Conservancy (TNC) and to meet the group's operations director, Stefan Kratz. TNC was one of the international groups that had played a significant role in convincing Beijing to institute the Nu moratorium and it was developing conservation plans across the Three Parallel Rivers region.[3] If I wanted to understand the central government's sudden move toward slowing down development, I would need to know what this and other NGOs' presence really meant for Yunnan. Stefan could point me toward the political players who were shaping conservation and development.

"You say you're going up the Nu?" Stefan eyed me carefully. "It's pretty sketchy if you don't speak Mandarin."

"Well, I don't have any maps either," I pointed out. "You can't get any. But I still have to visit the Nu. It's going to be gone soon."

Stefan understood my fascination with the river, but he also appreciated that the moratorium was about more than nature—it was about culture, politics, and power.

"I'm not a biologist," he said. "I run this office and do fundraising. TNC's goal is protecting biodiversity, but in China, you have to deal with people, too. The local officials in the Nu believe that dams are the only way to get rid of poverty and they'll do anything to get them built. Beijing supports the dams, too, but the central government is worried about how the rest of the world will view China if development wrecks such a special place. So you get a 'moratorium.' You've got different levels of the government arguing over how to handle this issue and I can relate; not everyone agrees with TNC about our plans for nature reserves."

For a better picture of what was happening on the ground, Stefan suggested I talk to one of TNC's field staff, fungi expert Dr. Zhou Dequn. He worked in Three Parallel Rivers and was in town that day, so later that evening I met Dr. Zhou for dinner in the courtyard of a quiet, two-hundred-year-old building.

"Kunming wants to be like the rest of China," Dr. Zhou smiled. "But it's very different in the villages. People are poor and they're mostly not Han [China's dominant ethnic group]. In Lijiang where I work, it's Naxi country. In the Nujiang, you have a mix of Nu, Lisu, and Tibetans, almost no Han except for government officials.

"Do you like fat?" Dr. Zhou gestured toward a dish in the center of the table. "Try this—it's traditional Yunnanese." He took a sharp knife and sliced a wedge off the side of a large pyramid of roasted pork fat. He inserted the fat into a steamed bun and chewed.

I followed his lead, then drank more tea—oolong helps the body digest rich foods.

"What about the Nu dams?" I asked. "Is Beijing's moratorium going to hold?"

"It's difficult in China," Dr. Zhou replied. "I'm not sure about the Nu; Beijing is in control of hydropower development. In China, we are just beginning to create a rule of law, environmental regulations, and a court system to back them up. China has solid environmental legislation, but enforcement isn't as tight as you would expect. Beijing is far away and local governments sometimes do things differently. Current law allows for some citizen access to plans and public input, but this hasn't happened so much with the Nu dams."

I told Dr. Zhou that I didn't understand why China's national environmental laws weren't being enforced in the Nu.

Dr. Zhou smiled. "If you push for change too hard, it can be bad for you, but it's much better than it used to be." He paused. "It's hard to understand China from the U.S. perspective, Ed, so be careful when you look around. I have trouble understanding the U.S.—I mean, how could you folks have elected Bush twice?"

We laughed and drank a toast to more responsive governments. Dr. Zhou set his cup down. "I can see that you understand how important it is to protect the Nu, and we both know that China cannot have as many cars as America. The only way to go is friendship between us. Otherwise, it will be the end of the world."

🐉

Stefan and Dr. Zhou's insights reinforced my sense that the complexities of conservation and development in China couldn't be understood fully from just an NGO standpoint. Like TNC, many international environmental groups had been active in Yunnan for over a decade. While they brought tremendous knowledge and resources, they also brought assumptions, and at times, plans that didn't meet local needs.

Yunnan was one chapter in a contentious history of conservation exported from the world of wealth to the world of poverty. The challenges were manifold. First, not all conservation work is altruistic; what the poor need doesn't always equal what the wealthy want to give. NGOs no doubt assume that rural people will benefit from nature reserves, but it is unclear whether there is any difference between imposing reserves and imposing tourism, roads, and dams. Second, the slender chance that biodiversity has to survive in Yunnan depends on international groups working in partnership with their PRC colleagues. There must be give and take between different groups of players who do not always share common cultural values or visions. Third, community-based conservation, where local people are involved in project planning and execution, is more likely to succeed than most brands of top-down planning imported from the outside. Evidence from conservation work around the world shows that success is more likely when villagers are participants. Fourth, every action in China is constrained by what central and local governments allow—but that space is expanding.

Mulling over these ideas, I finalized plans to travel with Albie from the bright lights and digital displays of Kunming to the Nujiang, where electricity existed in the form of low-watt light bulbs dangling from slender cords. I wanted to try to see Yunnan not just from the vantage point of an American environmentalist but through the eyes of a villager struggling to scrape a subsistence living from the land. I imagined that neither government-mandated dams nor NGO-designed nature reserves could provide enough for all the people in the Nu. Were there other alternatives? There was only one way to find out. So, two days after my abstract discussions in sleek high-rises and expensive Ming dynasty–era courtyard restaurants, I found myself bumping through another washout along the Nujiang's single main road, the roar of the river ringing in my ears.

After six hours of bone-jarring bus travel, we took a break in Fugong town. Albie and I hiked away from the busy market in the center of town through winding lanes of low wooden farm buildings past groups of shy, barefoot children. I wondered how many of these kids went to school. How would their world change as they grew older?

As we ascended into the emerald hills east of the river, every scrap of arable soil was terraced and planted with subsistence plots. It was late September, and the rice was turning ripe. We followed a water ditch past clusters of thatch-roofed houses, climbing into a narrow canyon draped with cascading ribbon waterfalls. Men carrying heavy sheets of corrugated roofing with tumplines passed us on the trail. There was no "forest," only the rank growth of recent fallows. The pressure to grow food was palpable—on the far side of the canyon, corn patches were planted on thirty-five-degree slopes.

"That's why the Nu's so muddy," Albie observed. "There's no way this corn can keep the soil in place. There's only two reasons why people would plant up here—their population must be pushing the limits, or government policies are forcing them to expand into marginal lands."[4] But there was no obvious answer that we could detect on the slopes above Fugong, and the bus was waiting to take us upriver.

Back on the bus in the valley above Fugong, there were no billboards, scenic pullouts, or visitor services, nothing to distract me from watching the Nujiang rage through more monster rapids. As the river sheered across huge talus blocks, remnants of a recent landslide, I considered Dr. Zhou's admonition, local peoples' lack of adequate food, water, and waste systems, and the imminent arrival of the dams. All of these are linked to "development," but what is that?

Rivers embody development through flow. For a river, development is complete when nothing impedes water's inevitable response to gravity. The ancient Chinese recognized a connection between water and human character. In China's oldest text, the *I Jing* (Book of Changes), the image of water under mountains signifies youth. The *I Jing* suggests that human maturation results from cultivating "a thoroughness that skips nothing, but, like water, steadily fills up all gaps." And in the 2,500-year-old *Daodejing*, the foundational text of Daoism and the third most translated book in the world, Lao-tzu wrote that "water gives life to the ten thousand things and does not strive."[5] To Daoists, flowing waters are the roots of growth and change.

For the ethnic nationality peoples of the Nujiang, development is more complex. What do they want? What do they need? Dr. Zhou cautioned against jumping to conclusions about anything in China, so I want to be careful here. I expect that villagers want adequate food, clean water, and the freedom to pursue their livelihoods. But immediately, a host of questions arise. There are nine ethnic groups living in the Nujiang watershed and I can't believe that they all want the same things. There's a history here, too, one with many inequalities. Some local people are better off than others, but all are seen as "poor" and "backward" in the government's eyes. Yunnan is a borderland region, on the periphery of the Middle Kingdom as it has been since imperial times. The state did not seek the locals' permission when the first regional nature reserves were set aside in the 1980s—they simply imposed them.

Nor is the government seeking permission for the dams. In China, however, even this single issue is multilayered. The dams are one piece of a much larger central government drive to *xibu dakaifa*, "develop the west," or the so-called Go West strategy—but does this mean that Kunming is destined to become another Shanghai?[6] If so, then

I wonder about the fate of both Yunnan's local people and wildlife. There is a reason why China's primates, bears, tigers, and elephants no longer live across most of the country—their habitat has been obliterated.

Ecosystems, ethnic nationality peoples and their cultural values, conservation plans, and government policies are all in flux. Like the Nujiang, everything is in motion, cutting deeper into the bedrock that upholds the land and the people.

Reaching Gongshan, we crossed the Nujiang a final time. The road deteriorated rapidly, the last thirty-two kilometers (twenty miles) taking almost an hour and a half to travel. The track petered out in Dimaluo.

Dimaluo is a Nu nationality village, inhabited since people moved south from Tibet at least a thousand years ago.[7] The Lisu joined the Nu in the Dimaluo region some five hundred years later when the Ming dynasty ruled China. In the nineteenth century, Tibetan herders drifted in from northern watersheds bringing yaks, cows, and a herding economy that the locals adopted. Today, almost everyone grows corn, buckwheat, and barley and grazes goats, yaks, and cattle. Life is not so easy in a land where slopes are steep and money is tight.

Since the PRC banned commercial logging twelve years ago, there is little cash in Dimaluo. The locals substitute yak butter and chickens for small change. Most people also gather edible mushrooms and rare orchids for a bit of money. But the government nature reserves have restricted gathering and grazing. In Dimaluo, the average villager earns the equivalent of about USD fifty cents a day.[8]

It didn't take us very long to find the newly opened guesthouse run by Alou, a local Tibetan guide—it was the only place to stay in Dimaluo.

"Nice to meet you," Alou greeted us in halting English. He spoke five languages but knew English the least. Smoke drifted out from under the eaves of his cookhouse—there was no chimney. Alou's wife was making dinner with the help of her mother and young daughter. Several chickens and a piglet scrounged in the corner; the kitchens in Dimaluo were open range. The hearth was the center of the home everywhere in rural Yunnan and people ate and socialized next to open fires. Cooking was done in a wok supported by an iron tripod over a fire built on a rough concrete slab set in the wood floor. Houses had few windows—light entered from under open eaves and through the doorway along with the animals. It didn't freeze very often in subtropical Dimaluo.

Alou offered to take us after dinner to Bai Hu Luo village, five kilometers (three miles) up the mountain from Dimaluo. He had a meeting with Shen Shicai, a worker from the Chinese NGO Center for Biodiversity and Indigenous Knowledge (CBIK). Alou was helping Shen interview villagers about what could be done to improve crop yields and control the spread of weeds in mountain pastures.[9] We finished our potatoes fried with chili and garlic, drained cups of salty butter tea, and followed Alou out the door.

Narrow footpaths, clouds hugging ridges, small, steep plots of corn and amaranth nearing harvest. After recent rains, all the streams were roaring. The trail went up and up through young forests of Yunnan pine, scrub oaks, twisted rhododendron. Bamboo, bracken fern, and wild ginger thrived in the late-summer understory. These mountains mixed subtropical and temperate vegetation in a botanical blend that was almost unimaginable.

The first thing I noticed upon entering Bai Hu Luo was a large satellite dish. The second was a concrete basketball court, and the third was a Roman Catholic church bearing an improbable Chinese-style façade. We were miles from the nearest road and 450 meters (1,480 feet) up a steep ridge. No village thereabouts had indoor plumbing. I knew that the government had promised to electrify every village in rural China, but why did TV take precedence over sewage treatment?

Shen wasn't going to answer my question. "Every village has at least one TV," he explained. "Some villages over in the Lancang even have vineyards. French missionaries were here in the nineteenth century. Basketball is big, too. I don't know when people put the courts in, but everyone plays. Just say 'Yao Ming' to anyone."

Shen outlined the issues the villagers confront. The government wants more stock animals raised, roads for tourism, and, of course, the large Nu dams. They also want to develop small-scale hydropower.

"You saw that construction below Dimaluo when you drove in? That's supposed to supply electricity to the villages right around here, but the people don't want it—they say it makes the river unhappy."

There are other problems. The government's agricultural agents only count the number of animals sold, but the villagers value animals in more ways than just money. Shen described a classic rural cycle: nutrient-deficient soils resulting in low production and people too poor to buy better seeds and fertilizer, leading to an exodus to town for cash jobs. But with people working away from home, there were fewer hands available to manage the fields and take care of the animals.

"And neither big dams nor new nature reserves are going to solve these problems," Shen concluded.

When Albie asked about government programs designed to help villagers, Shen mentioned that the severe soil erosion we first noticed in Fugong also plagues this area. Local people are paid to replant steep plots with fruit trees, but sometimes the government provides seedlings of species that don't grow well in the area.

Shen frowned. "The government doesn't always ask the villagers about what they need. They already have a plan. What I'm doing here with CBIK is finding out what the people want, and so far it looks like they want better vet services for their animals more than a bigger cash economy."

After returning to Dimaluo, Albie and I took our last walk of the evening to the dam construction site below the village. The roadside was a riot of ten-foot-tall thistles, flowering orchids, and ginger. About a mile from the village, the Dimaluo stream had been channeled off to one side. Across the river, two large power shovels were gouging out the mountainside. We walked through the camp that had been thrown together for the laborers: tilting, tarp-roofed shacks, broken equipment leaking oil, shiny pools of dark water, shirtless workers in flip-flops. It was an uninspiring sight.

But inspiration takes many forms. Though we would not find out for another month, the day we visited Dimaluo a letter from sixty-one Chinese NGOs arrived in Beijing, petitioning the PRC to follow its own environmental laws and allow "law-based, science-based, and democratic decision-making" to inform the Nujiang dams planning process.[10] Chinese law mandated access to data along with formal public hearings. But despite the moratorium, no environmental impact analyses had yet been released.

Was the letter a breakthrough or an illusion? Chinese and international NGOs were asking for something new—adherence to the rule of law. The PRC might respond positively—or it might view the letter as evidence of organized resistance against the state.

Chapter 2

The Frontier and
the Middle Kingdom

The mountains are high and the emperor is far away.

Chinese proverb

*T*HE OLD WOMAN wove across multiple lanes of stalled traffic hawking strings of fresh gardenias. My taxi driver rolled down her window, offered a few kuai, and looped a garland around the rearview mirror. The street was packed with people—businessmen in Armani, vendors selling peanuts and melons, women carrying kids on their backs, teenagers talking on cell phones. Bike lanes were crammed with hundreds of cyclists hauling chickens, ladders, boxes, and baggage. A chaos of cars and buses packed the center of the street.

Kunming, capital of Yunnan Province, embodies urban China. Vegetable vendors sell in front of Mercedes dealerships, new car owners duel with one-speed bikes for space, and city street maps are out of date a few months after they are printed.

But for all its development, Kunming is not mainstream China. The region was not brought under the sway of Han emperors until the Ming dynasty in the fourteenth century. Yunnan remains peripheral—

it shares a 4,061-kilometer (2,523-mile) border with (from north to south) Tibet, Myanmar, Lao People's Democratic Republic (PDR), and Vietnam (see map, page 10). From the perspective of those in power, this frontier has been problematic for seven centuries. But the state has a plan.

A year had passed since my first visit to the Nujiang. The dam moratorium continued to hold, but the Chinese government still refused to release its environmental reviews, claiming them as "state secrets." In the meantime, the Angry River raged on, environmentalists like Stefan and Dr. Zhou of TNC struggled to find a fit between people and nature, and development in Yunnan proceeded at a breakneck speed.

At home in Prescott, I devoured every scrap of news from China and wondered if Beijing could go green before the world's athletes descended on the capital for the 2008 Olympics. But after trekking through Yunnan's emerald mountains and confronting so many conservation issues, news coverage was simply not enough—almost as soon as I left China, I started making plans to return.

Over the next four years, I would visit Yunnan as many times, each trip bringing me a little closer to understanding the thicket of contradictions that defined the region. In the summer of 2006, before heading out into a remote area of northwest Yunnan, I intended to explore two of China's urban power centers, Kunming and Beijing. I hoped that some clues from the past might help me make sense of today's PRC.

With hours until my next appointment with NGO leaders, I decided to visit an unfamiliar area of Kunming east of downtown. Stepping out of a cab, I crossed a busy thoroughfare, browsed through some shops, bought roasted peanuts, and then ducked down an alley to explore.

The passageway opened to a residential lane that soon ran along a concrete-channeled watercourse. Decrepit apartment blocks lined the far bank. The water in the channel was blue-black scum, a new category of liquid for me. Kunming's population is approaching four million, but little of the city's waste is treated. No one drinks tap water.

Kunming began to modernize in the 1990s and many old quarters were torn down, replaced by wide streets and high-rises. The metamorphosis continues: I passed entire blocks of rubble, piles of old tile, brick, and wood, the bones of nineteenth-century buildings. Wrecking cranes and bulldozers swiveled through clouds of dust, chewing into crumbling walls. Chinese construction sites do not feature public safety barriers or crowd control—in the midst of the din, an elderly woman holding a piglet sat on a pile of bricks smoking a cigarette, unperturbed.

I entered a warren of cobbled lanes and sweep-eaved wooden houses with roofs growing thick beds of grass and moss. Hundreds of street vendors hustled tobacco, turtles, fish, neon-painted chicks, cameras, buckets of lizards, black slippers, and pirated CDs. At the far end of the street, a covered food market featured a great variety of wild mushrooms, melons two feet in diameter, pails of pickles and chili paste, and every cut of fresh meat imaginable. Walking out of the back of the market, I was surrounded again by cacophony—heavy equipment tumbling down the next old building. China was changing right before my eyes.

Renewal in Yunnan had not always been so rapid. Eons before humans arrived on the scene, the crustal plate upon which India rides slammed into ancient Asia, and the landscape we recognize today as the Himalaya, Tibet, and western China began to form.[1] For millions of years as India pressed onward and down, crust scraped off the plate's leading edge, and ancient rocks melted, rose, and cooled into hardened granitics—the Himalaya were born. India kept pushing and plunging, and eight million years ago the Tibetan Plateau began to loft rapidly, boosted by hot injections of the planet's melting mantle. Mountains all the way to China's present-day border with Russia and Mongolia lifted into the sky.

These fresh uplifts changed the climate. The Himalayan front blocks waves of moisture lifting off the Indian Ocean, leaving Tibet dry as well as high and creating the great Taklamakan and Gobi deserts beyond the plateau. At the eastern edge of the Himalaya, complex crustal folding and warping bent the ranges of the Hengduan Mountains southward, creating valley passageways for the summer monsoon to flow north and drench the land. Three great rivers, the Nujiang, the Lancangjiang, and the Jinshajiang, finished the job, sculpting deep, parallel, north-south canyons. Plants and animals from the southern humid tropics and temperate Eurasia began to migrate and mix in both directions, and Yunnan's rich flora and fauna started to evolve.[2]

Today, Yunnan is one of the heartlands of Earth's biodiversity. In the southern hills and lowlands of Xishuangbanna Prefecture, where the Lancang flows into Laos, elephants trumpet through old-world primary rain forest and people grow tea, rice, and rubber. Eight hundred kilometers (five hundred miles) upstream in northwest Yunnan, the river carves a deep trench below sacred Kawagebo, the 6,740-meter (22,110-foot) peak that anchors the eastern margin of the Tibetan Plateau. Yunnan stretches over only eight degrees of latitude, but if you follow the flow of the Lancang in North American geographic terms, it's like traveling from Anchorage, Alaska, to the southern tip of Baja.

Geologists understand that "the remodeling of the face of the world that happens when crustal plates move is . . . a consequence of the power residing in the mantle." What energizes these shifting Earth forces? The ancient Han believed that Long, the all-powerful dragon, breathed fire and the Earth shook. For dragon breath, contemporary Earth scientists substitute deep convection currents of super-heated minerals that flow like toothpaste under intense pressure.

The people of the Middle Kingdom believed in the auspicious character of Long; the emperor embodied the power of the dragon. The Son of Heaven represented the glue that cemented strong bonds between Heaven, Earth, and Man in the Confucian system. Rulers mediated between people and nature, and social cohesion was crucial to maintaining order. Despite tremendous upheaval over four millennia, this pattern gave Han China a remarkable resiliency that created the longest continuous expression of one coherent human culture.

But maintaining dynastic power required pragmatic considerations as well. Food for a burgeoning population and a large army had to be grown. Given China's geography, this meant creating an intensive irrigated agriculture, fed by large-scale canals and dikes. These systems, the most complex in the world, in turn demanded labor for building and maintenance. This toil formed the daily reality for Chinese peasants and had its consequences; historian Mark Elvin notes that large-scale grain growing and the brute labor of construction work were tasks that people chafed at: "Fields end freedom."[3]

China began losing its natural ecosystems well before 1 CE, as forests and wetlands disappeared before the ax and the plow. Yet the Han were masters of creating a political bureaucracy to run the country, conscript peasant labor, and collect taxes and tribute to pay for it all.

As Chinese power consolidated, securing the frontiers of the realm became paramount. When the Han looked outward, they saw "barbarians." These peoples might become genuine threats (the Mongols), or they could simply be different, without the splendid achievements of textile manufacture, paper making, printing, the compass, and gunpowder that made the Han so proud.[4] Depending on the dynasty, frontier peoples might be subjugated, assimilated, or merely subject to tribute payments to the Son of Heaven.

Yunnan remained on the margins of dynastic China for fifteen centuries. The region was simply too far removed from the central plains and east coast heartland of the Middle Kingdom. For centuries, the pattern remained the same: when imperial power gained strength, ethnic peoples from central China were pushed west and south into Yunnan before the expanding Han, trade would increase, and local rulers might pay tribute to the emperor. When conflict sapped dynastic power, border regions would revert back to local rule and trade.[5]

These patterns changed forever in the thirteenth century when the Mongols swept south through Yunnan and marched east to defeat the Song dynasty and establish the Yuan dynasty (1279–1368), the largest empire in history. The Mongols were the world's best warriors, but they were less competent as administrators. After only a century, a blink of an eye in Chinese terms, the Han returned to power, formed the Ming dynasty (1368–1644), and finally brought Yunnan under imperial rule.

The Ming governed Yunnan directly, established administrative bureaucracies, encouraged Han immigration, and built the basic road and bridge network that people travel over today. Yunnan thus became the southwestern border of the Middle Kingdom, but Ming influence waned rapidly as one moved away from Kunming into southern and northern regions where local peoples retained power. The center finally ruled the frontier, but control was another matter.

It is difficult, if not impossible, to grasp the history of Chinese power without visiting the city that has been the capital for over seven hundred years: Beijing. Other cities have been the seat of the emperor for longer periods; Xi'an was the capital of China for several centuries before the founding of Rome. But for all of "modern" history, Beijing has been the center of the Middle Kingdom.[6] A week before leaving for Yunnan and the rural west, I needed to undertake an errand in Beijing: a search back into the past so I could better comprehend the present.

It's a blazing hot day, approaching 40° C (100° F) and there is no shade in the symbolic center of modern China. I'm passing through Tiananmen Square, the largest public area in the world. Tiananmen can accommodate a million people, but today under the noon sun it's deserted. Hundreds of people are hanging out in the cool subterranean underpasses that link the square with streets north and south.

I stroll through the northern tunnel, emerge into white glare, and confront the Gate of Heavenly Peace and the Forbidden City. For five hundred years, this imperial palace was the heart of dynastic China, though it was not erected initially by the Han. In 1267, the Mongols under Kublai Khan began building his palace on this site. After the fall of the Mongols, the triumphant Han began a massive fifteen-year reconstruction using a million laborers, and the Forbidden City was born. Aligned along north-south feng shui lines, the palace has 8,700 rooms and measures 900 by 750 meters (2,953 by 2,461 feet) with a full moat surrounding its high walls.

Today, along the Forbidden City's south side, I wander through the shady willow gardens of Changpu River Park. A friendly Han woman walking to work at the new history museum invites me in for a brief tour in English. Inside the air-conditioned main room spreads a scale model world, a reproduction of Beijing during Ming times when the Forbidden City was surrounded by walls twelve meters (thirty-nine feet) high. The Ming workers who labored on the Forbidden City were citizens of a single dynasty that lasted a generation longer than the entire history of the United States. When America was born in 1776, the population of China was approaching three hundred million, the current census for the United States. After contemplating the structural details of the ancient capital, I thank the woman and exit. My destination lies elsewhere; I'm headed farther back in time, to the center of Beijing before the rise of the Ming.

🐉

Ethnic peoples living in Yunnan did not comprehend that the emperor residing in the Forbidden City was the Son of Heaven. Nor did they consider themselves to be "barbarians." Yunnan was not a frontier, it was home. Over time, however, the Han solidified the boundaries of the China that we know today, incorporating fifty-six officially recognized *shaoshu minzu* (ethnic nationalities), within the borders of the PRC. China is 92 percent Han, but the western borderlands are predominantly minorities. Yunnan's population is 33 percent non-Han.[7]

In the years after the 1949 Communist Revolution, the frontier was stabilized and its people were encouraged to identify with the PRC. Unlike U.S. government treatment of indigenous peoples, however, the Communists did not attempt to herd *shaoshu minzu* onto reservations. Nor did they demand immediate assimilation. Instead, with the exception of two periods of turmoil, border peoples have been able to pursue their livelihoods relatively unimpeded. The first time of strained relations was the Great Leap Forward (1956–1959), when Mao instigated policies across rural China that led to the largest famine in history. Then during the Cultural Revolution in the late 1960s and early 1970s, the Red Guards moved through Yunnan, attempting to stamp out "little nations chauvinism" and many temples and traditions were battered. Most often, however, Yunnan's ethnic nationalities were too far removed from the mainstream to suffer as much as other Chinese.[8] Even after the new leader of the Communist Party, Premier Deng Xiaoping, decided in 1979 to open China to the global market economy, rural Yunnan was too backwater to join the rush for profits. Foreign travelers have only been allowed unrestricted access to Yunnan since 1992.

That initial trickle has since become a flood. A million foreigners visited Yunnan in 2005, along with sixty million Chinese. Provincial officials would like to see a hundred million tourists by 2020. The very attributes that have kept Yunnan "stuck in the past"— intact forests, spectacular mountains, ethnic peoples who have retained much of their culture—now attract visitors from all over the world who are beguiled by a land so different from the rest of China.

Yunnan is special. The province is both real and symbolic for the Chinese. The reality seems straightforward—Yunnan is singular within China because of its biological and cultural diversity. It is also economically depressed. Outside of a handful of cities, the Yunnanese are extremely poor, with three-quarters of the population getting their living from subsistence agriculture. The income gap between urban and rural China is more than 3 to 1 and is a volatile political issue throughout the PRC.[9] The gap in Yunnan is almost 5 to 1—one of the highest in the country.

These visions of Yunnan the beautiful as well as the backward are layered with cultural symbolism for the Chinese. As an outsider, I am still attempting to unravel the many nuances. Visitors from eastern China are often aware of the social tensions generated by wealth gaps. Given recent Chinese history, anyone over the age of forty probably has their own memories of want. Yunnan also looms large as the wild west frontier of the PRC. To the average Chinese, the province is like Yellowstone and Yosemite national parks are to Americans. As a kid in the late 1950s, I remember attending a rodeo with "real" cowboys and Indians in Cody, Wyoming, outside Yellowstone. In Yunnan today, one of the tourist highlights is watching ethnic nationalities dancing in traditional outfits. In fact, many modern Chinese still view *shaoshu minzu* as "little brothers and sisters," whose achievements pale in comparison to those of the Han.

There is also a economic layer to this cultural attitude—the provincial government and commercial tour groups market Yunnan in very specific ways. Since the late 1990s, they have created a brand for Yunnan, *minzu wenhua dacheng*, "Great Ethnic Culture Province," that highlights cultural exoticism and scenic allure. Official documents are clear: "Let culture merge with economics . . . to build Yunnan into an economically prosperous, culturally developed, ethnically united . . . province".[10] The provincial government has determined that one good way to grow Yunnan out of poverty is by making ethnic nationality cultures turn a profit.

🐉

Beichang jie, the shady street below the west wall of the Forbidden City, is a quiet place on a hot day, but not because of the heat. The street runs alongside Zhongnanhai, the sprawling administrative compound of the Communist Party. The complex is off-limits to visitors; in China, building sites and structures have always represented power. Kublai Khan constructed his main palace just a few blocks from here, on the eastern shore of Beihai Lake at Tuancheng. Following the traffic flow, I head toward the ancient seat of Mongol power.

Walking to a remnant palace in a country layered with deep time, I wonder about my own status as a foreign guest, what I may take, what I might leave behind. I wish to take the pulse of conservation in Yunnan, to calibrate the odds that remaining wild places and minority peoples will somehow pass through the development dynamo that is twenty-first-century China. But my cultural predilection for nature and the chance to encounter wild China before it disappears sets me apart. Wildness and wilderness, as understood by Americans, have little cultural traction in China.

Like those in the United States, the tales the Chinese tell about "nature" are both ancient and modern, always complex, and often contradictory. The puzzle begins as soon as you attempt a basic translation of the term. The Mandarin word for "nature" is *ziran*, but its modern meaning dates back only to the early twentieth century.[11] *Ziran*, "self-so" or "spontaneously," has an ancient lineage, but it doesn't cover much of the territory that people in the West consider part of nature: the physical world, the opposite of culture, the essence of things.

Peering back into Chinese history, other words connected to "nature" stand out. *Tian*, "heaven," originally referred to "sky." The emperor was the Son of Heaven. Clearly, nature is a different realm for the Chinese; Americans, in contrast, have no tradition of expecting their leaders to embody the cosmos.

Then there is *qi*, the flow of energy that runs through everything—mountains, rivers, and humans. *Qi* goes well beyond a foreigner's conception of nature; to the Chinese, its universal force flows through all elemental matter.

In the West, much has been made of Daoism and Buddhism as

sources of environment-friendly values, but these traditions, though influential, have always been minority streams in China.[12] There are probably more Chinese Christians attending Western-style church services on Sunday mornings today than there have been practicing Daoists for the last several hundred years. Daoism and Buddhism have influenced classical poetry and painting more than they have guided how the majority of Chinese live their lives. If you pay attention to daily behavior instead of philosophy, what people do as opposed to what they say they value, actions often conflict with beliefs.[13]

A brace against disorder, Confucianism, the third great Chinese tradition, has always been the most influential path defining people-nature relationships. Confucian scholars have outlined eight steps that link *tian* directly with human affairs. Individuals are connected with the cosmos in a well-ordered humanist hierarchy that begins with personal cultivation and extends through family virtues, a well-ordered state with wise rulers, to *tian*.[14] This is yet another notion of nature missing in the West. Confucianism also puts great stock in *tuanji*, "unity," and tends to idealize wild nature as the opposite of urban life. This is about as close to Western Romanticism as Chinese tradition gets.

Other meanings of nature in China are mostly twentieth-century accretions. Important for older Chinese who remember Mao are slogans like *Ren Ding Sheng Tian*, "Man Must Conquer Nature." The Great Helmsman believed that nature's limits could be overcome by socialist labor and productivity. In the PRC today, expectations of personal wealth hold greater allure than conservation. For most younger Chinese, the Party's rhetoric about a "harmonious society" and national unity combine with international standards of market consumerism to overwhelm most environmental urges.

Nature in today's China is a polyglot in transition, a mélange of *qi*, landscape painting and poetry, Confucian humanist harmony, and strong market behavior with some borrowed international environmental standards floating here and there. What foreigners won't find is much consideration of wildness or wilderness. This may not be a defect but it is a difference. After working in the PRC for the past twenty years, wildlife biologist Richard Harris says, "I know of no context in which *ye*, 'wildness,' is used [to describe] a generally enjoyable experience."[15] China has never had a Henry David Thoreau, John Muir, or Terry Tempest Williams. The country was shut off by the Party from most international influences during the formative decades of the U.S. wilderness movement. Nature protection in China is rooted in a different soil.

There is scant evidence for a home-grown conservation with Chinese characteristics based on protecting wild nature, biodiversity, or ecosystem services—yet. Many citizens want to reduce pollution and enhance environmental quality for people, but few connect these concerns to China's endangered species and their shrinking habitats. Nonetheless, maybe Chinese and American attitudes are, finally, not so far apart. People in both countries believe in "using" nature over strict "protection," even as there is some movement toward defining conservation in a manner that does not set these two notions against each other. After all, utilizing mountains and rivers without attention to the long run often means that future use will be reduced.

While the future of "nature" in China remains unclear, the central government knows exactly what kind of vision it must offer to the rural people of Yunnan. When Deng determined that China's future lay with a state-directed market economy, he also realized that the PRC would have to begin the transition where development was most likely to succeed. The eastern and southern coasts of China already had much of the basic infrastructure for global communications and commercial exchange—this would be the place. Western China would have to wait.

Yunnan waited twenty years. During these decades, economic growth in China pulled hundreds of millions of people out of poverty and created a rising world power. Some 150 million rural residents moved to east coast factory jobs, the largest human migration ever recorded. But this loss of labor from the country to the cities only added to east-west social disparities.

In 1999, Beijing announced a solution: *xibu dakaifa*, "great western development strategy," or the Go West policy. Then-Premier Xu Rongji summed up the plan: it would "strengthen national unity," "safeguard social stability," and "control border defense".[16] But what did Premier Xu's rhetoric really mean?

For Yunnan, Go West means the end of the frontier. The margin will become modernized, poverty will shrink, incomes and education levels will rise. The provincial government has no intention of stimulating economic development just for tourists. For China, Go West will reduce the east-west wealth gap, slow down the stream of migrant labor, and spur a domestic market of consumers that will make the PRC less dependent on selling computers, toys, and furniture to the rest of the world.

While the domestic benefits of Go West are many, China is also looking beyond its borders. From the times of ancient emperors to the Communist Party, frontiers have always insulated the Middle Kingdom from foreign influences. The traditional role of government has been to seal frontiers; Go West punches holes in them. By constructing a vast array of road, rail, and hydro/powerline links to its Southeast Asian neighbors, Yunnan is joining the global economy.

I have a difficult time grasping the sheer scale, speed, and style of Go West in Yunnan. Let's start with roads. From 2006 to 2010, the PRC national road plan calls for building and paving 180,000 kilometers (111,850 miles) of all grades of roads each year. For comparison, the U.S. interstate highway system is about 76,000 kilometers (47,000 miles) long. In Yunnan, I have witnessed three villages make the transition from "roadless" to "connected." Imagine going from walking, biking, or maybe hitching a ride on a *tuo luo jie* (a village tractor) to continuous paved road access. You can now negotiate a better price for your tea or vegetables. Your kids can go to school beyond sixth grade because you no longer have to be concerned about boarding expenses.

The environmental consequences of all this road building are another matter. The government is spending tens of billions on roads and, within a decade, Yunnan will be linked by modern highways with Tibet, Myanmar, Vietnam, Thailand, and India. Yunnan will soon have direct road access to saltwater ports in three separate countries. Bereft of access to the sea for its entire existence, the province will be landlocked no more.

Railroads have always been expensive to build in Yunnan. The mountainous terrain keeps construction costs high. But now China is flush with cash. When Go West is complete, there will be three new rail lines connecting Kunming with Singapore, India, and Lhasa. Some of the new rail cargo will be precious metals and industrial minerals. Yunnan has China's largest lead, zinc, and phosphate deposits, most of which still lie underground. There has never been a modern transportation system to haul them to market.

As for dams, there are thirty-three separate hydro projects proposed for Yunnan's three great rivers.[17] Any observer can do the math—Yunnan doesn't need that much electricity. Why build so much hydropower capacity? In the mid-twentieth century, one could have asked the same questions about the Colorado or Columbia rivers in the American West. Much of the electricity generated by damming these rivers is shipped to California. Without this power, California could not have created the eighth largest economy in the world.

Go West hydro companies will sell a portion of the energy of Yunnan's rivers to power growth in Bangkok and Hanoi. The rest will be shipped to southeast China. The next chapter after the Go West strategy is implemented is to link Yunnan with Guangdong and the industrial supercities of the Pearl River delta on the far side of China. This will create a European-style common market powerhouse across the southern half of the PRC. Designs are already being drawn up to construct twenty new shipping ports the size of Seattle or larger on China's eastern seaboard. The irony is inescapable: the ultimate goal of Go West–style development is to "Go East."

How will the ethnic nationality peoples of Yunnan survive the coming transitions? How can conservationists support people and nature in Yunnan when Go West development is "reinventing another China"? The PRC has already answered this question. Go West will stop ecological degradation and foster *shengtai jianshe*, "ecological construction". But this Mandarin phrase is vague; I believe it masks more than it reveals.[18] "Ecological construction" is so broad that it can mean building thirteen dams on the Nu, or it can mean erecting only a few. In China, building no dams at all is not an option.

The question is not whether to develop, but how. One way to proceed is to embed basic environmental planning practices into Go West projects, but this is not happening on a large scale. Of course, there is the political problem of gaining access to information about the dams. Details about road construction projects are also lacking. Though Chinese law is clear, none of the new roads that I saw opening up access to villages came with environmental reviews. And it shows—design and construction are so shoddy that many roads are impossible to keep open year-round.

Basic conservation biology principles could also guide Go West. Ecological planning could influence where a railroad or highway gets sited, thereby reducing habitat loss so that an elephant or monkey population might not be eliminated. But as with integrated environmental assessments, conservation biology is not yet featured in large-scale Chinese planning. The roads, dams, and powerlines are simply getting built.[19]

At the conclusion of *The Retreat of the Elephants*, his magisterial survey of environmental history in China, Mark Elvin searches for reasons why unique Chinese attitudes about nature might have dampened the drive toward environmental destruction over the course of three thousand years. He can't find any that worked for very long.

What Elvin does discover is that the impetus to compete for scarce resources is common throughout human history and that, in China as elsewhere, "what might have been more viable long-term patterns counted for little or nothing faced with short-term choices for power." After nations gain strength and influence, pressures to reach outward to control more resources almost always swamp long-term environmental protection.

Maybe it can be different in Yunnan. Maybe Go West can yet be steered toward keeping Yunnan ecologically intact. The only way to find out is to search for what is happening on the ground in the backcountry villages and the protected areas, to meet people in the growing group of Chinese conservation leaders, and, when an opportunity arises, to offer assistance.

Tuancheng, the Circular City, sits on a small knob of lowland projecting out into Beihai Lake in central Beijing. It was from this place that Kublai Khan ruled his vast empire. Rising immediately to the north is the white dagoba spire of the Miao Ying Temple dating from the 1270s. The temple was reconstructed in 1651 to honor the Dalai Lama, when China's relations with Tibet were friendlier.

Beihai is my favorite park in Beijing. Like all open spaces in the capital, Beihai is often crowded, but there are quiet nooks behind groups of venerable upright stones and secluded corners in a temple's dusty outer rooms where one can escape the pressures of a city of seventeen million people.

I've come to Tuancheng to visit an urn made of a single piece of solid jade. The vessel weighs close to 340 kilograms (750 pounds). Encased in protective glass, the urn is inscribed with sharp-clawed *longs*, hundreds of dragons that dart around its circumference. Scores of red Chinese prayer tags are clipped to the copper rail that circles the enclosure. Used for ceremonial drinking during parties at the emperor's palace, it held a thousand cups of wine at one filling.

Today, all the urn contains is dust and memories. After conquering much of the known world, Kublai Khan's Yuan dynasty did not even last a century. The only material remains of the great Khan's court, here at the heart of the greatest empire in world history, is this beautiful jade urn.

Chapter 3

Under the Jade Dragon

When there's no tiger on the mountain,
the monkey becomes king.
Chinese proverb

FOOTSTEPS ON COBBLESTONE echo down narrow passageways, damp dawn air is scented with wood smoke, a black-
caped Naxi nationality woman in a blue Mao cap carries a sack
of mushrooms to the morning market. Arriving early, she spreads
a tarp on the smooth cobbles, dumps the fungi out. Fresh *Coprinus*
mushrooms from Yunnan pine woods. She removes a thin metal
hand-scale from her bag and sits to wait for the first customer. Soon
the haggling will begin.

Late afternoon a few blocks away in Dayan, Lijiang's old town, the
centuries-old capital of the Naxi ethnic nationality, tourist hordes
block every lane. It's chaos, a madhouse of commercial tour groups
in matching baseball hats queuing at every shop and clogging the
streets. It's almost impossible to walk. Nor is it easy to wield a camera;
there are too many people in the way.

There are over two thousand shops packed into the 2.7 square
kilometers (1 square mile) of Dayan. I've never seen such concentrated consumerism. The shops sell "authentic" Naxi crafts—silver
jewelry, wooden flutes, jade ornaments—as well as the usual tourist

kitsch—t-shirts, soft drinks, and film. Few items are made anywhere nearby.

These are two faces of Lijiang: the city is a regional service center and a world-famous tourist destination. While in 2005 almost three and a half million visitors besieged Dayan, by the end of 2009 that number had shot up to almost six million. The growth of tourism here has been spectacular, even for China.

In fact, Dayan itself is growing. The old town is expanding as new quarters are constructed in the same architectural style, adding more square blocks of shops and restaurants to accommodate the crowds. This might raise questions of authenticity to some, but it doesn't seem to matter to the local authorities or the tourists.

Dayan is, nevertheless, extraordinary. The old town is one of the few remaining places in China where you can glimpse remnants of an ancient way of life. Looking down on Lijiang from the heights of Lion Hill, you see morning mist drifting among thousands of wood-beamed eaves. The architecture is Naxi, not Chinese; a maze, not a grid. Late at night, after the bars have shut down, the water in Dayan's famous canals shimmers red in lantern light. In residential old town, those waters are still used for washing clothes and vegetables; the canals' upstream sources in Black Dragon Pool have never run dry.

I'm not sure how long this influx and reshaping will last. Visitation is still growing and at some point it will be difficult to distinguish the real from the reconstructed.[1] The manic growth is driven by several factors. Dayan was declared a UN World Heritage Site in 1997 and this dovetailed neatly with the government's program for crafting Yunnan into a "Great Ethnic Culture Province." Yunnan is the only province in China where tourism is promoted as a primary economic engine. In 2006, almost RMB 50 billion (USD 6.2 billion) was added to government coffers by visitors, up about 17 percent from 2005. Nine of every ten tourists are Chinese. They are able to travel because they have disposable income for the first time in their lives. The Chinese middle class, practically nonexistent fifteen years ago, is approaching the size of the U.S. population and is expected to double by 2020. You probably don't want to visit China during one of the national holidays when upward of two hundred million people try to get from A to B.[2]

Chinese tourists used to favor traditional historic sites like the Great Wall and Beijing's Forbidden City. But, as the economy exploded in the 1990s, a range of new attractions became popular. Today, nature reserves are big draws, and so is "folk tourism." This includes Disney-like theme parks displaying "authentic reproductions" of ethnic nationality village life complete with costumes, singing, and dancing.[3] Commercial tourism is spreading out from places like Lijiang and beginning to penetrate into rural areas. Whenever a new road is punched in, the tour buses are not far behind.

Go West development and the constant crush of visitors will undoubtedly change Yunnan over the next ten years or so. The question is whether the province can preserve its unique cultural and natural heritage while taking advantage of the benefits of modern China. Ecotourism is currently fashionable and some international NGOs believe that it can bridge the divide between past and future, conservation and development. But how much "eco" does such tourism really contain?

He Lushan smiled as she poured green tea into an enamel cup. We were sitting in TNC's visitor center in a traditional Naxi courtyard home in Dayan. Lushan has been managing the center since it opened in 2006 with funding from General Motors and Cargill. That first season, she hosted four thousand visitors a month—now, two years later, that number was closer to nine thousand.

Lushan is Naxi, born and raised in Nguluko, immediately below the southeast face of Yulongxueshan, the 5,596-meter (18,359-foot) Jade Dragon Snow Mountain that hulks just north of Lijiang. Since 2004, Nguluko has seen the creation of a thriving home-grown tourist cooperative that offers horse-riding day trips to Chinese tourists.

Lushan's parents started the first guesthouse in the village and the plan was for me to travel there that night. I wanted to see how the co-op was doing and to hike up Yulongxueshan, famous for its rich botany.

I also wanted to visit Wenhai, another village about four hours' walk farther back into the mountains. It, too, was the scene of eco-tourism activities, only these had been supported by TNC and several other NGOs. Unlike Nguluko, Wenhai's nascent eco-lodge had a Web site and had been written up in the *New York Times*. But I had heard that not all was going well with the project. All told, the distance between Dayan, Nguluko, and Wenhai is less than twenty kilometers (twelve miles). But these three places are worlds apart.

As soon as I arrived in Nguluko, I felt the altitude. The village is perched at about 2,800 meters (9,200 feet), near the top of the sandy outwash basin that spreads from Yulongxueshan all the way down to Lijiang. Stepping out of the taxi, the manic energy of commercial Lijiang began to fade away. About fourteen hundred villagers live in Nguluko; maybe twenty of them own cars.

Most of Nguluko's houses are built of solid limestone, the bones of the Jade Dragon, but there is also much new construction throughout the village. Many families clearly were doing well, but this has not always been so. Fifteen years ago, researchers from the Yunnan Academy of Social Sciences and the University of California, Davis, came to Nguluko to canvas the Naxi villagers about their interest in small-scale tourism.[4] The team found people living in poverty with no plumbing, little electricity, open sewers, and a per capita income of RMB 442 (USD 54). No tourists visited Nguluko. Despite some funding and much enthusiasm, none of the pilot projects worked out, and by 1997 the researchers had left. More than a decade later, the locals seemed to be succeeding where the academics had failed.

Lushan had warned that I needed an early start if I wanted to hike in front of the horse-riding day trippers, and she was right. People were already queuing for mounts when I headed up the single trail toward the Jade Dragon.

Above Nguluko, the braided path rose through potato patches, ripening barley plots, and heavily grazed goat pasture. The fields at my feet were carpeted with familiar late-summer flowers: asters, peas, and cinquefoils. I glanced up; beyond a huge, descending ridge arm of Yulongxueshan, four successive needle summits swept up into the sky.

The pastures ended abruptly in a wooded ravine where the trail steepened and became a deep gash in the earth. The erosion was severe. Where the route became a trench too deep for horses, multiple tracks spread into the thin pine woods. While horses were boosting Nguluko's economy, they were also bleeding mountain soil away.

Climbing from gully to gully, I reached a muddy flat. A shack sheltering vendors selling snacks for riders sat in the middle of bare ground, trash strewn everywhere. The horse tourists throw whatever candy wrappers and soda bottles they have into the woods—even if trash were collected, there is no place to dispose of it anywhere nearby.

After I traversed another flat with more tourists and trash, the trail steepened into a serious ascent. Clouds closed in on the crags, patches of fir and azalea leaned out of rock walls, and I began to feel like a figure in a Tang dynasty painting: "A thousand peaks: no more birds in flight. / Ten thousand paths: all traces of people gone."[5]

I couldn't miss the irony. Here I was, an American day-hiking in China, a speck of dust on the flank of the Jade Dragon, worrying about litter and erosion and recalling classical Chinese poetry, while the Han horse riders, wearing business casual and skirts and heels, were wondering why their mobile phones didn't get coverage up here.

Sheer cliffs signaled the end of horse travel. Far above the tourists, I scrambled up to a narrow limestone col thick with krummholz. Yunnan's famous blue poppies scattered across a rock-chip slope as darker clouds moved in. Yulongxueshan was hiding and it was time to leave. I skidded down seven hundred feet of crushed rock and landed near three grinning Chinese hikers. The tourists took my picture and proffered a smoke.

———

Back at the He family guesthouse, I contemplated two spread-winged stone bats, their arms arched into a circle of cobbles that defined the center of the courtyard floor. Bats, *pi-fong*, symbolize supreme good luck in China.

Bearing more green tea, Lushan explained how the co-op works. It's managed by a village committee that schedules households with horses or mules so that business is shared equally and each family earns a portion of the fees. The fees also pay for insurance and management costs, and some is set aside for school scholarships, road maintenance, and the ticket center. About three hundred riders visit the mountain each day, and villagers earn around 11,000 kuai (USD 1,333) a year for each animal before expenses.

Like many in the community, Lushan was hopeful about what that extra income could do. "You've seen how it's improving Nguluko."

I did, but I also remembered those eroded trails and mounting trash. Unlike some other ecotourism efforts in Yunnan, the co-op wasn't partnering with a nonprofit, but one of its stated goals was environmental protection.

"You work for TNC, can't you talk with the committee?" I asked.

"I know it's a problem, but the co-op doesn't have much training. They're still learning about conservation." Lushan told me that most of the erosion began when the forest was cut down in the 1980s. "And the trash isn't good, but people have jobs cleaning it up in the village."

I suggested various alternatives—trash bags for each rider, hiring workers to restore the trails and clean up the gullies. Lushan smiled. "These ideas might work, but it takes time when so much needs to be done at once."

It was late and the stars wheeled above the walls of the courtyard. As I climbed the stairs to bed, I recalled a comment from an American researcher about tourism in Nguluko: "Tourists arrive in large groups, overwhelm the town, commoditize everything in sight, and depart." That was written seven years ago, long before the co-op formed, when visitation was relatively low. In 2007, thirty-three thousand people visited Nguluko.

The following morning, I left the horse tourists behind and climbed four hours through cut-over pine woods to Wenhai. The village sits at 3,100 meters (10,170 feet), in a broad limestone basin hidden by the southwest ridges of Yulongxueshan. Wenhai means "dry lake"; during the summer rains a shimmering lake fills the bottom of the basin, only to partially drain away after the monsoon. The lake attracts winter water birds, including endangered black cranes and black-necked storks; it is part of the Lashihai Alpine Wetlands Nature Reserve.

From the ridge above the basin, Wenhai conjures peace: two small villages, lower and upper Wenhai, are surrounded by green patchwork fields; a lake reflects summer clouds, with the Jade Dragon's forests and ice flows hovering above. The road into Wenhai is only seven years old.

Upper Wenhai is the site of another co-op, this one centered around an eco-lodge, a Naxi farmhouse renovated for trekkers that would be my base camp for the next several days. When I arrived, no one was around, so I took off my backpack and sat out of the wind within the walls of the courtyard. I looked up to see solar panels on the rooftop. The shell of a defunct greenhouse flapped shredded plastic in the afternoon breeze. There was a biogas digester below the building that looked functional, and the yard was freshly swept, but the place had an air of neglect.

Feeling the uphill climb from Nguluko, I pulled out a book but I was too tired to read. A dog barked down the lane. The plastic snapped against the guesthouse wall. I leaned back, shut my eyes, and drifted.

I was alone in backcountry China, deep in the hills under the Jade Dragon. I imagined a valley in winter, a lake in the sky, crane wings flapping . . . Long ago in the time of an ancient dynasty, a fisherman bushwhacked up a wild stream, lost track, couldn't remember the way back home. He came upon a valley thick with blooming peach trees that soon led out onto a broad plain. There were rich fields, settled by ageless people of an unknown race. The inhabitants greeted him with a feast, explaining that in this valley they had all the food and wine they wanted. The fisherman stayed many days but then became homesick. As he prepared to leave, the people reminded him: "No need to share our secret." As he left, the fisherman remembered every landmark, traced each turn in the trail. Back home, he told his tale and then set out with his neighbors to find the lost valley. But memory plays tricks, forests grow old and wild, streams change direction over time. The fisherman never found the valley again.[6]

"*Ni hao*, hello, hello! *Ni hao ma?*" I woke to find the host of the eco-lodge, a smiling Naxi man clad in a threadbare jacket, offering me a cup of tea. He didn't speak English, but behind him stood two young Chinese women who did.

Spring and Lucy were tourists from Hangzhou in eastern China, where they taught primary school. Spring seemed delighted about their initial voyage to the "wild west," proclaiming, "This is our first time in beautiful Yunnan," and she offered to translate for me whenever I needed help. I wondered what these thoroughly urban "easterners" would make of Wenhai and suggested hiking together the next day.

"This is the first hike in my life," Spring commented the next morning as we crested the low pass north of Wenhai and left the lake basin behind. "Yunnan is so beautiful, I want to go very far today." I shared Spring's enthusiasm, though I wondered what "far" might mean to a Chinese schoolteacher from a megacity of six million people.

We followed a rutted track through green pastures dotted with clumps of trees below the snows of Yulongxueshan. The view was spectacular: ice mountains, Alp-like gardens, and, to the north, the dark gash of Tiger Leaping Gorge, where the Jinshajiang (upper Yangzi River) carves one of the deepest canyons in the world.

What were these Chinese women seeing? Was their experience similar to mine?

"Yunnan has so much nature compared to Zhejiang Province." Spring raised her arm and swept it around the valley. I followed her gaze. Where she saw healthy pasture, I saw heavily grazed fields fretted with erosion. Spring's "forests" were my "goat-hammered woodlands." Asian black bear, rhesus macaque, and an endangered pheasant had been seen in this area in the past, but it was difficult to imagine how they could survive under current conditions. Maybe Lucy and Spring saw some version of Peach Blossom Valley from the Chinese story I had dreamed about. My ecologist's eye revealed a land hard-pressed by humans. But the day was undeniably beautiful.

Xuehua nestled under a high ridge of the Jade Dragon, a poor village in a postcard setting. We were thirsty, so we stopped at a farmhouse and asked a child for water. He didn't speak Chinese, and he ran away, ducking into a courtyard doorway. I peeked into the compound: a few pigs sleeping in the sun, chickens, washing on a line, and a wood-framed house with smoke hazing the eaves. A girl in a ragged denim jacket stepped out to greet us, followed by her mother. The older woman spoke only Yi, so Lucy queried the girl in Mandarin, and soon we were sitting in the sun, drinking tea and chatting.

Lily was eleven and went to school in Wenhai, a three-hour round-trip walk. She was very lively; her mother and the other kids gathered around us were more hesitant. Lucy and Spring talked with Lily about school, but I was curious about the contents of the storage shed across the courtyard. It was stacked to the rafters with charcoal fagots. A large woodpile in a corner told me that the charcoal was not being burned to heat this farmhouse.

"Lily wants us to take her picture in her Yi clothes." Lucy was pulling a camera out of her daypack. The girl had disappeared. I reached for my camera, too, though I wanted a photograph of the charcoal. Lily soon reappeared dressed in the traditional women's clothing unique to the Yi. She curtsied in the sunny courtyard as we snapped her picture. I asked her about the charcoal; she glanced at her mother and didn't answer. I photographed the woodpile and the charcoal and then handed out pens and stickers of the Beijing Olympic mascot animals to the children.

On the trail home, Lucy related what she had learned about Lily's schooling. "If Lily goes to middle school, she'll have to board in Baisha down in the valley, because it's too far to walk there every day."

Spring calculated the costs. "She said it costs her family 800 kuai (USD 107) a year for school, plus 75 kuai (USD 10) in book fees. Her family can barely afford it. If she had an older brother, she wouldn't go at all; there would only be enough money for him."

"What's her chance of going to high school?" I asked.

Spring's bright faced clouded as she told me that she didn't think this poor rural family could afford their daughter's education beyond middle school. In China, the state mandates schooling through grade twelve, but there is a great disparity between funding for urban and rural education.

Lucy and Spring departed Wenhai the next day, and I decided to hike back toward Xuehua by a different route. I wanted to see how China's tangled history of environmental management had shaped the land in this region.

Since the 1949 revolution, rural people across China have been subject to dramatic, unpredictable swings in government land-use regulations. Events in Wenhai are typical for northwest Yunnan.[7] Prior to the PRC, there existed as many systems of land stewardship as there were ethnic nationality groups. Lands could be held in private, managed by family clans or village councils, or be subject to diverse common property arrangements. But as the Communist Party consolidated power and began to push for co-ops in line with the Party's political vision, local traditions were disrupted.

With the mid-1950s Great Leap Forward, the Party co-ops expanded into large-scale collectives at the expense of most remaining customary arrangements. Diverse and local land management, mandatory cooperatives, large state-controlled collectives—in less than ten years, Wenhai's people and forests bore the brunt of contradictory policies that resulted in little forest protection and less certainty as to what might happen next.

Into the 1970s, the large collectives held sway but China's economy stalled out. Then came the shift that led the PRC away from state socialism toward markets and the global economy. In the early 1980s, the Household Responsibility System was introduced, placing production back in the hands of villagers and opening rural China to the rest of the world.

Imagine that you're a villager in Wenhai. For three centuries, your ancestors created unwritten rules around how to use and care for the land. After the 1949 revolution, your father was forced to adjust to a variety of state-imposed management schemes, often to the detriment of the land. For the next thirty years, he had little voice in decision making.

Then a measure of power was returned to villagers, but only a measure. Your family was ceded collective use rights to the fields and forests adjacent to Wenhai while the government retained control of many state forest lands. Now your household cared for (but did not own) specific fields for farming, and you could grow and sell for personal profit.

But the new system lacked essential ingredients. While state lands were sometimes demarcated clearly, collective land boundaries were not. Where was the line between lower and upper Wenhai's shared forests? Who controlled what? What group adjudicated inevitable disputes—the village? local government? Beijing?

In Wenhai, the Household Responsibility System did little to slow poor forest management. You could labor all year growing vegetables and your harvest might yield a surplus to sell. Or not. If you cut down trees beyond your small allotment from collective forests and sold them on the black market that fed the reconstruction of Dayan in Lijiang, you could pull in RMB 75 (USD 10) a day.

PRC policies also steered villagers toward logging. Keep in mind that in China, there is little private land; the state owns everything. The government can and does confer collective use rights, but the law is murky, corruption abounds, and the state can extinguish rights without due process. In Lijiang County, 77 percent of all land is "collective," but few villagers are clear about what can and cannot be done with this land, and local officials take advantage of the system for personal profit.

With Reform and Opening, the PRC also decentralized decision making and funding. With paltry funding, however, the Lijiang County Bureau of Forestry had little means for enforcement. If you and your neighbors decided to do some logging, you probably wouldn't get caught. And for the bureau, one easy solution to the lack of funds was to log the forest itself. After all, the central government provided a handy role model. Between 1985 and 1998, the state cut forests in Yunnan as fast as possible to reap cash in the booming market economy, even as they restricted local people from doing the same. No wonder I couldn't find any older trees in the hills around Nguluko or Wenhai.

Then, in 1998, disastrous floods scoured the upper watersheds of northwest Yunnan, raging downstream over an area larger than New England. The floods caused over RMB 150 billion (USD 20 billion) in damage. In response, the PRC banned all logging in upland western China. The benefits were obvious, but the downside was that in one fell swoop, the central government eliminated the main source of cash for many villagers and tax revenue for most local governments.

I looped up the ridge above Wenhai into the forest. From a distance, standing at the eco-lodge, this area appeared dense with trees—healthy forest. But up close, I could see trails heading off in every direction and scrubby brush sprouting up where tall oaks used to stand. Despite the ban, this forest was being cut heavily.

A column of smoke rose into the air a few hundred yards up the hill above me. I immediately thought of campfires and then realized almost no one camps for recreation in China, and the fires were too close to the village. I climbed toward the smoke, then stopped. I didn't need to find the source of the fire to solve this mystery. The answer lay ten yards to my right. Dug into the hillside was a yard-high black hole streaked with soot. In front of the hole was a pile of oak trunks. The "campfire" plumes came from villagers burning trees in primitive earth ovens, roasting the wood into charcoal.

I sat down and pulled out my notebook. Lily's family in Xuehua had reminded me how expensive it was to put a child through school. In Nguluko, members of the co-op were making good income from tourism. In Wenhai, it looked like charcoal was filling the gap. But working this hillside was a far cry from guiding a horse and rider up to a snack stand in a scenic meadow.

If you traded charcoal for schooling, the numbers just didn't match, and the forest wasn't going to last either. A year of school fees for one child cost about RMB 900 (USD 120). What potential cash income was available to villagers that might offset this burden?[8] They could sell a few goats for RMB 225 (USD 30). That still left RMB 675 (USD 90) to come up with for school. Making charcoal in a hillside hole in the ground is incredibly inefficient. One hundred kilograms (220 pounds) of fresh oak yields only 5 kilograms (11 pounds) of charcoal. A villager makes about RMB 5 (USD 0.60) selling 100 kilograms of charcoal down in the valley (there is no market for charcoal in Wenhai). If you had to meet school costs solely from selling charcoal, you would have to cut down 13,500 kilograms (29,760 pounds) of live oak every year. Multiply that amount for each school-age child in Wenhai, and you have seriously degraded forests.

Glancing back up at the plume, I stood up and headed back to the eco-lodge. I was beginning to see why conservation was losing out to development in Lijiang County.

The Wenhai eco-lodge was created in 1995 with funding from a Ford Foundation grant. It was designed for foreign ecotourists, hikers, and climbers; Chinese tourists were not part of the plan. The idea was to keep development small-scale and in local hands. But the co-op's luck was poor. The Lijiang earthquake in 1996 shook the regional economy during the first year the eco-lodge was open. Visitors were few and villagers squabbled over work roles. Through 2000, only twenty-two guests a year used the facility.

In 2002, the co-op was revived with help from TNC. The lodge was renovated and alternative energy systems and a greenhouse were installed.[9] TNC's vision was based on the Northwest Yunnan Conservation and Development Action Plan that the organization had crafted working with the provincial government.[10] The plan identified major problems in the region: population growth, logging, overgrazing, and uncontrolled tourism. The solution was to think strategically, identify critical conservation needs, and target several "action sites" such as Wenhai, where pilot projects could be launched to link conservation with local livelihoods. Biodiversity conservation and ecotourism were going to protect northwest Yunnan from large-scale development.

When I visited Wenhai five years after this revival, the eco-lodge's greenhouse was defunct, co-op membership had declined, visitation averaged a handful of people every few weeks, and charcoal burning was unabated.

What happened? Let's begin with ecotourism. Say the word anywhere in the world and you will soon be embroiled in debate. The term has many definitions, but most agree that ecotourism is small-scale visitation that has some conservation value while also providing economic benefits for local people.[11] But what do *conservation*, *economic benefits*, *local*, and *small-scale* really mean? And who gets to decide?

All these terms have to be defined for specific projects in local places. What works in Wenhai may not be successful in a nearby village, another region in China, or a different part of the world. In Lijiang County, TNC adopted solid ground rules. They surveyed biodiversity, met with local governments, the tourist board, and tour operators, and conducted many meetings with villagers. TNC provided workshops for villagers in ecotourist guiding, business accounting, and how to run a guesthouse.

Most environmentalists reviewing these accomplishments would feel that TNC was on the right track. But numerous studies have shown that ecotourism in the world's remote, poor, and beautiful places remains problematic. As visitation rises, market forces tend to combine with government boosterism; Lijiang's old town becomes Disneyland, Nguluko is thronged on a daily basis, and Wenhai becomes just another commodity in the "Great Ethnic Culture Province." The only unusual element in this story is the amazing speed with which it is unfolding in China.

When TNC came to Yunnan in 1998, the organization was beginning from zero in China. As an international NGO, TNC was required to partner with the provincial government; all NGOs working in China must register with an official agency.[12] This arrangement automatically creates some tension; what if your goals and methods do not match those of your Chinese partner? TNC, the wealthiest private conservation organization in the world, also brought a track record to China based on work in thirty countries, along with a commitment to its own brand of conservation science. But does experience derived in, say, Venezuela or Guatemala translate to a Naxi village in Yunnan?

From the beginning, TNC committed to a huge undertaking—the Yunnan Great Rivers Project—covering an area of 66,000 square kilometers (25,480 square miles), 17 percent of Yunnan. There are over three million people living in thousands of villages across this region. Like Wenhai, many places face imminent development threats to both local culture and global biodiversity. Despite its wealth and influence, TNC could not be everywhere at once.

Even in the areas where TNC concentrated its efforts, there were enormous economic pressures. The high costs of schooling, humping loads of charcoal down to market in the valley— how does an international organization account for these village realities? TNC's plan for Wenhai placed the market squarely in the mix: "[We work] with our local partners to give them skills they need to interact with a global marketplace while not changing them in any fundamental way . . . we hope to enable [villagers] to . . . compete with larger, non-local tourism enterprises." These well-meaning statements from TNC suggest that markets are benign, that level playing fields exist in China, and that a few months of workshops can somehow raise villagers' skill set up from subsistence agriculture to ecotourism.

These goals are chimeras in Wenhai. If I were a Wenhai villager, I would have to eat and I would want to send my kids to school. China's entry into the global marketplace would not have helped me here, as local prices for vegetables and animals are down. Valuable lands that I would have once controlled have been taken away, and corrupt local officials and some of my neighbors cut down trees despite the logging ban. If I were one of the handful of remaining co-op members, I could split a years' scarce profits from 150 paying guests. Or I could leave Wenhai and work in Lijiang in a tourist shop for RMB 3,600 (USD 480) a year.[13] As a rural Naxi, I would probably be at the bottom of the economic pecking order in a market saturated with unskilled labor. But what I could get in Lijiang would be decent pay compared to my other options, and chances are I would take it.

What about the government's role in tourism? The original partnership goals between the province and TNC appeared sound: modest economic growth and ecosystem protection. But the government wants things both ways. In 2004, officials signed off on a Further Fast Development of the Tourism Industry Plan, with the strategy of "whoever invests, whoever develops, is the one to profit."[14] Sixty-one million visitors to Yunnan in 2005 will become one hundred million in 2020 as tourist revenue ratchets up to RMB 115 billion (USD 15 billion).

Beginning in 2008, "high-end international leisure" development is coming to the watershed just below Wenhai. The corporate Shui On Group is partnering with the government to raise "the sophistication of tourism, . . . [and] leisure facilities, enhancing the ethnic experience, and developing ecotourism."[15] But what does a Hong Kong property development company know about ecological issues in Yunnan, or about "the interests of indigenous residents" in Wenhai?

The following morning broke clear. Backpacking out of Wenhai, I waded through a field of brilliant yellow mustard. Yulongxueshan danced in the waters of the lake as I ascended into the hills.

Solo on the trail in backcountry China, I felt edgy and excited. I had no map, just directions that a villager had shared in halting English. My goal was eight miles away in Suhe village where I could catch a cab to Lijiang. I would have to remember the twists and turns of the route. If I lost the way forward, I needed to be able to retrace my steps back to Wenhai.

The country was a confusion of trails, "a road of ten thousand rivers / and a thousand peaks."[16] I was walking through lands far removed from villages, and the dense Yunnan pines were taller than I had seen before. But there was no way to tell whether the forest was collective-use, state-run, or part of the Lashihai Nature Reserve.

As the route began to bend toward the lowlands, Naxi voices floated up from the trail below. I slowed my pace; three young men, all carrying rifles, were walking in my direction. My heartbeat quickened. Personal firearms were banned in China and the government had rounded up all guns some years ago. I suspected that these villagers knew that this foreigner with a backpack in the middle of nowhere understood that they were breaking the law. The men didn't smile or respond to my "Ni hao," but we passed without incident.

Minutes later, I took a break by a stream twisting through a gully. The sound of the water settled me down. I hadn't seen any animal sign all day. Despite hiking for a week through two "nature reserves," there was little evidence of the land in Wenhai or Nguluko being protected. Those villagers out hunting were part of the reason why. China was challenging my assumptions about how to conserve nature and culture. While I rested by the water, I sorted through my thoughts about the major conservation actors in the PRC.

The central government embraces global markets and also retains a strong nationalist vision of "one China." The Party cares about conservation, but there are conflicts: economics often trumps ecology, and decentralized authority limits implementation of national environmental laws.

Local governments in China are branches of the Party. Yet they often receive minimal funding to meet state targets. So they use their decentralized authority to secure funds through public-private partnerships, increasing the potential for corruption.

State and private corporations drive economic growth, and wealth is accumulating in China at a rate and scale never seen before. If you work in commercial tourism, during a single holiday you can profit from a mass of Chinese travelers equal to the combined populations of France, Spain, and Italy spending a collective RMB 70 billion (USD 8.7 billion). Conservation will never match these monetary incentives.

Over the last decade, the Naxi, Yi, and other ethnic nationalities in Yunnan have become linked to TV, roads, and tourists in a China ever more dependent on a globalizing world. Given the rapidity of this ongoing assimilation, villagers with low levels of education, skills, and political power cannot be expected to weather these forces without conflicts.

The Chinese Han majority are also being challenged, but they are often privileged, not disempowered, by their social status. The constraints of Maoism have evolved into a heady "capitalism with Chinese characteristics," as the government likes to say, and the new middle class is flexing its economic muscle.

Conservation NGOs like TNC, the World Wide Fund for Nature, Conservation International, Greenpeace, and many others have helped bring international environmental standards to China. Foreign NGOs in China also make mistakes as they learn to work in new cultural and political milieus. Unlike computers and flat screen TVs, environmental norms are never easy to export.

As I encountered all these actors throughout Yunnan, I reminded myself to distinguish what they say from what they actually do. There's a Chinese saying: "don't take your shoes off until you come to the riverbank." I needed to keep my shoes on and my eyes and ears open.

I, too, have my own biases and goals. I want Yunnan to prosper economically, but I don't want unbridled development at the expense of the land and traditional cultures. I believe many of the PRC's conservation efforts are well-founded, but I worry about how the state commodifies nature and ethnic peoples through its top-down authority.

Despite the PRC's puzzling systems of land management and the NGOs' uneven efforts at ecotourism, I still believe Yunnan—and the country as a whole—can develop and implement successful conservation strategies.[17] But China needs to evolve its own brand of conservation, one that blends the country's ancient traditions of working with nature with the smartest ideas from the outside. The central government takes pride in describing China's economic success as "capitalism with Chinese characteristics"; what would a "conservation with Chinese characteristics" entail?

I shouldered my pack and began a long traverse up what I hoped would be the final ridge between me and Lijiang. I crested the grade up into pastureland and there it was—flat agricultural fields and, in the distance, sun glinting off glass and steel. The Lijiang basin. After all the twists in the trail, I could only go forward and down, "forever wandering, a sand gull, winging between the sky and the earth," back to modern China.[18]

The trail soon became a dirt track sloping down through meadows and small patches of corn and sunflowers. Then I hit a new concrete road; the plots grew into fields banked with irrigation ditches, clusters of houses, people on bikes. Looking back for a last glimpse of the Jade Dragon, I saw only green ridges rising into the late-summer sky.

I thought of Lily, Lucy, and Spring, the people working at the eco-lodge, the tale of Peach Blossom Spring, and the lingering question that concludes that famous story: "Wandering in the world, who can fathom what lies beyond its clamor and dust?"

"Is this Suhe?" My question startled a lone German tourist with a large digital camera dangling from his neck. He nodded and pointed down a lane.

I walked a few more blocks and turned a corner into a clamor of construction, whining power saws, crews of men hoisting wood beams, children watching from the shade of spindly young trees. Suhe was no longer a village. The Chinese were replicating Dayan, building another Lijiang old town for tourists.

Chapter 4

Old Mountains, Young Parks

Once a two-inch nail is hammered into wood,
even nine oxen will have difficulty pulling it out.
Chinese proverb

WO HUNDRED THOUSAND villagers live *around* Laojun reserve. That means for every golden monkey I am supposed to be protecting, there are six hundred people!" Dr. Zhou Dequn, the TNC field manager who first warned me to check my American assumptions at the Chinese border, was pacing around his office in Lijiang.

Dr. Zhou was just back from Laojunshan, a remote mountain area home to the highly endangered Yunnan snub-nosed monkey—known to local people as the golden monkey. A little-known upland of broad peaks and narrow valleys spreading across 131,427 hectares (324,763 acres), Laojunshan was proposed as a provincial-level nature reserve in 2000. Then in 2003, the United Nations, with PRC approval, included Laojunshan within the Three Parallel Rivers World Heritage Site.[1]

Nature reserves don't exactly fit China's well-earned reputation for development at any cost, but Laojun is actually one of over twenty-five hundred reserves created by the PRC. In fact, reserves cover almost 16 percent of the country. This is impressive; since 1956 when the first reserve was established, China has protected more land than the United States has designated over the course of 137 years. The growth rate of reserves in China has been rapid as well; more than half date since 1995.

These reserves offer a chance to protect the wildlife, rare plants, and unique ecosystems that make Yunnan so extraordinary. And after seeing the struggles with ecotourism in Nguluko and Wenhai, I was ready for some positive news. So I had planned to visit Laojunshan and then Pudacuo, a new reserve near the northern city of Xiangri-la that was billed as China's first national park. I was eager to discover a path toward conservation success in Yunnan. But so far, Dr. Zhou was dampening my hopes.

"It's just a waste of my time!" He threw up his hands, leaned back in his chair, and looked at me as if I was supposed to have the answers to his problems.

The issue wasn't just people in the reserve—it was the nature of the protected area system itself. While the PRC has done an excellent job of designating land as "protected," it has been far less successful at determining what that designation really means. Simply put, China does not have a comprehensive protected area law. Multiple government policies work at cross purposes, providing no clear direction about exactly how the land should be managed and for what purposes. The central government would like to create new authoritative legislation but no one expects this to happen anytime soon.[2]

Protected-area policies have never been well coordinated nor have they remained consistent over time. The earliest reserves were simply created by central-government fiat with little on-the-ground assessment of what might really work in China. Next came the PRC's 1980s economic and political reforms; reserve designation was decentralized along with the economy. But Beijing provided few rules and less funding. Local governments, operating in a statutory vacuum, were given quotas and that was about all.[3] Finally, in 1994, the central government issued specific guidelines under a Protected Areas Ordinance, resolving some but by no means all of the problems.

One issue the 1994 regulation did not clear up was who managed nature reserves. Nine different agencies—including the ministries for forestry, construction, and the environment—share responsibilities. Just a glance at their names makes it obvious that these bureaus have conflicting goals. It is almost impossible to understand the complexities of the relationship between the State Forestry Administration (SFA), which manages the greatest number of reserves, and the Ministry of Environmental Protection, which manages far fewer areas but retains significant oversight authority over SFA.[4] There are also major disconnects between Beijing's goals and those of China's provincial governments. Plus, there are disagreements between local bureaucracies.

Dr. Zhou explained how each local bureau held a completely different view of Laojun. One supported national park designation, another preferred mass tourism à la Lijiang, and a third wanted to open the area up for large zinc and copper mines.

"Some officials want to shrink Laojun's boundaries rather than work with partners to create a plan we can all live with. Two years ago, TNC sent a letter to the Yunnan provincial government to find out what was going on and we haven't got an answer back yet."

Despite the bureaucratic chaos, TNC had made some progress. Poaching of the golden monkey had significantly decreased and a solid plan for managing the reserve had been drafted.

But Dr. Zhou wasn't satisfied. He stood up and looked down into TNC's office courtyard. On the ground floor, a cluster of blooming orchids spilled from a red-glazed vase. "Right now, nature reserves do not match China's situation. Go to Laojunshan, Ed. Visit Mr. Zhang; he's the top local leader. Go see for yourself."

"Slow down, please. Now." Deb Jin spoke the words forcefully in Mandarin, but she cast a harried glance in my direction. Our driver downshifted his late-model four-wheel-drive Bronco into a lower gear and threw his half-smoked cigarette out the window. Deb, a graduate student pursuing a thesis on the politics of conservation in Yunnan, spoke Mandarin fluently and was translating for us on this trek into the proposed park. Rounding out our party was Luisa Walmsley, one of my students at Prescott College on her first trip to China. Luisa was investigating potential national parks in northwest Yunnan.

I didn't mind the driver's speed; unlike many roads in the mountains of Yunnan, this one didn't feature a sheer drop-off immediately next to the right of way. But there were obstacles.

We skidded to a halt behind a stalled-out truck, severely overloaded with sheaves of freshly harvested wheat. Three Naxi were pounding on the underside of the chassis with a blunt iron bar. The one-lane road was too narrow for passing; we were stuck until the farmers fixed the truck.

Our driver got out, lit another cigarette, and leaned against the hood. Usually, no one has automotive repair tools in rural Yunnan, but we were lucky. After only ten minutes, the farmers gave a shout, climbed back into the cab, and their truck lurched forward.

The road bisected fields where hundreds of villagers were busy harvesting wheat with hand-scythes. From their dress, I could tell they were mostly Naxi and Lisu. The road was lined with walnut trees bearing young green fruit the size of marbles. Low ridges of scraggly pine forest hunched down to the valley floor. Up-valley, early summer haze obscured the high country where Laojun lay.

"Ask the driver how many people he brings up here, would you, Deb?"

"He says only TNC people and researchers. He knows Laojunshan is protected, but he says there isn't anything to see or do. If he wasn't working, he would never come here."

By late afternoon, just as the sun was gilding the bellies of billowing clouds with a deep golden hue, our driver pulled into a lane that led to the farmhouse of Zhang Zhiming. The tidy courtyard, double-wok tile stove, and extra rooms for guests told us that Mr. Zhang was relatively well-off. It was obvious, too, that he had extensive experience dealing with foreigners—he was welcoming and full of authoritative information yet somewhat deferential and reserved. Mr. Zhang also had an impish grin that crinkled the corners of his eyes in the fading light.

"The mountains in Laojun are old, but conservation here is young," Mr. Zhang sipped green tea and looked me in the eye. "My family has been here for two hundred years, but I didn't learn about conservation until 1989 when I guided a scientist to study the golden monkey."

Several years ago, Mr. Zhang had quit herding to guide researchers full time. He also formed a grassroots co-op called the Shitou Guide Association. Made up of twenty villagers, including four women, it provided visitor services for Laojunshan.[5] But despite Laojun's status as an official reserve, the government had provided almost no support for the co-op. Instead, the group received money and training from TNC and the Global Environmental Institute (GEI), a Beijing NGO. The previous year, GEI had given the co-op a loan to build a monkey observation station.

Lack of government funds has always been a problem for nature reserves in China. Since the 1980s, provincial and county governments have been expected to provide financial support, but this has amounted to an unfunded mandate. At times, NGOs like TNC and GEI have stepped in, but often reserve managers have taken to working with private entrepreneurs. Commercial development pays for reserve "protection" but because there is little oversight and less transparency deal making abounds. The resulting hotel, road, and cable-car construction, air and water pollution, and litter have caused considerable damage. Anywhere from 20 to 80 percent of reserve funding comes from such projects; nobody really knows. Some Chinese research has suggested that most of the proceeds from these activities do not fund conservation activities or help support local communities.[6]

I explained to Mr. Zhang that we had come to Laojun to see how Chinese protected areas worked, especially since this particular area might gain national park status and hadn't been developed yet.

"There're two routes we could travel." Mr. Zhang spread a TNC map on the table. "How much walking can you do?"

"We're used to heavy packs," Deb told him. "We can walk all day long."

Mr. Zhang didn't believe us so we made plans to take the easier route. We visited a bit more and then we retired to our rooms. Before turning in, I gazed down-valley into the darkness. Orion was standing on his head in the summer sky. Despite sleeping in a farmhouse with chickens, dogs, and pigs nearby, I couldn't hear a single sound.

Midday found us deep in the mountains climbing up through logged-over forests with little regrowth. Mr. Zhang gestured across the slope. "The state cut all this down in the '80s and '90s. Before logging, there weren't any roads here."

By the time the state's chainsaws were stilled, the upper Yangzi watershed (of which Laojun is part) had lost 85 percent of its old-growth forests.[7] But the PRC took no responsibility. Instead, the government blamed the erosion that led to the destructive 1998 floods on the "backward" land-use practices of Yunnan's ethnic nationalities.

"My turn to deal with the smoke, I'll get more tea." Deb left our room and went over to the shack with the open fire inside, "kitchen" at our camp, which was a collection of herder huts perched at the edge of a huge mountain meadow. Chill mist cut to the bone up here above 3,900 meters (12,800 feet). Mr. Zhang and the co-op porters were cooking dinner, a process that takes hours, with a rock-walled indoor fire providing little heat and less ventilation. What was normal air quality for the guides was borderline asphyxiation for us. So we huddled in our unheated sleeping quarters, taking turns fetching tea to fuel our conversation.

"Do you know what zone we're in?" Luisa asked. She was referring to the fact that many Chinese nature reserves are based on a bull's-eye-like management-zone model borrowed from the United Nations' biosphere reserve program.[8] According to central-government policy, the inner core of many protected areas is inviolate, with people strictly prohibited. A buffer zone surrounds the core and allows for some human use. A third experimental zone provides for a broad range of activities.

"But people are everywhere," Deb observed. "It's like the government regulations were written as if villagers didn't exist in China."

"No one even knows how many villagers live inside reserves," Luisa offered. "I've read anywhere from one to three million *inside* cores and thirty million in and around reserves all over China."[9]

There were other Chinese laws that might help—the PRC has a species protection statute similar to the U.S. Endangered Species Act, and the country signed the biodiversity protection covenants that came out of Rio in 1992. I reminded my companions that Beijing, unlike our government, had also set specific targets to add protected areas to the national system through 2050.

"OK," Luisa conceded, "so China's going to protect a few million more hectares with reserves. I just think it's weird that when they do create a reserve, the local government remains in control instead of the management staff."[10]

"Well," Deb pointed out, "there's no nature reserve *law* in China, no single Park Service, no coordination . . . "

"Let's go, let's go!" Mr. Zhang stuck his head into the room. "Dinner's ready, you better eat a lot, we're going to walk a long way tomorrow."

On the trail early, it didn't take long for the sun to burn the morning fog away. We climbed over a ridge, following sketchy herder tracks past a quiet lake that breathed mist from its mirror-still surface. Tangled gardens of fat-budded rhododendron kept us on a route edging open pasture. Then we climbed a long slope of slippery talus to a pass where the track petered out.

The route was difficult but not dangerous. We tip-toed across a cliff face while balancing on small shelves of rock, rounded a ridge, and entered a centuries-old stand of large trees. The forest was multi-layered: soaring, lichen-draped firs and a subcanopy of treelike rhododendron. Deep centuries of stillness haunted the space between the trees. Snub-nosed monkey habitat.

Like many nature reserves, Laojun was first set aside to protect the habitat of a single charismatic animal, but scientists still don't understand much about the Yunnan snub-nosed monkey. There are twenty wild primates in China, five of which live nowhere else. The golden monkey has the smallest population of all, maybe two thousand animals scattered in fourteen isolated patches. Infrequently encountered below 3,000 meters (9,840 feet), it is the highest-dwelling primate in the world.

No one knows how long golden monkey subpopulations have been isolated. But population genetics and conservation biology suggest that their numbers must rise and reproductive exchange become established between the groups, or inbreeding will edge them further toward extinction.

Mr. Zhang stopped and pointed into the canopy. "The golden monkeys must have old forest because they eat lichens and bamboo for their main foods. They also need lots of habitat so they don't eat everything from one place.[11] The golden monkey is the symbol of Laojunshan."

Listening to Mr. Zhang, I was struck by the scientific and political parallels between the snub-nosed monkey and the northern spotted owl of the Pacific Northwest. Both species are endangered and the subject of environmentalists' attempts to capitalize on their charismatic appeal for use in conservation campaigns. In the United States, ten years passed before the government created an owl conservation plan. In China, after scientists called for protecting the monkey, it took only six years, with TNC helping to broker a formal management agreement.

But while reserves have been around for decades in China, the science behind designing them—conservation biology—is a new field just becoming influential. It takes time to establish a biological basis for protecting nature; after fifteen years of field research, scientists are only now beginning to get a handle on the golden monkey. Even China's most revered animal, the giant panda, has lost some ground and become more isolated since conservation efforts were initiated.[12]

Every biologist working in China is also aware that protected areas alone cannot do the job. Studies suggest that habitat corridors linking animal subpopulations must be created for wide-ranging species like the wild panda and golden monkey. But how can this be accomplished here in Laojunshan across a Balkanized management landscape that frustrates a scientist as even-tempered as Dr. Zhou?

"Laojunshan is still unknown." It was difficult to hear Phoe Yong. The four of us, along with Mr. Zhang and several co-op members, were crowded into a small room at the monkey station. His voice competed with a crackling open cooking fire, blaring satellite TV, and a radio turned up loud.

Phoe was a PhD student at Sun Yat Sen University in Guangzhou who had been hired by GEI to design a trail system for Laojun.[13] The goal was to build a five-day loop for visitors, attracting hikers over the four-month season, maybe three thousand people a year. Mr. Zhang and the guide co-op had done some test treks the previous summer, but it was still a small market in a country where the very concept of recreational hiking was new. And Laojun was less scenic than Tibet, the current tourist hot spot.

"Chinese are like Americans," Phoe commented. "They want to go to lots of places and they don't have much time. But Lijiang is overdeveloped, there's no hope there." In Laojun, Phoe hoped to highlight conservation and environmental education.

He lowered his voice. "The problem here is that the guides aren't modern, they're backward. They have no training. They don't know how to act around foreigners. See how they always eat off by themselves? I don't think a co-op with local people fits the government's plans for Laojun."

Phoe's complaint is echoed by every NGO study conducted over the last decade. Each review portrays not just guides but even reserve managers as poorly equipped to do their jobs. The most recent research shows that only about a third of staff have adequate professional training.[14] Lacking trained managers, it is not surprising that many protected areas don't have solid management plans; if staff do not have the skills to craft them and the government doesn't fund the work, then how can adequate plans be produced?

For our final day in Laojunshan, Mr. Zhang wanted to hike to a ridgetop vantage point where we could see much of the western border of the proposed national park.

"It's very steep, but you people can hike anywhere," Mr. Zhang laughed. Then he broke into his favorite (and only) English phrase, "Let's go, let's go, let's go!"

Everyone took off up the trail, but I lagged behind, revisiting last night's conversation. It was easy to disparage poor villagers' attempts to adapt to the coming tidal wave of tourists, just as one could complain about the government's inadequate policies. After only a few visits to reserves in Yunnan, how could I even begin to grasp conservation in China?

One reason why conservation issues are complex is that nature reserve planning across the developing world has become internationalized.[15] China has so far depended on imported nature reserve models because the PRC has never had the wealth (or political inclination) to create its own. This is sometimes difficult for Americans to grasp, but imagine if significant portions of the environmental work done in the United States were funded and carried out by NGOs based in Germany and Japan.

China welcomes international conservation groups into the

country and these groups collectively deliver tens of millions of dollars to Yunnan. But while NGOs must engage the government, they cannot challenge it. Each group also brings its own agenda—there are biologists, community experts, and donors, each holding a definition of "success" and each learning how to operate in the institutional ambiguity and messiness that is today's China.[16] One lesson everyone learns quickly in conservation work: political expediency is a valuable commodity in the PRC.

A stiff breeze was blowing when I caught up with the group at the top of the climb. Bands of high overcast filtered shadows and sun shafts across the land. Old growth crowned the near ridges; in the distance, patchwork fields and mixed forests stretched west into the spring haze.

"The border of Laojunshan is where you see those fields way over there." Mr. Zhang pointed west. "Right now, the golden monkey is living in the forest below us, only two ridges away."

A zephyr blew across our perch, forcing us to retreat behind a thick patch of blooming rhododendron. "Are the monkeys safe up here? Is Laojunshan large enough?" Luisa asked.

"I think so," Mr. Zhang said. "But Laojunshan must be strictly managed. The government must act, and villagers must act, too."

Keeping up the dialogue among the villagers, the government, and the NGOs was a constant struggle. Some years TNC sponsored environmental education about the golden monkey in local schools, some years they didn't. And while TNC organized a single meeting every year to get feedback from the community, Mr. Zhang argued that more input was needed. But first, everyone needed a common language.

"TNC's been here since 2000, but people are still unclear about what they do," Mr. Zhang smiled. "I've read the plans, TNC's very good at plans, but most villagers don't understand them."

I suggested the co-op could be a good way to bridge the gap between TNC, the villagers, and visitors.

"The co-op may work. You're real hikers and conservationists, but many people in China have no contact with nature. So for success with protected areas, everyone has something to learn." Mr. Zhang chuckled as he stood up. "The problem in China is, you never know what you're going to get!"

Mr. Zhang looked at me steadily. "Laojunshan will be different."

After taking our leave of Mr. Zhang and Laojunshan, we sped north over just-completed highway toward the city of Xiangri-la, gateway to Pudacuo National Park. The country was colder, higher, and drier, composed of big valleys and broad-shouldered mountains. And the people were different; northwest Yunnan is culturally aligned with Tibet.

"Mystic lands and exotic ethnic culture await your visit": I blinked in the bright glare of the windswept valley as a garish color photograph of long-haired Tibetan men on horseback reared into view. Then our car swept past the outsized billboard. Beyond the sign, groups of women wielding hoes worked young barley shoots in a huge basin below snowcapped peaks. Miles ahead at the far end of the valley, I could just make out a cluster of tall buildings.

Xiangri-la is a Tibetan town, at the doorstep to Yunnan's piece of the Himalaya. It's the northernmost place you can fly to in the province; the airport is only nine years old. The city has always been a trading center for the subsistence pastoralists living in the outlying mountains, but not long ago the Chinese changed the town's name from Zhongdian to Xiangri-la in an attempt to lure tourists to this rapidly developing part of Yunnan's "Great Ethnic Culture Province."[17] I hadn't been in Xiangri-la for three years; given the pace of the PRC's Go West policy, that might as well have been three decades.

"Welcome, nice to see you again." With his compact build and lustrous black ponytail, Gezu fits the stereotype of a strikingly handsome Tibetan mountain guide. It had been a year since we had last met in Lijiang, and Gezu's business was booming. He had another client, so his cousin Tsering would guide us through Pudacuo to Nizu village.

"You know the area all around Nizu has just been declared a national park?" Gezu asked. Not only had the village been surrounded by Pudacuo; it had also just become linked to the outside world by a new road.

Tsering stepped forward to shake hands. He was taller than Gezu, with the same handsome face and warm smile. "We'll stay with a family building the first guesthouse in Nizu, but they just started construction so we'll be sleeping in their house.

"There's one issue about the new park," Tsering continued. "They're charging 190 kuai to get in. That's a hundred U.S. dollars for the four of us. It's for the commercial bus tourists; no local could ever pay that much. If you're up for it, we can hike in on a different route, but it'll be harder. You OK with that?"

That was fine with us. We set up a departure time for the following morning, wished Gezu good luck on his trip, and left to buy food for the trek.

Pudacuo National Park is the most recent model for the future of protected areas in China.[18] The 2,000-square-kilometer (772-square-mile) area was a provincial-level reserve until June 2007, when it was declared a "national park." The trouble is, though Beijing has blessed this designation, the central government still hasn't passed any new law to codify basic definitions and standards, which would enable managers to create common ground. Until this occurs, no one in China can really say what a "national park" is.

Much is at stake in Pudacuo. The central government does not want conservation to fail for at least two reasons. First, biodiversity values are high: there are important montane wetlands, rare subalpine lakes, much old-growth forest, and many endangered species. According to surveys conducted by Chinese scientists, 20 percent of plants and 30 percent of all animals in China are found here.

The second reason may be more important. Pudacuo is the government's first full test of the concept of a twenty-first-century national park in China. Visitors cannot drive into Pudacuo; they must travel on natural-gas-powered green busses on new roads that are well-constructed, the best I've seen in China. Bus stops feature solar-powered buildings and composting toilets. Few U.S. national parks have these innovations. Local Tibetan herders living in and around Pudacuo get preferential hiring for jobs in the park.

Pudacuo represents a pragmatic shift away from Chinese policies borrowed from elsewhere that declare nature reserves inviolate; the state is learning that it cannot uphold such standards. Pudacuo's management is also innovative because decisions spring from a partnership between the province, TNC, Southwest University in Kunming, and Deqing Autonomous Prefecture. This structure should be more flexible than the old state-dominated command and control approach, given the complexities of conservation in the PRC.

"The farmer says we can hike up this hill to the next ridge and down the other side to the new park road," Tsering returned from a Tibetan farmhouse with directions. "Then we can catch the green bus to Shudu Lake. I've never done this route before, but once we get to the lake I know the way."

All of us were excited to be walking into new mountains, but the slope, covered with young Yunnan pines and blooming pink and white azaleas, was unremittingly steep. After hours of strenuous off-trail climbing, we found ourselves in open scrubland below a ridge-line summit *lartse* (a Tibetan Buddhist cairn honoring local deities). Snowy ranges sailed across every distant horizon.

"This is just like working for Outward Bound," Deb chuckled. "You take your group out with topo maps and go for it."

"The only difference here is that we don't have maps," Luisa observed.

We turned east into steep fir forest. Some of the larger trees had been cut recently. Tsering explained that they were destined for the new visitor center being built near the park entrance. "The big beams in the lobby will look good for the tourists."

Tsering came to a halt at the head of a rocky chute. "I think the best way down is to go the way they took the logs down. They shot them through this gully and hired villagers to pull them off the sides when the trees got stuck. They used yaks to haul the logs out at the bottom."

Down we went. The gully was steep and deep, a rough channel of eroding stones and soil. Trees along the sides showed fresh scars from the butt ends of hurtling logs. With our heavy packs, the climb down was brutal.

The road was only a mile away, but it took almost an hour to descend 700 meters (2,300 feet). At the bottom, we felt battered, as if we, too, were bruised timbers. We just managed to catch the last park bus to Shudu Lake.

Given the improvisational nature of the first day's route, all of us were looking forward to a less-demanding hike on trails. After a fresh-stewed yak and noodle breakfast, Tsering led us up into fir woods until we topped out at the edge of a huge open alp land at 3,850 meters (12,630 feet). Meadow stretched away for miles, with a jumble of rusty peaks carving the skyline far to the north: the Yunnan-Sichuan border.

We made our way across the highlands. After an hour, we edged off meadows into a young forest of larch trees and then the trail torpedoed deep into a sharp fold in the hills. Altitude, humidity, vegetation—everything telescoped down within a short distance. I didn't have to think about diversity; I could feel it all around me.

"*Ni hao ma?*" Luisa greeted a middle-aged Tibetan woman weaving at a makeshift loom set up in a grassy clearing. The woman smiled broadly; she didn't speak Mandarin, but she gestured for us to sit. Her daughter, shy and studying a schoolbook, sat nearby under the shade of a spreading maple.

"This is their summer camp," Tsering translated. "They have yaks up high and she's taking a break from her farmwork so she's weaving this blanket." The glade was idyllic, birdsong from the canopy, yellow meadow flowers, the soft *whap* of the loom's shuttle, and friendly smiles that transcended several languages.

What if I took a photograph of the woman weaving, or her daughter studying in the shade? How would my pictures be seen by friends back home?

Much would depend on the stories that accompanied the photos. Without context, most people would simply see an ethnic nationality woman making cloth by hand in a mountain meadow and would add their own interpretations—environmental sensitivity, living in harmony with nature, a rustic backcountry life. Being there in person, these were the impressions that welled up in me.

But I did have some context. I glanced from the woman to her daughter. The girl was studying Mandarin, a language her mother would never know. Because of this single fact, the girl's life would be dramatically different. Most Tibetan women in backcountry Yunnan are illiterate; they cannot read or write Mandarin or Tibetan. This family's cash income was probably minimal even by Chinese standards, and they had few choices to change this—hard physical labor as subsistence agropastoralists or menial work at the bottom of the economic scale in Xiangri-la.

Meeting the Tibetan family made me realize that Pudacuo was not only a new category of nature reserve for China; it also gave the Chinese a novel way of relating to nature itself. Instead of protected areas with inviolate cores, national parks welcomed people to come in and enjoy the experience. Like my pictures, however, whether parks better represented the relationships between people and nature in China remained an open question. Just as Americans had a tendency to romanticize Tibetans, poor subsistence farmers would never experience Pudacuo the same way wealthy Chinese visitors did.

From Deb's perspective, locals were being used more than helped by NGO visions of environmental harmony. At her research site up north, the local Tibetan doctors who had knowledge of medicinal plants were called "plant stewards" by TNC. But the doctors didn't want to be labeled as environmentalists.[19] They just wanted better health care, access to their plants, and maybe a village clinic.

Deb was right; the villagers I had met in Yunnan had no prior experience with which to fathom *environmentalist* or *national park*. Most farmers and herders didn't even have a concept of *scenic view*. But if labeling locals as land stewards helped NGOs gain support or financing, what was the harm?

Deb didn't agree. "Tibetans can describe themselves however they please, but I'm talking about transnational environmental NGOs making decisions about Tibetans *for* them. If villagers are just plant stewards, that makes them useful symbols for protecting biodiversity, but it also reduces real people down to some essential category."

"Wait a second," I said. "Didn't you just say transnational? The NGOs call themselves international.

"Who sets their agenda?" Deb replied. "Where does their money come from? *International* means state-to-state. TNC doesn't bring U.S. policy to China and the environmental NGOs working here aren't federally funded. They set their own strategies and the money they use here in Yunnan comes from Caterpillar, Cargill, Bank of America, and Morgan Stanley. That's 'Big Conservation.' That can work, but it doesn't work if the community is neglected."

"Your stories remind me of what the government is doing with Pudacuo," Tsering had been smoking a cigarette, listening to the discussion. "The government's focused on the numbers—tourists, number of trips, park fees, new roads. They're fencing off villages and sacred mountains, closing collective grazing lands, and requiring entrance fees that only outsiders can afford. The government's doing some good things, too, but I don't think the national park is designed to work for everybody."

The rest of the hike through Pudacuo to Nizu revealed striking botanical biodiversity: an old-growth streamside forest with huge poplars and birches, aspen groves, five species of pine, and several blooming orchids.

The mountains were spectacular along the entire route. Nizu was spread out in the upper reaches of a big whitewater river canyon below soaring rock walls that reminded me of a small-scale Yosemite. The village gets a few hundred visitors a year.

The very first house we came to turned out to be our destination— along the building's east wall, rough-peeled logs framed the new guesthouse. Two sprawling pigs guarded the front door.

"They only have enough food for us for tonight, so we'll have to move to the government place in the morning," Tsering informed us. "You folks like snuff?"

The oldest man in the household held out a hollow wild sheep horn tipped with brass fittings—a homemade snuff box. The tobacco mixed with wild herbs was potent and my tiredness melted away. Home-brewed rice liquor soon followed, along with a feast of tsampa (toasted barley flour mixed with water), dried yak stir-fried with vegetables, rice, and lots of beer.

After the feast, I pulled Tsering aside. "How much should we pay them for dinner and the night? They're really poor and incredibly generous."

"In Tibetan communities, it's not good manners to ask directly. In the morning, I'll try to find out, but we might just have to leave something for them."

I thought about all the people living in and around Laojun and Pudacuo; even the Chinese government couldn't count how many there were. But backcountry farmers and herders throughout Yunnan know exactly where they live and who their neighbors are—they depend on these relationships. A new national park wasn't going to replace community lifeways built up over generations. Unless the Tibetans living in and around Pudacuo became more involved in management. And that would require managers to ask some basic questions about people as well as protected areas.

What's a "community"? The answer is complex and varies from one village to the next in Yunnan. But there are several essential ingredients.[20] Every community is located in a specific place that anchors inhabitants to ecosystems. It's impossible to build a guesthouse out of local logs if there aren't any forests nearby; you can grow rice near Laojunshan, but not in high elevation Nizu.

Social structures also define communities. Do you grow your own food, barter, or work for cash in town? Shared values anchor community norms. Is your village for or against road access, state-defined national parks? Do you and your neighbors use money or some other metric to value a festive meal and a night's lodging for guests? Would you want to represent your culture by dressing up as a tour guide on one of Pudacuo's green buses?

People in Nizu may not be well-educated, but they can sense dynamic forces around them and are attempting to adapt. What they lack is a voice in pending decisions and a big-picture view beyond their village. They have no idea how many Chinese tourists are about to descend on Pudacuo National Park and their tiny community.

For their part, NGOs may believe in community-based conservation in theory, but they are still figuring out the practice. NGOs in Yunnan (and in China in general), often find themselves caught between community values, their own norms, and government targets. Most village environmental rules focus on fair sharing and reducing conflicts that stem from using local land, trees, and water. International conservation norms are based on protecting nature, not using it.

And while environmentalists may want to honor local definitions of community, they are acutely aware that biodiversity conservation often demands regional coordination. For example, Tibetan medicinal plant doctors in one village cannot by themselves ensure the survival of any endangered plant whose range spreads across distant lands. All of the wide-ranging large mammals in Yunnan require actions that go beyond any single valley or small set of communities

Another problem is time. Building community conservation takes years in a country where collaborative decision making, transparency, and accountability are rare.[21] Yet roads and powerlines are fragmenting habitat so rapidly in Yunnan that environmental groups often feel pressed to act, whether the community is involved or not.

Of course, Beijing has never based land-use policy on local community values. Villagers had little say about the Nizu road; with the coming of Pudacuo National Park, local government wanted to stimulate the economy and so the road was built. In a one-party state, there are few incentives for the government to share power: elections are rare, opposition groups don't really exist, and transparency is ephemeral at best. Since the 1980s, the government at all levels has almost always said "economic development first, social and political reform later." But in Yunnan and the rest of western China, this means that villages in the deep countryside, often the least likely places to experience economic growth, may also remain the last locations where local officials embrace anything approaching community conservation values.[22]

After saying goodbye to our Tibetan hosts, we packed through Nizu past ripening winter wheat and young potatoes to the government-run guesthouse at the far end of town. After lunch, Luisa and I interviewed Mr. Zhu, an official in the local government.

"People support the Nizu road," Mr. Zhu asserted. "It's not just about the park and tourists. Nizu makes the best butter and cheese in the area, but people have trouble getting them to market. Plus it will take less time to get to the clinic down in Luoji town—there's no health care here in Nizu."

"Do young people return after they're done with school?" I asked.

"Yes, almost everyone comes back, including me. People love Nizu, but we're still poor. The government plans to increase peoples' income 200 kuai every year through the new road and more visitors to the park."

Luisa had noticed the Three Parallel Rivers office next to the village bureau and asked if Mr. Zhu worked with the World Heritage Site program managers. But it turned out Nizu wasn't technically part of Three Parallel Rivers or the new national park. Instead it had been designated an "ecological village," devoted to environmental protection and visitor services. There were new logging restrictions, and Three Parallel Rivers was funding some forest restoration nearby.

"The park is financing more lodging here to help us welcome tourists. Nizu will become a gateway for Pudacuo and Three Parallel Rivers—the ecological village is the future of the countryside everywhere in Yunnan."

The day we left Nizu, our hiking route climbed out of the valley without switchbacks, as if it was designed for stock animals, not human backpackers—which it was. Sweating at the top of a particularly grueling grade, we passed a Tibetan on horseback who muttered something to Tsering in passing.

"What'd he say?" Luisa asked.

Tsering grinned. "He said 'you guys are crazy to walk with such heavy packs, you should hire a mule.'"

The trail led into a canyon shaded by an incredible diversity of trees: cherry, maple, walnut, buckeye, oak, and occasional giant firs. We passed waist-high wild peonies, their silken petals the color of dried blood. I looked up from the flowers—the sound of tinkling bells floated through the forest. Six heavily laden mules tied in a train were headed down the mountain toward Nizu, their hooves striking sparks on the rocky trail. An old Tibetan man smoking a cigar and sporting a neon-pink sash around his waist followed close behind. The caravan clattered past and disappeared.

"What was in those crates?" Deb had worked with pack stock one summer in Idaho.

"Everything you'd need in Nizu that you couldn't grow or make," Tsering replied. "That's how things came in before the road."

We continued up and over the alpine pasture, through dense fir and spruce, and down the mountain on the other side—late in the day, we were back along the new road in Pudacuo National Park. Five minutes later, we were cruising at fifty-five kilometers (thirty-four miles) an hour on a natural-gas-powered green bus with twenty-four Chinese tourists. A guide dressed in Tibetan garb droned into a microphone. The tourists napped. Many sported matching baseball caps, a diagnostic field mark of Chinese commercial tour groups. A few people breathed bottled oxygen, which seemed unnecessary at 3,000 meters (9,840 feet)—unless you had just flown in from sea-level Shanghai.

The bus pulled over at a rest area overlooking a velvet-green yak pasture. I disembarked and shot pictures of the beautifully designed site—interpretive signs in Mandarin, Tibetan, and English, solar-powered buildings, wood-plank trails elevated across moist meadows. No one hit the boardwalk; instead, the visitors crowded Tibetan vendors selling roasted corn, peanuts, and soda. People took photographs of the pasture, the buildings, the vendors, and each other. I felt like I was in Yosemite Valley with a tour group from Los Angeles, minus the oxygen bottles. Then the driver hit the horn, people hustled back on the bus, and we drove away toward Pudacuo's new big-timbered visitor center.

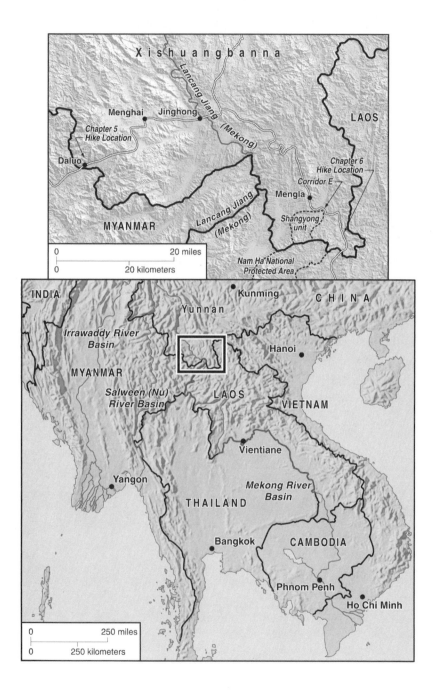

Chapter 5

In the Land of Twelve
Thousand Rice Fields

I live in the upstream and you live in the downstream.
Our friendship flows in the river we both drink.
M. CHAN Y (former Chinese foreign minister)

S WEATING IN THE blistering tropical heat, I slowed my three-speed rental bike and swung off the paved river road down a rough dirt lane. An hour outside of Jinghong, capital of Xishuangbanna Dai Nationality Autonomous Prefecture in southern Yunnan, I was following the Lancangjiang (Mekong River) as it flowed down the length of the province and out into the belly of Southeast Asia.

While the Nujiang turns west into Myanmar and the Jinshajiang twists north and east out into the fertile Sichuan plain, the Lancang cuts due south into Xishuangbanna and then through five countries before it is swallowed by the South China Sea. It is the twelfth-longest watercourse in the world and the most international of China's three parallel rivers.

Tracing the Lancang from northern Yunnan into Xishuangbanna, a traveler passes into a different world. Without leaving the province, you swap snow leopards for elephants and tigers, fir trees for rubber and rice, the Himalaya for the old world tropics. Xishuangbanna's seasonal rain forests are unique, the northernmost extension of tropical Asia in China.[1]

The peoples of northern and southern Yunnan are also very different—none of the ethnic groups overlap. Thirteen nationalities make up over 75 percent of the one million people living in the south, each group with its own language, architecture, and distinctive dress. The Dai in the lowlands with their paddy rice are the largest group, having lived in Xishuangbanna for well over a thousand years. Dai kings controlled Sipsongpanna, the "land of twelve thousand rice fields"; the local rulers were never subjugated throughout all of the Han dynasties until several years *after* the 1949 revolution.[2]

Culturally, geographically, and now economically, Xishuangbanna is a gateway to the rest of Asia—and to the world beyond. While northwest Yunnan may be modernizing under the influence of the PRC's Go West strategy and mass tourism, the south is undergoing radical change as it becomes directly linked to global commodity markets.

Xishuangbanna is in the midst of a profound makeover, driven by its unique position as the main tropical region in China. You can grow crops here that cannot be grown elsewhere. Since the 1950s, the Chinese government has invested heavily in rubber plantations in southern Yunnan, first to feed its political vision of productive workers creating a new socialist order and now to provide tires to the hottest vehicle market in the world.[3] In the last decade, rubber and other commercial monocrops have transformed the region's landscape. The benefits of rubber are obvious to any automobile owner; I wanted to find out the costs.

"Albie, make a left!" I was screened by huge-leaved banana trees, but my partner was close behind. Framed by palms a hundred yards away, the Lancang flowed swollen and muddy from the summer monsoon, the color of café au lait.

"It's good to get off the road, I don't trust Chinese drivers," Albie remarked as we biked down the rutted lane. "I'd rather be in a boat on the river." Well off the beaten track, we pedaled through a narrow crease in the hills into a small valley. The sun blazed down, melting the afternoon into radiant heat haze. Rows of rubber trees stretched away in geometric lines.

Avoiding large puddles, we biked around a bend and a building came into view. A cacophony of shouts and grinding metal rose above a tall fence surrounding some sort of compound. All we could see was a corrugated roof with bands of heat pulsing off metal into the sky. We leaned our bikes against the wall, found a gate, and walked back into the nineteenth century.

The building inside the compound was an open-sided foundry that melted recycled scrap metal. Eight shirtless Chinese workers wearing plastic flip-flops bent to the task. One worker wheeled a barrow of scrap to a huge bucket and dumped his load. The bucket was then winched by hand into a blast furnace where the metal melted down into an orange stew crusted with black slag. Two workers slowly tipped the molten contents by hand into rectangular molds where it bubbled and popped. After the metal cooled, other workers, balancing the molds between stout bamboo poles, carried them out into the yard and dumped the ingots in a glowing heap.

The heat in the yard was insufferable, but the workers smiled at our approach and gave us thumbs up as they continued with their labors. It was too stifling to stick around, so after taking some pictures we retreated to our bikes.

"The forest is gone, but these guys will never lack scrap metal. Did you see what they were wearing on their feet?"

"I guess the government doesn't worry about worker safety standards," Albie replied, "as long as the business adds to the economy."

As we rode back through miles of plantation, Albie spoke aloud what I was thinking. "What about growing food? What about functioning forests? It's always about the lowest price, never about all the social and ecological costs. I just wish you could make a profit from a viable population of elephants."

Rubber trees have played a major role in transforming lowland Xishuangbanna from a wild landscape into a fragmented illusion of "tropical." Between 1976 and today, rubber plantations increased from 1.1 to 20 percent of lands across Xishuangbanna.[4] Rubber is now dominant below 800 meters (2,620 feet), replacing much of China's unique seasonal rain forests. While all types of forest across Xishuangbanna have shrunk since the 1970s, the rain forests have been reduced by some 70 percent.

Ecologically, rubber is a nightmare. Plantations have shredded southern Yunnan, leaving rain forests in fragments. The land has been carved up even *within* Xishuangbanna's "protected" nature reserves. Immediately outside most reserves, there is little natural forest left. Tigers and elephants, two of the most endangered and culturally significant animals in China, no longer maintain viable populations in Xishuangbanna. Yet the government maintains that rubber monocrops are "forests."[5]

Rubber plantations do not exist in a vacuum. Ethnic nationality peoples have been greatly affected by the transition from tropical forests and traditional slash-and-burn swiddens to monocultural cash crops. Since rubber came to Xishuangbanna, many local people have been forced to leave their homes in prime lowland areas and move up into the erosion-prone hills.

The way food is grown has also been transformed. Traditional swidden agriculture requires farmers to wield a complex knowledge of a host of crops in patchy fields, fallows, and secondary forests that also yield wild crops. Rubber, in contrast, is a simple system demanding little but manual labor and an eye toward global markets.

The economics of the transition to rubber are complex. The good news is that villagers' incomes have increased dramatically; rubber can provide a path out of poverty. Rubber is so hot right now that

Chinese entrepreneurs are investing outside of Xishuangbanna in northern Laos and Myanmar where growing conditions are better—and environmental regulations nonexistent. If the price of rubber continues to go up and demand remains high, more plantations will certainly be developed.[6]

The downside is that Xishuangbanna's landscape is more homogeneous and ecosystems less diverse. And rural people are becoming more dependent on global commodity prices over which they have little understanding and less control.

It's unclear whether China's rubber plantations can remain competitive over time. The growing season is already shorter in Xishuangbanna than elsewhere in Southeast Asia; rubber-killing cold snaps occur about every eight years. However, new, hardier rubber strains capable of growing at higher elevations are being tested to solve this problem.

After pedaling through miles of lowland plantation, Albie and I headed into the hills to see how these changes were playing out in southern Yunnan's upland communities. What was happening above the reach of rubber trees? Were slash-and-burn agroecosystems history? To find out, we hired Ainipa, a local Bulang nationality man to guide us along a route into Xishuangbanna's far southwestern interior near the Myanmar border.

From an open bus window, water buffalo in the far distance appeared as dark abstract forms sprinkled across green rice paddies. Up close, I found them to be doe-eyed beasts, with smooth gray skin and rippling muscles. The animal I was touching tilted his hand-carved wooden yoke against the paddock wall.

We had been hiking for an hour in low mountains on village trails through second-growth forest, irrigated paddy, and cornfields bearing ripe cobs. Skirting our first settlement, we came upon a garden of young tea.

"How old are these?" I pointed to the knee-high shrubs.

"Four, maybe five years old," Ainipa replied. "People are planting more and more for cash."

We descended into a wide valley. Local land uses still displayed a rich variety: wet paddy, tea plantation, secondary forest, patches of fruit trees, bamboo thickets, fish ponds. The Lancang watershed has the most diverse array of crops in China. Twenty percent of the world's rice strains originate in the PRC; the majority come from southern Yunnan. But even here, we could see that the land was changing. There were no older forests, not even remnant patches. The tallest trees were less than fifteen meters (forty-nine feet) high. While we were too high up for rubber, I could sense a shift under way as villagers, responding to government policies and market incentives, traded their subsistence swiddens for fixed fields of commercial cash crops.

In late afternoon, we crossed the border of a rice paddy that expanded into a standing-water wetland. At the far end of the marshy ground, sunlight glittered off a gold pagoda. "This is Zanlan village," Ainipa explained. "It has the most beautiful Buddhist temple in the area and we're staying here tonight."

Zanlan, a large Bulang village, sits at the head of a small mountain valley, filling up a hollow in the hills with traditional wood buildings pitched close together. We stayed in a home near the top of the canyon; from the porch, a river of thatched roofs flowed downhill, framed on either side by thickly forested ridges.

We greeted our hostess and her young daughter and went to the market to buy food for dinner. The "market" was a few piles of vegetables spread on tarps on the ground in front of a small dry goods store. An elderly woman, wearing the traditional black headscarf and the beaten silver elbow bracelet of Bulang females, sold us scallions, fresh dofu, Chinese cabbage, and wild oyster mushrooms.

Back at our lodging, our hostess fired up her wok. We thought we were providing supper, but we were in for a surprise—and a treat. The woman stir-fried the dofu with red chilis and stewed the cabbage with the mushrooms. Then she stoked the fire, tossed in garlic and more dried chilis, and then reached into a sack and threw handfuls of pale wasp larvae into the mix. In minutes, we were sitting down to a three course feast featuring one of the most unusual dishes I had ever eaten.

"This is a special dish for guests," Ainipa explained. "There's only a short window when you can gather them." The larvae were delicious, nutty and crisped with garlic. Everyone had seconds except for Albie, who was not at all convinced that immature insects were a delicacy worth savoring.

After dinner, we sat on the raised porch and stared into the darkening evening. We had only hiked here a day but could already feel the effects of growing rural populations and government policies to replace food plants with cash crops. To us, it all felt tenuous, like the ecological slack in the system was being removed.

"I just wonder what's going on that we can't see," Albie pondered. "These ecological changes must be affecting social relations and eroding traditional agricultural knowledge."

"I know the Bulang believe that rice has a spirit, they have festivals around it," I offered. "I wonder if tea or sugar or rubber have souls to them?"

Albie sat back. "The Dai have been Buddhist for twelve hundred years. They used to protect tens of thousands of hectares of forests.[7] And now, in two decades, the forests are gone and we aren't even sure what rice means to them anymore."

We left Zanlan early the following morning, stopping at the temple on the way out of the village. A new road ran above the temple and curved up a hill. Ainipa told us it was only a year old. "There's a government plan for Zanlan. This road goes to where they're building a visitor center for bus tourists. The temple and the village are going to become big attractions. They're thinking about charging an entrance fee."

The morning's hike took us deeper into low subtropical mountains through a patchwork quilt of crops. We saw a few swiddens, but the dominant pattern was obvious: permanent plots had replaced shifting agriculture. Tea plantations were everywhere.

By early evening we were in Manmai, Ainipa's home village. "I know you guys don't like new roads, but you don't have to worry about that here; this is just a farming village. Come and meet my family." Ainipa's father was friendly, but quiet. His wife smiled and queried Ainipa in Bulang about our trip.

The Bulang are a small group in Xishuangbanna, around ninety-five thousand strong.[8] They are midslope farmers who share cultural characteristics with the lowland Dai and upland Akha peoples. The Bulang combine animism with Theravada, the dominant Buddhism of Southeast Asia. They never developed writing; instead, the Bulang have a rich oral tradition in a language related to Thai. Ainipa's mother cannot read or write in Mandarin; his dad can only write his name. Like the other two hundred people in Manmai, the family makes their living as subsistence farmers.

"I went to school here till I was ten," Ainipa replied in response to my question. "Then I went to high school in Jinghong and that kept me away most of the school year, but I could work on my Mandarin and English there. I'm the first person from Manmai to graduate from high school. I want to go to university and that costs around seventy-five hundred yuan [USD 1,071] a year. But my parents don't even earn half that, so I'm doing guide work and saving."

Dinnertime signaled a party to friends and neighbors, and people dropped by to check us out. Besides Albie and me, two village products were center stage: strong tobacco and numbingly potent corn liquor home brew.

After a while, all shyness fell away, with people laughing and asking us questions in rapid-fire Bulang. Raucous conversation, drink, and tobacco smoke filled the house. An older man, his head wrapped in a black scarf, climbed up the ladder and entered the room. He walked right up to me, touched my head, then gestured for me to sit down next to him on the floor. The elder wished to massage my head and legs, Ainipa translated as he stir-fried supper. That was fine with me. The man rubbed me gently and concluded by blowing lightly in my ears. He performed the same ritual with Albie and then sat back, lit a cigarette, and spoke in Bulang to Ainipa.

"He says you're the first foreigners he's ever seen. He's seventy-four and doesn't get out of the village much. He just blessed you and wants you guys to have a good time with us."

So we smoked more local tobacco rolled up in corn husks till I got so dizzy I almost fell down the ladder exiting the house in search of fresh air. No one went to bed early that night.

It was pouring rain the next morning as we said goodbye and hiked back into young forest. We climbed high, tracking a network of ridgetop trails through cornfields and what Ainipa called "dry rice."

The hike was short, which helped us deal with the downpour. By early afternoon we were in Manlin, another poor Bulang village. Ainipa steered us to the local tea factory so I could interview the manager about his business.

There's a Chinese saying: "Seven things in the house: firewood, rice, oil, salt, soy sauce, vinegar, and tea." Yunnan has a millennia-long tea tradition; it is the only place in China where the glossy-leaved shrub grows in the wild. The region produces eighty-six thousand tons of *Camellia sinensis*, the third most of any province in the country.[9]

The tea factory wasn't much—a long open-sided building with few lights and lots of floor space. "You've come at a good time, we're harvesting," Manager Wang said.

"How much do you process?" I inquired.

"Between 32,000 and 42,000 kilograms [35–45 tons] a year. It all goes into *pu'er* [a fermented black tea that is highly prized on the international market]."

As we were talking, a woman entered the factory's courtyard, a woven basket full of shiny leaves on her back. Mr. Wang spoke to her brusquely and she lowered the basket onto a scale. After weighing, the load was dumped on the floor, and a worker quickly pawed through the leaves, assessing quality. He spoke to Mr. Wang, then returned to his work sorting dry leaves into different grades. Mr. Wang peeled a few bills off a thick roll and paid the woman. She hoisted her empty basket and walked back out into the drizzle.

"It takes three to four hours to fill a basket, about seven kilos [fifteen pounds] is the average," Mr. Wang explained. "But people here are lazy. Not many bring in more than one basket a day."

Mr. Wang gave us a tour but there wasn't much to see. Several huge woks fired by bottled gas were used to toast the leaves. A heated drying room finished the process. After a few minutes, we shook hands and left to find our night's lodging.

The rain had ceased and the village was wreathed in clouds. We stopped by a man selling snacks from an open window in his house and bought some stale cookies.

"No one's getting rich picking tea at ninety cents an hour, Albie, but that's better than the urban minimum wage.[10] I bet people don't pick many baskets because they've got more important things to do."

Albie shrugged. He didn't see anyone in the village except Mr. Wang making enough profit from tea to send their kids to middle school. "There's not even a primary school here, right Ainipa?"

"That's true." Ainipa bit into a cookie. "Tea is a good thing, but I don't like what it's replacing, and that's food." He also didn't like all the fertilizers and herbicides being used on the cash crops.

"Don't you guys see where this is going?" Albie crumpled a cookie wrapper. "The global market's driving all these changes and the government is happy to watch it happen. Down in the lowlands, they protect a few nature reserves and promote rubber everywhere as if conservation was some kind of random exercise. Up here, they undermine the one food-growing system that's ever worked in these mountains, and villagers have no choice.[11]

"If Ainipa is the only person with a high-school degree, what are most villagers' chances for success in the cities? Meanwhile, you've lost your forests, knowledge of swiddens, and your food security.

"This is going on all over southern Yunnan, the Mekong, Southeast Asia, all over the world. It's all about the China price, because you and me and everybody else wants it as low as possible."

🐉

Twenty-four hours later, we were descending a curving ridge toward Myanmar. We broke out of old fallows into emerald rice. The air was languorous and paddies curled away in sinuous waves following the line of the land. Reentering forest, the path shrank to nothing, a dark line through dense growth. This was cobra habitat; I took every footstep on faith, following Ainipa as he sped down the hill.

Then we were back in rubber. Regimental gray trunks stretched away as far as I could see, and that was it: few other plants, little birdsong, just ghost trees growing in the open air.

Stopping at one tree, I touched my finger to the sticky liquid oozing from collectors' cuts. Tasting the bitter latex, I saw the tires on my pickup truck back home. I remembered the Chinese foundry men melting rebar. I heard my tea kettle whistle as the water boiled just before I poured it over dark green leaves, and I pondered the mysterious transformations at the heart of people living in the world.

We jumped a concrete drainage ditch, walked into a village, and caught a bus to Jinghong. Albie was headed back to the United States, Ainipa to Jinghong to fill out a school loan application while he waited for another group to guide. I was going to visit the place in Xishuangbanna where tropical forests were making their final stand.

Chapter 6

Into the Great
Green Triangle

To raise a tiger is to bring trouble upon oneself.
Chinese proverb

FROM MY PERCH thirty meters (ninety-eight feet) in the air, I could barely see the forest floor beneath me or the sky above. I was surrounded by a tangle of leaves and limbs. Wrapped in a cocoon of steel cables and nylon mesh, I shuffled slowly along a pathway strung between small platforms straddling giant trees. Near Mengla in southern Xishuangbanna, this nature trail is the ultimate tree fort of any child's fantasy. The translation from the Chinese captures it well: "Aerial Walkway between Sky-Towering Trees." There is no other trail like it in all of China.

And there is no forest in China like the tropical seasonal rain forest protected in the Mengla unit of Xishuangbanna National Nature Reserve. Sky walking gave me the perspective of a gibbon cruising through the treetops. It also allowed me to see beyond this particular protected stand out into the greater landscape where the rain forest has disappeared. From a gap in the canopy I caught a glimpse to the west outside of the reserve; all I saw were rubber trees marching in rows to the ridgetop and beyond.

Since a scientific paper published in 2007, no peer-reviewed update has appeared to track how fast rubber is replacing rain forest in Xishuangbanna. The government released the figure of 166,666 hectares (411,840 acres) of plantation lands in 2005, but a 2008 Reuters news release quoted a number more than double that amount, concluding that "the real figure may be much higher."[1]

I had witnessed plenty of rubber on previous trips to Yunnan; this time, I wanted to explore the government-supported biodiversity corridors. These thin green linkages offer the only alternative to the wholesale destruction of tropical Xishuangbanna.

The Biodiversity Corridor Initiative was launched in 2005, the brainchild of Greater Mekong Subregion (GMS) policy makers at the Asian Development Bank. For the bank, it is a visionary project with two mandates: to "restore ecological connectivity and integrity in a selected set of important biodiversity areas" while "improving livelihoods of peoples living in and around the biodiversity conservation corridors." The thinking was that if the GMS was going to become a Southeast Asian economic powerhouse with transnational highways, rubber farms, and hydropower dams, then ecosystems would also need to be protected. Five countries had established five pilot corridors in key regions across the GMS from Yunnan to Thailand.

I wanted to see what this experiment looked like in southern Xishuangbanna. Like pearls that a jeweler forgot to string together, five subunits of Xishuangbanna Nature Reserve sprawl across 230 kilometers (143 miles) from Myanmar to Laos. When the PRC set aside the reserve twenty-nine years ago, the majority of land between the pearls was not yet plantation. Today, Chinese biologist Li Hongmei and her colleagues describe the reserves as "virtual islands" in a sea of rubber with "little or no appropriate habitat connecting them."

Functional biodiversity corridors could change all this. The Ministry of Environmental Protection in Beijing and the Yunnan and Xishuangbanna environmental protection bureaus have already signed agreements to support the corridors.

And there's more. By 2016, if the pilot corridors prove successful, they could serve as a template for regional transboundary land management across the entire GMS, providing an international model of how to sustain economic development without compromising biodiversity protection.

Corridor E, the smallest pilot corridor in the entire plan at a mere 2,471 hectares (6,105 acres), would link together two of the larger pearls in southern Xishuangbanna where China dips down far enough to be surrounded on three sides by Laos. Corridor E was where I wanted to go. But not because of its size.

"The only hope for tigers in Xishuangbanna is to make a serious conservation effort in Nam Ha reserve in Laos," Dave Smith emphasized to me, "because that is where most of the contiguous forest habitat is." Smith, a wildlife biologist at the University of Minnesota who has studied tigers in Nepal and Thailand for many years, is working with a Chinese team to keep the Indochina tiger alive in Yunnan. No one knows how many cats still prowl the border region, but in May 2007 Feng Limin, a doctoral student from Beijing Normal University, took a camera-trap photo of a female tiger fording a stream in Shangyong Nature Reserve on the Yunnan-Laos border.[2]

This is where Corridor E comes in—it would connect Shangyong with the rest of Xishuangbanna's reserves to the north. To the south, Shangyong is already contiguous with Nam Ha National Protected Area in Laos (see map, page 82).

On the ground, the boundary between China and Laos is poorly marked, in deep forest. Most important for tigers and the other species that depend on Southeast Asia wildlands, Nam Ha is large. At 222,400 hectares (549,560 acres), it stretches from Yunnan fifty-five miles south into Laos, one of the biggest protected areas in subtropical Indochina. If diminutive Corridor E becomes healthy habitat again, then China's most revered animal might be able to reestablish a viable population.

Corridor E is critical, and not only because of tigers. Asian elephants could also use this linkage to move back into their former northern ranges. Altogether, the Nam Ha wildlands in Laos and in Shangyong Nature Reserve in Xishuangbanna provide habitat for at least seventeen mammal species on China's national Red List of endangered animals.[3]

An additional part of the plan would reconnect Xishuangbanna's fragmented landscape. Looking forward to 2012, Chinese scientists in cooperation with conservation staff in Laos and Vietnam, hope to lay the groundwork for a truly transnational system of linked reserves: the Great Green Triangle. If the necklace containing all five pearls of Xishuangbanna Nature Reserve were to be successfully restrung with Nam Ha in Laos added as a sixth pearl, only 30,000 additional hectares (74,130 acres) would be needed to create another linkage from Yunnan due east across far northern Laos to bring in two additional protected areas lying on the Laos-Vietnam border. This would create a Great Green Triangle of wildlands, by far the largest protected area system in Southeast Asia, Alaskan in scale at 1,189,400 hectares (close to 3 million acres).

For an area intended to shelter wildlife, I found Corridor E extremely easy to visit. In fact, thousands of travelers pass through Corridor E each month; Route 3, China's newly built transnational highway linking Kunming with Bangkok, runs through the corridor on its way to the Laotian border and points south. Route 3 is the centerpiece of economic development in this part of the GMS.

Looking out a bus window at eighty kilometers (fifty miles) per hour, I noticed rubber, secondary forests, and patchy fields of corn. Sixty percent of Corridor E remains forested, good news for tigers and elephants. There are also plenty of people; eight villages with some 2,300 residents.[4] People living in and around reserves are the norm throughout China. Route 3 only makes management harder; how are large animals supposed to cross busy highways?

Despite the inherent conflict, Corridor E does offer some hope that wildlife and people can coexist. Dr. Hu Huabin of the Xishuangbanna Tropical Research Garden is working to create a functional conservation landscape; in two short years, he has already made Corridor E a healthier place for local villagers. Farmers have helped to demarcate corridor boundaries on the ground. There is a new source of small loans and credit set up in each village. Multiple workshops have been held to solicit peoples' ideas on how to replant formerly forested areas with tree crops that could also provide cover for migrating mammals. An agroforestry nursery has been established. To better understand how animals might move through Corridor E, Dr. Hu is monitoring elephants and gaur, a large, wild cow that is prey for tigers.[5]

In May 2008, Dr. Hu received a letter from the prefecture government that officially designated Corridor E as the newest protected area in Xishuangbanna.

After scoping out Corridor E but unable to secure a permit to hike into Shangyong reserve, I found myself one of eight passengers along with six cases of beer and several sacks of rice bouncing in the back of a packed *tu luo ji* (tractor) headed for the Han village of Mengyong.

Not too far from Corridor E, Mengyong lies in a small river valley just below Xishuangbanna's eastern border with Laos. Mr. Luo, my interpreter, had a friend living there and knew that I wanted to survey how the ongoing advance of rubber in the lands surrounding Corridor E might affect the success of the pilot project. Mr. Luo also promised access to uncut primary forest, though I knew it was located outside any reserve and therefore not strictly protected.

"I hope you're prepared to push," Mr. Luo commented as we negotiated another mud pit. The recent rains had torn up the road.

I wrestled a rice sack back into an upright position and then looked around. Most of the watershed we were bouncing through was new rubber plantation. Our tractor was overloaded and the road offered no respite. The track was little more than short stretches interrupted by morasses. The journey was brutal; it took two hours to travel ten kilometers (six miles). At least when we jumped out to push, the knee-deep mud cooled everyone down in the late-afternoon heat.

When we arrived, the sun was slanting deep shadows across the curving rice paddies surrounding Mengyong. Above the small cluster of houses, a huge moon lifted above the wooded eastern ridge where China met Laos.

Mr. Wang, the villager guiding tomorrow's hike, eyed me skeptically as we drank tea after supper and made plans. "I guess you're strong enough to do this hike with us," he cracked a grin. "We've never had a foreigner visit Mengyong before. There's nothing here to see."

But for me it was enough to see the rubber that was devouring the landscape. Mr. Wang explained that the plantations were only a few years old—most of the area around Mengyong would have been counted as "rain forest" in the most recent scientific study of the area.

Five years earlier, the valley had been thick with large trees. Then government laborers cut the forest down and burned it, hand-digging the slopes into terraces for the rubber. Mr. Wang wasn't mourning the loss. "We did the planting. We do all the work from now on, and then we'll sell the sap to the state and get rich in a few years. I'll be able to build a better house, maybe buy a car."

"The road's pretty poor," I remembered the afternoon's uncomfortable journey. "So how . . . "

"The road'll be paved in two years," Mr. Wang interrupted.

When I asked about changes since the forest had been destroyed, he admitted that less corn was grown now that villagers spent more time working the plantation, but he maintained that rice still yielded surpluses. He also allowed that the climate was warmer and water supplies had decreased.

"What about forest animals?" Mr. Luo asked.

"Well," Mr. Wang measured his thoughts before responding, "there's still bear and monkey near the border. But the hunting's not as good as before."

"You hunt?" I was surprised. "What about the government ban?"

"We still hunt. People hide their rifles when the government comes around. The fine is five thousand yuan [USD 700], too much for anyone to pay, so we're careful. Maybe we'll find animals on the hike tomorrow."

The following morning before the sun crested the border ridge, we were headed into the hills. We crossed the river and meandered through paddy interspersed with dry plots crowded with soybean plants. After twenty minutes the slope steepened and we entered young rubber. The trees were planted on narrow terraces that broke the steep hillsides into a series of risers, as if the ridge had been reconfigured into stair steps for giants. In gullies too steep to plant, the charred remains of the most diverse forest in China lay in twisted piles of trunks and branches.

We climbed upward, terrace after terrace. Then it was dark and cool. A green canopy of buttressed trees blocked the sun and the smell of water thickened the air: uncut rain forest. Just out of reach, a brown and white butterfly bigger than my hand floated by. Unseen insects drilled the air with metronomic clicks.

We slid into a wet ravine and the path became a stream. Walking in water, we angled upward past small cascades and huge-leaved wild bananas. Mr. Wang handed his ancient rifle over to his neighbor, Mr. Ang, and pulled a machete from his pack. "From here, it's very steep and there's no stream or trail. Be careful to follow me."

Mr. Wang grabbed a clump of bamboo and swung up the slope between the streams, making a mockery of the angle of repose. Everyone fell in behind. For the next hour, we labored upward, slipping on the steep ground and hoisting ourselves over trunks and branches. The trees shrunk in stature, and I recognized subtropical montane forest. We were well above 1,000 meters (3,280 feet).

Laos greeted us at the top of the ridge in the form of a faint track through dense forest that even Mr. Wang couldn't find at first. Five minutes down the path, he stopped and pointed at scruffed up dirt and leaves.

"Bear," he grunted. "But it's an old track, he's gone."

There was a break in the canopy eastward, but summer haze obscured the view. Using its yard-long barrel as a sightline, Mr. Ang pointed the rifle toward Laos: "See? Away out there—plantation."

Squinting down the length of the gun barrel, I could just make out a clearing in the green forest blanket maybe seven kilometers (four miles) distant, new plantations marching up toward the ridge from the opposite direction. The border ridgetop was state forest, not linked to any reserve but off-limits to logging. For now, it remained intact (except for the illegal hunting) and still offered a solid chunk of healthy habitat.

"The government says there won't be any more plantation on our side." Mr. Wang stubbed out a cigarette and rose to move on. "We can still get fuelwood and some logs for construction from this forest, but that's it."

The tread turned into a trail as we walked south, one foot in Laos and the other in China. Up here, nobody needed a Laotian visa.

At a low gap under tall trees, we passed a little-used camp festooned with sheets of cast-off plastic, a rotting rubber boot, and several spent rifle shells. "Smugglers' camp," remarked Mr. Wang. You couldn't blame them for littering; the nearest trash collection was at least sixty-five kilometers (forty miles) away.

After another half an hour downhill, we broke out of cool forest into an open furnace—young rubber planted on steep slopes near 1,200 meters (3,940 feet). The plantation contoured all the way down to Mengyong shimmering in the distance. This plantation was clearly *liang chao*, Mandarin for "two exceeds": too high and too steep for the standard variety of rubber to flourish.

I asked Mr. Wang if he planted a different type of rubber up here. "No, the only choice we had was how much land we wanted to work, and many people took on a lot. High or low is no big deal; what matters is our income."

Back in Mengyong that evening, we celebrated the Autumn Festival with Mr. Wang and his wife and many friends and neighbors. For these poor farmers, the food was plentiful—red chili dofu, braised squirrel, fresh bamboo shoots with ginger, chicken blood stew and bean sprouts, and a special dessert of sugary sticky rice. Beer and home-brewed corn liquor flowed freely.

Late in the night, I stumbled out of the cement-block kitchen and looked up. The border-ridge rubber plantations glowed eerily in full moonlight. This is the new Xishuangbanna landscape, the matrix surrounding Corridor E and the nature reserves, made over by the state to produce rubber for tires and cash for villagers. But the reality isn't win-win; water tables are dropping, less food is being grown, and the price of latex (and villagers' future incomes) will rise and fall with the global economic tides.[6] Neither monkeys nor Indochinese tigers have much use for rubber. They will leave Yunnan, fade south into Laos, into their Nam Ha stronghold, and wait for better times, or . . .

Plantation under moonlight—standing in the soft night air, I squinted south down-valley in the direction of the Great Green Triangle wildlands that flowed across that distant border. Compared to Xishuangbanna, northern Laos is lower in elevation and less developed. Land is cheaper, people are poorer, and the government is weak. China is strong, wealthy, and has a great appetite for rubber-tired automobiles. How likely is it that lands in Laos will protect China's endangered animals?

Laos could be a saving grace for Indochina tigers. The cats are getting hammered throughout their dwindling global range. Maybe three thousand to five thousand animals remain alive in the wild, and almost every population is plummeting.[7]

China is no exception. The State Forestry Administration says that there are no more than fifty wild Chinese tigers, far below a viable population size. Dave Smith estimates that sixteen cats may call the Xishuangbanna borderlands home. He is currently advising Chinese biologists as they complete the first assessment of Yunnan tigers' range requirements and prey base.

Smith's work is timely. Indochina cats require plenty of habitat.

Tigers also need healthy populations of prey, but plantation lands are not useful to the wild deer, wild pigs, and guar upon which the cats depend.[8]

Beyond the basics of food and habitat, tigers in Yunnan have three additional needs. The first is Corridor E. Managing for connectivity will help tigers, but such planning also must provide for people living in tiger habitat. This is no simple task—tigers are the only large carnivore that regularly prey on humans. The Chinese revere the cat as the most potent of all animals, but this is easier to do while drinking black-market tiger-bone wine in Jinghong than it is to do walking home from work through tropical forest in fading evening light.

The Great Green Triangle is the second requirement for a healthy future for Indochinese tigers in Yunnan. If all the corridors in the PRC's plan function well and weave Xishuangbanna Nature Reserve back together again, habitat will be available for anywhere from 63 to 212 animals, not necessarily enough for long-term viability but still a solid start. Only by extending corridor connections east into Vietnam and south into Nam Ha in Laos to support all three sides of the Great Green Triangle will tigers have a fighting chance over the long term.

Tigers must benefit from local and regional management in Yunnan and its immediate neighbors, but the cats also need help globally. Tiger populations have declined precipitously—between 1997 and 2006 alone, the animals lost 41 percent of their global habitat. International trade in tiger parts and products was first restricted in 1975, but poaching remains the other major factor in the tiger's decline. Since the mid-1990s, the price of a tiger skin on the black market has increased twenty times.

China is the number one market for illegal wildlife products (the United States is number two), and the government has worked hard to eliminate this trade. But tigers need more. In June 2008, a month after Chinese authorities declared that Asian big-cat skins were not being sold on the black market, undercover investigators in China found one whole tiger skin along with twenty-six skins of two endangered leopard species. If China and the international community do not create and enforce tougher measures against the USD 10 billion illicit wildlife trade, conservation projects like Corridor E and the Great Green Triangle will end up protecting habitat devoid of animals.

Nam Ha: I had read about the southern leg of the Great Green Triangle. The reserve is the fourth-largest subtropical forest protected area in northern Indochina. In about 20 percent of all Great Green Triangle lands, eighteen endangered species call Nam Ha home, including tigers, bears, leopards, Asian elephants, macaques, and gibbons. There is habitat for almost three hundred birds, the highest avian diversity in the region.[9]

As in China, there are thousands of hill people living in and around Nam Ha, but their impacts on the reserve have traditionally been minimal. Hard against the Yunnan border, in the Laotian backwater northern province of Luang Namtha, Nam Ha was a classic example of a wildland core located in a region where a great diversity of local peoples scratched out a meager subsistence living.[10]

No more. Rubber has come to Luang Namtha. Before 2003, there were less than 1,000 hectares (2,470 acres) of plantation throughout the province. Five years later, rubber trees marched across a minimum of 16,000 hectares (39,540 acres). Or maybe they have been planted on 20,000 hectares (49,420 acres)—there is no accurate assessment.[11]

As in China, land tenure in Laos is contested: community, state, and private land boundaries remain unsettled. Unlike the PRC, Laos is one of the world's poorest as well as poorly managed countries: local government is severely understaffed and underfunded, and there is a general lack of accountability. There are reports of rampant corruption and cronyism on both sides of the border.[12]

Some of the new rubber plantations are inside Nam Ha National Protected Area. How could this be? Nam Ha has been a national-level nature reserve under Laotian law since 1993. Illegal deforestation rates would have to more than double to destroy Nam Ha. Off the record, one of my contacts who has worked in the area for ten years estimated that before the end of 2008 from 1 to 3 percent of the reserve had already been cut, burned, terraced, and planted. He admitted that "Nam Ha ranks very low on the province's priority list."[13] Another anonymous source was quoted in the *Asian Times* saying that "Nam Ha will be gone in ten years."

Nam Ha's fate is uncertain, and a glance at newly signed plantation contracts for the matrix of lands surrounding the reserve is sobering. Rubber concessions negotiated with Chinese investors already total anywhere from about 200,000 to 500,000 hectares (494,210 to 1.24 million acres).[14] It is impossible to track specific locations or the types of land to be converted.

Rubber is the largest driver of land use in northern Laos, but it is not the only force for change. Add up all the acres in just-inked contracts for food crops bound for China— corn, sugarcane, and cassava—and another 117,000 hectares (289,110 acres) come into production.[15]

The scale of land transformation on the Laos-Yunnan border is staggering. From Luang Namtha Province's total area, subtract Nam Ha and other protected lands and you are left with around 600,000 hectares (1.48 million acres). For the new contracts for rubber and food monocultures, the acreage ranges from an almost-certain 319,000 hectares (788,270 acres) up to more remaining land area than the province contains.

This arithmetic undercuts the future viability of most large mammals in the region. The best-case scenario for Nam Ha is that it becomes another wildland island surrounded by a sea of plantations with little to no conservation value. The worst case is that we will no longer be able to distinguish the island from the sea.

Chinese investment is the engine driving this wholesale transformation. If the PRC needs more rubber (and corn, and cane, and cassava) and Xishuangbanna has already been made over, then Laos is the nearest, cheapest, and least regulated place to go. The northern Laotian landscape is being transformed into one vast rubber farm in less than ten years. The same transition took fifty years in Xishuang-banna.[16]

There is some good news. Opium production in these borderlands is down. And, just as in Yunnan, local villagers have profited from rubber. Rural household incomes are up and poverty is fading. Future benefits, however, are uncertain for the same reasons I discovered in Mengyong—with an additional Laotian twist. There is a huge mismatch between rubber work and the local labor pool. In five years or so, when the scale of plantation harvests really begins to take off, there simply will not be enough people in all of northern Laos to harvest the latex. Where will the laborers come from?

Before I traveled Route 3 through Corridor E south to the border and gazed across the line toward Nam Ha, I believed that Asian Development Bank efforts to blend a major highway with biodiversity conservation corridors held some promise. Then I walked the plantations and forests, listened to villagers, read documents and NGO reports, and crunched contractual acres of rubber trees.

And I remembered where I was: in China at the boundary where the Lancang becomes the Mekong and morphs again through the language of banks and bureaucrats into the Greater Mekong Sub-region. In the GMS, economic development and interstate highways are the primary goals in all policy documents; biodiversity corridors are "pilot projects." Route 3 was funded at the rate of USD 90 million. Through 2008, all five of the biodiversity corridors have received USD 2 million. Plus, threats to biodiversity are found not just around but also within the corridors. Yet every GMS government has signed an Asian Development Bank document to protect them.[17]

Two forces in the GMS appear resistant to reform: weak national environmental regulations and the power of money. Five of the six

GMS countries have national biodiversity action plans, but they are "paper thick, action limited." The Cambodian, Laotian, and Thai plans are an average of six years old but they have never received funding. Vietnam had no approved biodiversity protection framework until mid-2009 and still has no environmental impact statement process. Myanmar, the largest and least developed Southeast Asian country, has nothing at all.

Yet development funds are flowing out of China and Yunnan down the Lancang and into the Mekong Basin. The two historical barriers to this movement, insufficient capital and poor roads, have been removed. In 2010, investment monies are easily available, new interstates shunt goods and services all around, local villagers bank their futures on rubber, and no GMS government appears willing to do much to enforce current environmental regulations. But how much regional trade can tigers and elephants stand?

A Han proverb says, "To raise a tiger is to bring trouble upon oneself." This isn't a warning about the danger of carnivores but about the future consequences of present actions. Despite the biodiversity corridor pilots, the Asian Development Bank's number one priority is to stimulate regional cross-border trade. By 2012, China's goal is to double its economic trade with Laos, Vietnam, and Myanmar.[18] Whatever the fate of the Great Green Triangle and the tigers and elephants of the borderlands, the PRC doesn't plan to stop there.

Chapter 7

The Dragon Meets the Angry River

When you break ice, the water beneath will also move.

Chinese proverb

WHEN I FIRST VISITED Yunnan and its three parallel rivers, my main focus was water. The rivers provide water and water is life. From my perspective, keeping the rivers flowing was paramount, and I saw the dam moratorium as a tentative sign that Beijing might be inching toward my way of thinking. I had yet to fully grasp the power of China's economic currents. My visits to the Nujiang up north and to Xishuangbanna's southern borderlands had shown me that, despite some efforts at conservation, development remained the national priority. Everywhere I went, water was being transformed from a commons into a commodity.

Of course, I wasn't wrong about the fundamental necessity of water and the rest of Earth's resources. Commerce cannot change the laws of the universe, and if its mountains and rivers are exhausted, even the Chinese dragon will not be able to sustain unending growth. But I hadn't seen a plan that could counter the relentless deforestation, pollution, and sapping of rivers that was taking place in Yunnan and throughout the country. One thing was clear: almost all of China's conservation and development issues have global roots. To understand them, I would have to do what the Lancang does: leave China and flow downstream into the Mekong Basin. I needed to go beyond visiting poor villages in Yunnan to surveying one of the world's fastest-growing economic regions.

Yet even this broader exploration had to begin with water in China. I started by attempting to visit the newest dam in Yunnan just outside of Jinghong. I had seen pictures of the dam—in a photo two years old, it was still low, squatting across the breadth of the Lancang like some bulked-up concrete animal. But a visit proved impossible; I was stopped at a police checkpoint well before the construction site. The guards weren't smiling, so I turned back toward town.

Jinghong is the third and newest dam in the Lancang's planned hydropower cascade. Upstream from Jinghong and due in 2013, Xiaowan dam will be iconic, featuring a massive wall some 300 meters (984 feet) high and producing 4,200 megawatts of power, second in size only to the famous Three Gorges facility on the Yangzi River in central China.

Yunnan already supplies 10 percent of China's hydropower. But the province holds the potential to more than double that amount. Besides the Nu, the PRC has plans for eight dams all together on the Lancang as well as at least twelve dams on the Jinshajiang (upper Yangzi). These new dams would generate 100,000 megawatts, about as much power as all U.S. dams combined.[1]

Why all this hydropower capacity? The answer might appear simple. China burns more coal than any country in the world and the resulting air pollution is dreadful. Every year, at least four hundred thousand Chinese, the population of Sacramento, California, die from toxic air. Clean hydropower offers a partial solution to China's air-quality issues, and the country's carbon footprint would also be reduced.

After these plain facts, however, the question "why dams?" turns political.

I had already discovered that the PRC plans to ship Yunnan-produced energy to eastern China, to use Go West hydropower to "go east." The PRC also wants to export power and political influence into Southeast Asia. I couldn't visit the entire region, so I asked around, made connections, did some research. This is what I found.

🐉

Leaving Yunnan, the Lancang forms the border between Laos and Myanmar. Then it bends east and south, picking up Thailand, Cambodia, and finally, Vietnam, where it sinks into a great delta sump. This is the Greater Mekong watershed, or, as it's defined economically by banks and bureaucrats, the Greater Mekong Subregion.

All of Xishuangbanna's waters gather downstream in the GMS—there are 70 million people living there. Forty million depend on the protein from fish they pull from the lower Mekong. In fact, more freshwater fish are caught here than any other place in the world.[2]

Fish are creatures of floods and flows. Standing on the banks of the Lancang, flow appears simple: I see moving muddy water, the sheer bulk of a big river doing its daily work.[3] What I can't see: organic sediments and dissolved nutrients, the reproductive and migratory behavior of aquatic animals, and the patchy distribution of all these facts of river life between shallows and shoals, from eddies to the mainstream.

I have never witnessed the Lancang at flood stage, but every Southeast Asian river responds to the pulse of the seasonal monsoons. The alternation of wet and dry periods means distinct high and low flows, and both fish and people have adapted accordingly. Every wet season, the Mekong spreads beyond its banks and inundates 84,000 square kilometers (32,433 square miles), an area about the size of the state of Maine. Aquatic lifecycles are driven by these hydrological pulses. For many fish, high flows mean feeding and spawning, while low flows signal upstream migrations. For Mekong farmers, floods bring sediments and nutrients that replenish floodplain gardens.

Now imagine immense shadow structures, a host of huge dams undergirding a future regime that wild rivers cannot tolerate: a power-shed.[4] Dams by their very presence reduce flooding, smooth out the difference between dry- and wet-season flows, trap sediments in reservoirs, and change water temperatures. Powershed management is not focused on the biological requirements of river dwellers; it is geared to guarantee that dams generate cheap electricity. Virtually every expert expects the coming hydropower cascades to affect most GMS inhabitants, from fish to fishers. To what degree remains unclear.

There are two reasons for this uncertainty. First, no hydropower cascade on any Yunnan river is fully operational yet. With only three out of eight dams built on the Lancang, however, dry-season flows are significantly lower.[5] Second, and more revealing, no scientist, individual country, or regional government body has modeled the consequences of the Lancang's looming powershed and its impact on livelihoods when *all* the dams are built.

So if dry-season flows are already falling under three dams, then what are politicians and policy makers planning to do in the future?

They are planning to build more dams. Outside Yunnan, the facts are sobering: eleven dams are planned for the Mekong's mainstem. Beyond the Mekong, throughout all of the GMS, the numbers are startling: seven dams in Cambodia, ten more in Laos, fifty-four in Myanmar, five in Vietnam, for a grand total of seventy-six.[6] In the coming years, powersheds will not be limited to Yunnan's three parallel rivers.

Information about dams is generated primarily by two regional bodies; the Mekong River Commission (MRC) and the Asian Development Bank's GMS program. With roots in regional development stretching back before the Vietnam War, the MRC's mandate is "to cooperate ... in sustainable development of the Mekong River basin ... in a manner to optimize ... benefits ... and to minimize harmful effects."[7] MRC members include Thailand, Vietnam, Cambodia, and Laos, but China and Myanmar are only observers.

The Asian Development Bank's GMS initiative shares the same

six countries with the MRC except that China participates fully. This is a large bank-lending project, yet the overall focus is remarkably similar to the MRC's: poverty reduction through sustainable development. The GMS initiative is a new Silk Road for the twenty-first century, a regionwide movement to increase people's incomes through the transborder flow of goods. Member countries, however, can't create profitable integrated markets without highways, bridges, powerlines—and dams.

Reading through official documents of the MRC and the Asian Development Bank, I saw the Mekong shrinking before my eyes. In 2007, the UN Environmental Programme published an environmental outlook for the Greater Mekong: biodiversity "faces many serious threats"; "there is evidence to justify" fisheries concerns; food insecurity is resulting from "concentration of the benefits of economic growth"; and, as far as dams, "much depends on how they are managed."

With billions of bank dollars, two regional groups supporting legions of environmental scientists, and a political framework that includes all the countries in the region, why is the outlook so uncertain?

An obscure NGO report provides one answer. In 2007, Eric Baran and his colleagues at the World Fish Centre in Cambodia published an exhaustive review of the Mekong fisheries literature. These scientists pinpointed several disturbing patterns. They documented a history in which all GMS countries have undervalued fisheries; and if the wild catch is portrayed as less valuable, dams appear to be more beneficial. Baran and his team also discovered that, more often than not, "the resources of the poor are not included in impact assessments". Overall, the researchers noted a "general disinterest in accuracy".

Clearly, the Mekong Basin policy makers need to commit to scientific accuracy. Recent progress is encouraging. Since 2004, the MRC has used more sophisticated models to better characterize the Mekong's hydrology, sediment movement, and fish migrations.

The MRC hired its first climate change program officer in 2008 and is reaching out more often to NGOs and local stakeholders. GMS countries have begun to use forward-thinking environmental impact assessments that look beyond national political boundaries.[8]

Despite this good news, I don't believe these reforms are sufficient to sustain the Mekong. The Asian Development Bank and the MRC have the reality of rivers backward: GDP doesn't come first. Regional economies will always be nestled within the ecological framework of the Mae Khong, the "mother of rivers." But science has not yet swayed the prevailing economic logic that motivates powerful governments, corporations, and private entrepreneurs.[9]

River ecology certainly does not dictate Beijing's priorities. Returning upstream to China and Yunnan for a moment, how can anyone evaluate the downstream impacts of hydropower cascades without basic information from upriver? The PRC has released some Lancang flow data, but little else; as with the Nujiang, China claims these data are state secrets.

It's no secret that dams are good business in Yunnan. The provincial economy is growing faster than China's. Yunnan expects to double its GMS trade to USD 60 billion in less than five years, and the Lancang dams will feed this surge. The ink is already dry on long-term electricity contracts with Thailand and Vietnam. The PRC wants to electrify Southeast Asia and it is "going out" with a low China price to do it—for profits, for resource control, for regional influence.[10]

Following the flow of the river southward where Lancang becomes the Mekong Basin, recall the horde of dams planned or being built beyond Yunnan. That total—seventy-six dams in the GMS—is actually incorrect; it refers only to those dams bankrolled by Chinese investors. Malaysian and Thai financiers are also active in the region.

Nobody knows what the ultimate tally of dams will be, but every GMS country is building them as rapidly as possible. With loans from the Asian Development Bank and the World Bank that almost equal the entire GDP of Laos, that country is constructing dams so that one of the world's poorest countries can profit from selling billions of dollars of power to Thailand. Partnering with Sinohydro, the largest dam-building company in China, Cambodia is constructing its first large hydropower project. It will flood thousands of acres of a national park. Every GMS country is "going out" as best they can; powerful China is merely leading the way.

Beyond the Mekong Basin, in forty-eight countries across four continents, China is using the immense profits generated by being the low-cost factory to the world to finance more than two hundred dams. These include a project in Borneo slated to become the largest dam in Southeast Asia. There is a dam in the Democratic Republic of Congo that would cost USD 80 billion and surpass Three Gorges to become the single-largest hydropower project in the world.[11] Details on most of these projects are not available because there is little government transparency in many host countries (think Uganda, Iran, Nigeria, Sudan), but the cumulative environmental and social impacts will be immense.

Some comparative perspective on China's international dam-building efforts is warranted. After all, before 2000 the hydropower track record of the United States and other countries was poor. In that year, however, the World Commission on Dams released a comprehensive critique that most observers expected would change the rules of hydropower development forever.[12] But a short decade later, China was stepping in to fill the open niche of global dam developer with few strings attached. Why stop at the Mekong Basin when you have the opportunity to wire the world?

Feeling the strain from my attempts to make sense of these daunting forces, I biked away from Jinghong until I found a quiet place to sit by the Lancang. The river thrummed between its banks, busy with the work of transporting water from upstream mountains to downstream sandbars, muddy riverbanks, and one megadelta where freshwater meets the sea. I wished for its current to drown out these problems, carry away the complexities, but that was beyond even the Lancang's power. I opened my journal to a jumble of notes about population growth, water stress, human hunger, and climate change.

Current population growth projections place another twenty-five million people into the GMS within the next fifteen years. Combine this growth with near-term economic expansion, and the MRC (2002) predicts that in less than a decade human needs for water will increase about 100 percent for industry and some 30 percent in agriculture.

To water stress, add food insecurity. Today across the GMS, some forty million people are undernourished.[13] By 2020, the number of those at risk of hunger could more than double. A 2004 study by Parry et al. predicted that the price of global cereal staples would triple by the 2080s; over the year it took to write this book, rice prices rose 160 percent while corn increased by 70 percent.

Carbon dioxide is also increasing in Earth's atmosphere. Factor in climate change on top of the stresses outlined above and life in the Mekong Basin will change forever. I think of the Yunnan and Tibetan glaciers feeding the Mekong; they may likely disappear by 2035, reducing the river's flow by at least 10 percent. Most difficult for me to digest is the news that global warming is so strong over the "Third Pole"—the Greater Himalaya and interior high plateaus of Asia where all GMS rivers originate—that the atmospheric gyres that generate the life-giving monsoons may be shifting into novel patterns that may lead to less rainfall.[14]

I set my notebook aside. Since humans settled Southeast Asia millennia ago, the Mae Khong has connected life to life. The "mother" river is still doing her job, but changes are imminent.

Xishuangbanna, the land of twelve thousand rice fields, is transformed into a land of fifty million rice farmers and fishers in Vietnam's

Mekong Delta. Climate change will catch these downstream people in a vise between sea-level rise with saltwater intrusions into their paddies, and less freshwater flowing down the river from its dammed headwaters in Yunnan.

Next upstream, Thailand sells surplus rice to more hungry people than any other country. Thailand expects to consolidate its economic trading position by withdrawing large amounts of water from the Mekong to irrigate vast new paddy fields. The Thai have not considered dams or climate change in their calculations.

Cambodia and Laos, very poor countries with governments not known for transparency, are absolutely dependent for protein on Mekong fish. Under most climate change scenarios, these countries remain relatively rich in water supplies. But they are building dams.

Farther upstream, Myanmar is an ecological and political crapshoot. Very little information is available from this country. All we know is that Myanmar, with financial backing from Chinese corporations, is constructing more dams.

Which brings me back to the Lancang, right here in headwaters China. Downstream flows and their timing, amounts of replenishing sediment, future electricity production—all depend on the Yunnan dams. Yet, as the Tibetan Plateau warms and dries and China's glaciers melt, Yunnan too could begin searching for water. China controls the spigot and therefore the destiny of the entire Mekong Basin.

To address these problems, virtually every Mekong Basin expert recommends the same solutions, and they all begin with strengthening the MRC.[15] Enhancing the MRC's clout means more country-to-country cooperation, a greater willingness to use science and to share information—and enrolling China. Imagine coordinating management across a huge transboundary basin with the upstream half disconnected from the lower portion—the PRC has refused numerous invitations to join the MRC. China believes that the price it would pay in reduced political leverage is too high.

Alternatively, China could work outside the confines of the MRC to become a regional leader, helping to move the Mekong Basin away from the piecemeal development that with every passing year looks more like water hoarding than water management. Beijing could help negotiate water-sharing agreements that take pending climate change seriously. With all the carbon storage and other environmental services that its forests provide, Yunnan would benefit greatly if China stopped acting like the Lancang disappeared when it flowed out of Xishuangbanna.

Biking back to Jinghong in the cool evening air, I remembered lingering on the banks of the Nu at the end of my first trip to Yunnan. Then I noticed a single, taut powerline strung between the road and the Lancang and I thought: "Two poles of influence, two price tags to consider, two vital needs: water in the river and light in the night."

These parallel rivers share so much more than currents and kilowatts.

🐉

In 1078 Song dynasty China, the poet Su Shih poled down the Ssu River and wrote, "Long rapids drop steeply, waves leap up . . . I see only the current boiling in a thousand whirlpools."[16] Nine centuries later, it is easy to be consumed by the economic currents of Asian markets and politics, simple to forget that China's rivers link this present moment to history's millennial sweep.

When Su Shih stared at the river rapids so long ago, the water alternately boiled and moved with "unspeakable slowness." Now, several years after my first encounter with the Angry River, I paced beside the Nu wondering if it was possible to slow the mad advance of dams, commerce, and development in Yunnan. And if not, I wondered what would happen to the people, animals, and plants that make their home in one of the most diverse watersheds on Earth.

Since my trip in 2005, the road up the Nu had been resurfaced, but the route remained a grind. Much energy had also flowed through PRC political channels concerning the Nujiang dams, though little had changed on the ground. The 2005 NGO letter asking for public environmental review was rejected by Beijing; the Nu was an international river and therefore development plans remained off-limits. A 2006 NGO lawsuit was put on hold when the Ministry of Environmental Protection promised that all Nujiang projects would meet legal standards—even if environmental documents remained unavailable for Chinese citizens to peruse as required by law. In 2007, the Chinese media brought charges that local governments were illegally engaged in dam-site preparations without state-level approval. The Ministry of Water Resources countered that "comprehensive environmental reports were being prepared."[17] Anti-dam activists celebrated at the end of that year when the government canceled what would have been the largest dam on the middle Jinshajiang. Did this cancellation portend the collapse of the dam-building movement on all of Yunnan's rivers?

It was impossible to know. The PRC manifests all the complexity of its symbol, the dragon. Long is a sign of male potency, a key element of the Chinese zodiac, and one of the creatures of the four cardinal directions. The emperor, Son of Heaven, was a dragon. There are spirit dragons that bring rain, dragons who guard treasure, and Di-long, the Earth dragon who rules over watercourses. Over the past few years in the Nujiang, manifestations of all these dragons could be seen at work.

Then the Earth lurched and buckled. In May 2008, a subterranean suture related to the fault system that also underlies the Nujiang shifted, and the Wenchuan earthquake wrecked havoc on the people of Sichuan Province north of Yunnan. Alongside the human tragedy, thousands of dams and reservoirs were seriously damaged.

In the aftermath of this disaster, a group of expert Chinese hydrologists sent a formal letter to Beijing warning of the risks of future hydropower development in seismically active southwest China. Scientists sought reassessment of all dam proposals in the region. Chinese Academy of Sciences researcher Yang Yong pointed specifically to all the proposed dams in the Three Parallel Rivers tectonic active belt. Fan Xiao, chief engineer of the Sichuan Geological and Mining Bureau, warned of "extremely unstable geological conditions." Fan wanted studies of the risks to be shared: "We hope the results of the investigation would be made public."[18]

Beijing did not immediately respond.

Bingzhongluo, the final outpost on the Nu before the road fades north into Tibet, has only one main street and it's just a few blocks long. The place is billed as the last town in the prefecture, the end of the road. But I wasn't so sure. There was new asphalt running east down toward the river. I decided to follow it.

Mountains surround the broad swath of ancient river terrace upon which Bingzhongluo spreads its bright green rice paddies. The icy northern reaches of the Gaoligongshan loom to the west. The town is enclosed on all sides by the Gongshan Scenic Area, part of the Three Parallel Rivers World Heritage Site, but the average visitor might never know. There are few signs to guide the way.

But I got lucky. On the road below town, I came across a World Heritage signboard pointing upriver and reminding me that this route was once part of the Cha Ma Gu Dao, the old tea-horse trade trail to Tibet. A thousand years ago, tea and silk from Xishuangbanna were traded via caravan north along the Nu for horses and precious stones coming south. You can still traverse this route all the way to Deqin town if you have a few days' time, a guide, and a backpack full of provisions.

I didn't. So I followed the road up the Nujiang as it narrowed down into a cliff-lined canyon, tucking itself in among towering rock walls. The road deteriorated into loose gravel with steep, unguarded drop-offs not for the faint of heart. The government plan is to upgrade this route into an all-weather road reaching out from the head of the Nu to create a modern version of the tea-horse trail. When this comes to pass, tourists won't have to retrace their steps back down the river highway. Instead, they will be able to visit Song Ta, at a capacity of 6,200 megawatts the largest of all proposed dams on the Nu. The thousands of villagers whose farmlands will be flooded will be less fortunate.[19]

Passing only an occasional four-wheel-drive vehicle carrying a few adventurous Chinese tourists, I turned around and left the road, searching for a footpath closer to the Nu. An hour back down-valley, I came upon a cable suspension footbridge spanning the river. Small rapids curled back upon themselves in standing waves downstream of the bridge. Crossing over to the Nu's east side, I found only trails through cornfields. Steep plots rose up the slope into frizzy low clouds. Development projects didn't appear to have reached this side of the river.

A narrow slip of thickly forested canyon bent down toward the river between two ridges. Scrambling into this dark cleft, I began climbing, looking for signs marking the Three Parallel Rivers boundary. The canyon's watercourse broke in steep falls over boulders, misting me as I passed by. Ferns draped everywhere under large broad-leaved trees.

Now I was far above the Nujiang. The forest was uncut but there was no telling whether it was officially protected or not. Assuming local people understood where their community-managed forest lands met the Three Parallel Rivers World Heritage Site, why search for boundary signs up here?

Since a series of decisions dating from 2003, the Nu, the dam proposals, and World Heritage Site protection have all become tightly linked. The process began when the United Nations accepted China's petition to protect Three Parallel Rivers. A short month later, Beijing tentatively approved Yunnan's provincial-level proposal for Nujiang hydropower development. Soon after, the PRC's first environmental impact law came into effect without any grandfather clause excluding existing projects from meeting the new standards. The upshot of these events was straightforward—almost in the same breath, the Yunnan government said "yes" to both large-scale hydropower development and sweeping landscape protection. And both plans lacked any provisions for environmental impact review.

But Yunnan officials were shrewd when they negotiated with the United Nations over the boundaries of the Three Parallel Rivers site. Despite the implications in the name, none of the rivers or their lower canyons, where biodiversity values are highest and the majority of local people live, are actually within the World Heritage area. Instead, to accommodate future dams, the boundary lines were drawn far above the Nu, beginning at 2,000 meters (6,562 feet).[20] This was why in 2008, I was high above the Nu, searching for a boundary that was never designed to protect the river.

These politically astute demarcations proved to be imperfect. On a 2006 site visit to check on allegations of threats to Three Parallel Rivers, UN inspectors discovered proposals for dams, mines, and tourism development that would "result in a 20% reduction in area of the original heritage site," directly affecting "the integrity and authenticity" of the World Heritage Site. Despite the scale of the proposed deletions (imagine shrinking Yellowstone National Park by 20 percent), local officials maintained that all development would follow national environmental policies. The UN team responded that "this view contradicts the reality of the situation" and listed the site as a candidate for the global list of endangered World Heritage Sites. The inspectors gave the Chinese government a year to explain their position.

"Still under study and not approved" read the Chinese government's 2007 report back to the United Nations on the status of the proposed dams on the upper Nu, the Jinsha, and the Lancang rivers. As for boundary reductions, none were "yet approved," "all questions are under examination," environmental reviews were in process, and the United Nations would receive results in due time as required by World Heritage agreements.

The dragon was meeting the Angry River—villagers, the hydropower corporations and their local government allies, and the UN

inspectors would all have to wait. Beijing, however, was in a tenuous position. If the Nujiang environmental review documents were
claimed as "state secrets," closed to Chinese citizen and media review,
then how could the government consent to share them with a group
of foreigners from the United Nations?

There were no boundary markers to be found in the canyon I
was climbing in, just mountain walls stretching up and up into gray
clouds. But as I scrambled back down toward the Nu, the overcast
began to lift. Soon, a gap in the forest canopy revealed the river and
I could just make out large rapids far below. From this height, the
standing waves appeared as small and still as dewdrops on a leaf
and I recalled Su Shih's vision of moving water that appeared to be
stationary.

Then the clouds dissipated, revealing a pale, high-altitude screen
bridging a vast space between my canyon and ice mountains in the far
west across the river valley. From my perch, heaven and earth shifted;
I felt like an ant on Di-long, the Earth Dragon's back. I sensed the
muddy Nujiang twisting through its sinuous gorge, glimpsed Bingzhongluo town perched on fertile ground, witnessed a glacial host of
blue mountains walking up into the sky. Di-long reared up, the river
bent unimpeded around another mountain wall and disappeared.
Was the water moving free or standing still? I couldn't tell.

By the time I worked my way back down to the water's edge,
Gawagapu Peak hung in the heavens 5,000 meters (16,400 feet) above
the Nu. I remembered that the highest headwall of any Nujiang dam
would be less than 100 meters (328 feet) high. I also understood that
Chinese dragons could choose to be visible or invisible and that, so
far, Di-long remained undecided about which form he was going to
assume.

Chapter 8

China 2020

The nation is ruined,
But mountains and rivers remain.
Du Fu, Tang dynasty
(translation by G. Snyder)

The Dream

ISITING CHINA, it is easy to be transfixed by the rush of development: the hullabaloo of high-volume traffic, the construction of seemingly endless rows of high-rises, the hopefulness of so many people bent on improving their lives. Every day, the PRC is working to transform itself into a modern, developed nation—an economic and political powerhouse in Asia and in the world.

But if you believe Beijing's rhetoric, it is also struggling to realize a more nuanced dream: the creation of a "harmonious society" that can bridge commerce, conservation, and human well-being. Meeting with a Taiwanese political leader in 2006, President Hu Jintao declared, "Frankly speaking, we do not want to pursue excessively rapid economic growth. What we are seeking is efficiency and quality of development, the change in the economic growth mode, resources conservation, environmental protection and improvement of people's livelihood." Hiking throughout Yunnan, from the raging water of the Nu to the rubber plantations of Xishuangbanna, however, I had witnessed more rapid development than resource conservation.

It wasn't until one evening when I was leaning on a rooftop railing in Kunming that I finally saw inklings of the dream becoming reality. In soft dusky light, my eyes swept out over a dense urban forest composed of more apartment buildings than I could ever care to count. I noticed no chimneys; Kunming's climate is mild, the city is known for its perpetual springlike weather, and few buildings have central heating. But every apartment in my view, old or just built, boasted an array of solar-powered water heaters and storage tanks. It looked to me like the future of China was already present, hidden away in plain sight atop every building in the city. As Earth spun on its axis into darkness, I suddenly became aware that almost every drop of domestic hot water in Kunming came courtesy of the sun.

Development and implementation of renewable energy—in Kunming and every other city in the PRC—will be critical if China is to "build a well-off society in an all-round way." While its record of land and wildlife conservation has often been spotty, the PRC has made tremendous progress toward at least one environmental goal: the transition to a "green" economy. Since 2005, Beijing has left the United States in the dust when it comes to clean-tech investment and manufacturing.[1]

Yet despite all the wind turbines and solar cells, China's goal of sustainable energy use will not be easy to achieve. Government forecasters expect that China will continue to depend on burning coal for most of its rapidly expanding energy needs. By 2020, oil imports will likely double, making China more dependent on foreign suppliers. In the same time frame, China's CO_2 emissions are also expected to double. Even as the PRC has become a leading producer of renewable technologies, it has also become *the* leading producer of greenhouse gases, overtaking the United States in total emissions.

Shedding that dubious distinction will require seriously ramping up every non-fossil-fuel energy source—from hydropower and nuclear to a broad mix of renewables. It would also mean revolutionizing land-use planning and building codes. With automobile purchases guaranteed to grow along with thousands of miles of new highways, strict standards will be needed to keep vehicle pollution from worsening.

Given these barriers, can China's dream come true? Forecasting is fraught with uncertainty. Look back twenty years—in 1990, what did we predict accurately? Few people back then expected that China would shake the world today. No one imagined that U.S. trade with the PRC in the single month of May 2008 would more than double all *annual* trade between the two countries in 1989.[2]

Fast-forward to China 2020. Follow all the predictions into the near term, the next decade or so. Begin with energy exchange as it physically exists: a smoky indoor cooking fire in rural Yunnan, all the automobiles idling in Atlanta and Beijing gridlock. Consider a shiny metal pipeline a yard in diameter stretching thousands of miles across roadless Siberia toward China to deliver thick black crude.

Don't stop there. Scale up beyond China's brave vision of efficient energy use. Gauge the social and political barriers that push China away from sustainability. Then place the country with the largest population in the world *within* the world—the global host of the wealthy and poor, developed and less developed nations, north and south.

Next, imagine an atmosphere ever more loaded with molecules made of two parts oxygen to one part carbon.

Dreams are mysterious and powerful, provocative drivers of human behavior. Our common bias is often toward outcomes we can measure, results that can be compared through counting costs and benefits. Yet in the Judeo-Christian tradition, Proverbs warns that "without dreams, the people perish." The Chinese might frame this insight another way: "without the skills to catch a dragon, one shouldn't go down into deep waters."

China certainly believes its vision is attainable. The country is growing, rising in importance and influence, *zou chu qu*, "going out": to Yunnan and the rest of western China, to the Mekong Basin and Southeast Asia, to energy-rich neighboring countries such as Russia and Kazakhstan, to South America, Africa, and the Middle East, and, of course, to the United States. The scale and speed of China's growing influence is breathtaking—China 2020 is only ten years away.

Growing the Dream

China's amazing GDP growth commands much of the world's attention. For many people, the main questions are, when will the PRC replace the United States as the world's number one economy and how can I get in on the action?

The answer to the first question is not immediately. Assuming that future growth proceeds at recent rates, projections suggest that China will overcome the United States between 2025 and 2035.[3] China's expanding economic power is big news, but questions focused narrowly on the size of any country's GDP miss critical points. The important trend is that the balance of global economic power is shifting toward China and Asia. By 2020, Asia's combined GDP is projected to be 50 percent larger than the United States or the European Union. This will be a world in which, as a recent *New York Times* article said, "America is not the engine of globalization anymore . . . it might be China, it might be Europe—but it's not the U.S."[4]

This is difficult news for many Americans to accept, and analyses that portray these trends as "threats" to U.S. interests are common. From a broader perspective, however, the point isn't who has the biggest GDP, it's what the combined impact of all that growth will be. China's vaunted development merely extends pressures on global ecosystems and resources that are already too high because of ongoing consumption by the United States and the rest of the industrialized world. The PRC is just now joining the show, raising the stakes in the process. India, Brazil, and the rest of the developing world are not far behind.

Emphasizing competition also ignores the fact that China produces for the world, and the world purchases from China. Forty percent of all U.S.-bought consumer goods are made in the PRC. The United States cannot simply "contain" China's rise because that would also require constraining American consumer spending. The PRC portrays this story as about the fairness and economic parity that would allow a less-developed country to join the ranks of well-off nations. But with its growing economic and ecological footprint, China is driving America and the world toward a global reckoning with the fossil-fuel-powered, high-consumption, industrial way of life.[5] There is a well-known Chinese proverb that cautions that an opportunity may provide a blessing or a curse. The potential boon here is that the scramble to make room at the table for China may wean all of us off coal and oil with utmost haste. The darker portent is that the world may not be willing to share, is inadequately prepared to do so, or simply will not act in time.

Whichever way the future unfolds, the path leads through China 2020.

Driving the Dream

When it comes to cars, China and the United States are very different and very much the same. From the backseat of a taxi, I could definitely appreciate the distinctions: my driver was speeding along at a hundred kilometers (sixty-two miles) per hour, passing an overloaded truck on a blind mountain curve. Two weeks earlier, stuck in standstill Kunming traffic, another driver had suddenly wrenched his steering wheel hard right, jumped the curb onto a crowded sidewalk, coasted down a block out of the road snarl, and then cut back left to the front of the line just as the light turned green.

Wild driving aside, the two countries' car cultures are pretty similar. We love to drive and so do the growing number of Chinese who can afford to own an auto. Middle-class Chinese are snapping cars up at astounding rates. Only eight million private vehicles were on the road in 2000; sixteen million were purchased in 2006–2007. Despite the worldwide recession that began in 2007, in 2009 over eleven million cars were sold. Sales are rising about 20 percent each year, and though the rate of ownership is only forty cars per thousand people (about the U.S. level in 1925), projections suggest that by 2020 from 100 to 130 million vehicles will be cruising on China's roads.[6]

Auto owners require roads to drive on and Yunnan's Go West highway growth is being replicated all across China. The PRC's target is a national system spanning fifty-three thousand miles, and construction is on schedule.[7] Only the Chinese are building their highway system twice as fast as interstates grew to become part of the American landscape.

Given the sheer numbers of new automobiles on the road today and the expected growth rate into the future, the question is whether *any* degree of vehicle regulation, no matter how stringent, can keep the PRC habitable.

Building the Dream

My friends call me crazy, but one of my favorite things to do in China is to traverse a busy city street. Crossing a road in Kunming or Beijing is like navigating a street in any Asian megacity. There are large trucks, cars and all manner of loaded carts, bicycles, and pedestrians, each moving at their own speed. The trick is to calibrate your movement to these multiple velocities as you momentarily enter the influence of each: speed up for cars, slow down for bikes, stop on a dime for trucks, even if you're temporarily stranded in the middle of the street. Then you're standing safely on the far curb.

Like pedestrians navigating a busy thoroughfare, people in Asia are in the midst of crossing a historic divide between urban and rural.

When I was a child, Tokyo and New York were the only places with ten million residents; by 2020, there will be twenty-five such mega-cities worldwide. China will contain eight.

It is difficult to grasp what this urban transformation means for China, when the east coast city of Shenzhen will have more residents than Sweden. There exist a range of estimates for the number of new city dwellers that China must accommodate over the next ten to fifteen years. The low end is somewhere around three hundred million, the population of the United States today.[8]

This leads me to consider square meters, cement, BTUs, and pavement. As you read this, China is erecting one of every two structures in the world. By 2020, this will translate into some five million new buildings, enough structures erected over a decade to house, service, and provide working accommodations equal to all the built space that currently exists in America. Unlike structures in the United States, most of these buildings will be made of inexpensive cement—now I can see why China is the world's number one producer of this product.

What I can't see is the gas emitted in the production process, up to 8 percent of the world's total CO_2 emissions. Nor can I detect the heat that escapes from these buildings due to poor design, inferior construction practices, and lax enforcement of building codes. The PRC may have excellent residential energy-efficiency regulations, but policies are poorly enforced.

Shoddy construction or solid, new urban buildings have to fit somewhere on the land. China's urban footprint is spreading outward, covering the ground with pavement and sprawling blocks of high-rise apartments, shops, and factories. Each Chinese city differs in details, but a general pattern has emerged—trading urban growth for arable land. Since 2001, Chinese cities have swallowed a large portion of food-producing land, an area about the size of West Virginia. A recent "best-case" projection, looking toward 2020, places future arable land losses at another 8 percent.[9]

China has never been well-endowed with agricultural land. The PRC has 22 percent of Earth's people but a mere 7 percent of the planet's arable lands. Or had—in addition to urban development, China has lost farmlands to pesticide and heavy-metal pollution. Farming has been part of the Middle Kingdom's cultural identity for millennia; twenty-five hundred years ago, the definition of an incompetent ruler was one who allowed "farmland [to lie] uncultivated," proving that food security was an issue even for Chinese emperors. No ruler, however, can produce food from land that has been paved over.

Even if the government is wise enough to conserve arable land, farmers cannot produce food without water. But in the PRC in 2010, water is no longer treated as the "highest good"; instead, it has become the lowest common denominator. Chinese agriculture wastes half of all water that is applied to fields. In cities, losses from leaky pipes hover around 20 percent.

Given that northern China has less water per capita than Morocco, and the Yangzi River in the south has the fourth-largest freshwater flow on Earth, moving water from the bottom to the top of China has become the 2020 plan.[10] The central government is spending a minimum of RMB 500 billion (USD 60.2 billion) on the South-to-North Water Transfer Project. And with this plan, the lack of water has met toxic water. Since the 1980s, when China prioritized economic growth over pollution control, 40 percent of all surface water in the country has become so filthy it "is of no practical or functional use." The south-north transfer can't be completed until polluted rivers are treated to become potable, and different levels of government are haggling over who will foot the bill. If the transfer is delayed for too long, half a billion people may run out of water—and luck.

Ancient levies on the Yellow River, the Yuan dynasty Grand Canal—through thousands of projects since before the time of Christ, Chinese engineers have plumbed the Middle Kingdom with complex hydraulic schemes. I have never drunk directly from a tap anywhere in the PRC, but I have washed my face in clean mountain streams in Yunnan where the land is still relatively healthy. Beijing takes water pollution seriously. The question is whether central-government commitments can filter down to local-level implementation in time.[11]

The 2008 Olympics focused PRC leaders on Beijing's ubiquitous air pollution. Coal burning and vehicle fumes drive up pollutant levels to some of the highest in the world. The resulting sulfur dioxide contributes to acid rain, there are extremely high ozone levels, and tiny particulates clog human lungs. Yet there is broad evidence that PRC pragmatism might counter air pollution trends. Sulfur dioxide levels have been falling since 2007. In only three years, sulfur scrubbers have been installed in over half of all Chinese power-plant smokestacks. To prepare for the Olympics, the government spent RMB 120 billion (USD 17.6 billion) on pollution control and met its "Blue Sky" air quality targets.[12] None of this would have occurred without the political resolve to deal with the issue.

International coverage of the Olympics and China's efforts at pollution control have helped to highlight the conflict between "Green China" and "Growing China" in the public consciousness. But the reality of building a harmonious society is even more complex. Even if you "green" the dream, you still have to share it.

Sharing the Dream

My education on the role of social equity in shaping China 2020 began in a Kunming park one stifling summer afternoon. Exploring an unfamiliar neighborhood, I spied a canopy of green trees amid high-rises—some city open space where I could escape the heat. But when I reached the park, I could barely squeeze in; the place was jammed with a mass of working-class people smoking, talking, gambling, just hanging out. I walked on by wondering if there was some holiday, but no—businesses were open as usual.

The following day, I returned to the park. The place was still crowded. Later, after a chance encounter with an English-speaking cabbie, I began to solve the mystery. "Those are migrants," the driver explained. "They come to Kunming for jobs but can't get hired, so they stay in the park till the police tell them to move on. I don't come from here, either, I'm from Sichuan, laid off from factory work. *Wo cao* [Chinese expletive], driving pays crap, but I'm lucky I'm working."

Where you come from and how you're counted makes a huge difference in the PRC. How the government deals with migrants is going to deeply influence conservation success in China 2020.

Some numbers illuminate this point. We already know that domestic migration from China's rural west to the urbanizing east has fed the largest movement of people ever recorded. Six years ago, experts suggested that about 150 million Chinese were on the move.[13]

They aren't going to stop moving. Just compare the annual income of a villager in Yunnan with factory wages in Guangzhou. Each year, anywhere from 7 to 12 million people are still relocating for work. That means that in 2010, there are anywhere from 180 to 200 million people in this huge, shifting pool. Even with the government's Go West development creating new jobs in western China, the megacities of 2020 will be fueled by migrants, not natural population growth.

A host of ecological costs come with migration at this scale. China is no exception to the worldwide rule that urban dwellers use two to three times more resources per capita than people living in the countryside. If the growing megacities of China 2020 are going to consist of up to 40 percent migrant laborers, the government might be able to mitigate urban ecological impacts if this influx could somehow be constrained. But the PRC of today and into the future depends on cheap migrant labor to keep the China price as low as possible, producing 75 percent of the country's GDP.

One major social barrier indirectly impeding social reform is *hukou*, the Communist Party's household registration system. Mao established *hukou* as a tool to limit people from moving freely around China. Market reforms loosened *hukou*; people have been able to migrate to cities for decades. Once they arrive, however, the system prevents them from gaining equal access to basic social services: health and unemployment benefits, subsidized housing, and education for their children. The PRC is reforming *hukou*, but urban migrants still form a vast underclass. City governments do not recognize them as residents; the shadow population of Shenzhen is at least 6.4 million people, while the official count is about 2 million.[14]

The primary reason why this social pressure cooker has not burst is that migrant laborers feel they are better off with city jobs relative to their prospects back home in the countryside. So they continue to pour into the cities and power China's economy. The cities expand outward—with serious environmental consequences. The question is, what will happen when economic growth slows? This leads deeper into other social problems: China's widening wealth gap, increasing unemployment, uncertain health care, and the general lack of pension and social security benefits.[15]

In China 2020, social issues will deeply influence environmental problem solving. It works like this: Beijing underfunds cities, expecting the ever-expanding market economy to provide capital in lieu of sufficient levels of taxation. City administrators, facing burgeoning economies and hordes of job seekers from the countryside, must find room for new factories and residential apartments. So officials condemn (or buy) property on the urban periphery at agricultural land prices. Then they sell development rights to investors at the commercial real estate value, pocketing immense profits that give them funds to run their cities. In China, these are not occasional or indiscriminate acts; estimates suggest that from 10 to 50 percent of city coffers are filled by profits made solely from real estate transactions.

There is a darker side to this story. I have seen calculations that point to forty million peasants over the last decade losing their lands through real estate fraud and collusion. In U.S. terms, this would be equivalent to all citizens who live from Massachusetts to Maine being swindled out of their property and forced to relocate. China's "enormous industrial metabolism" has not allowed local governments to reduce their dependency on illegal land acquisition and corruption. Even the central government admits to the problem. According to the Chinese Academy for Environmental Planning, from 2001 to 2005 only half of all funds allocated for environmental mitigation efforts were actually spent on their target projects.[16]

Chinese citizens react against corruption and environmental pollution with public demonstrations. There were 87,000 in 2005; that's 238 protests for every day of the year. The central government has responded by allocating more money for rural jobs and crafting a new land law in which farmers can lease their fields for profit.[17] But Beijing's influence on local government politics remains tenuous. If these issues aren't resolved well before 2020, it is difficult to imagine how China's megacities will continue to expand without social disruption.

Importing the Dream

Just as the PRC confronts domestic social barriers to realizing the dream of becoming a "well-off society," it faces basic physical constraints. China simply doesn't have the natural resources and energy supplies to quadruple the size of its economy, build megacities, satisfy the middle class, and provide hundreds of millions of poor people with a developed-world standard of living. So to comprehend China 2020, one must follow the flow of raw materials imported *into* the PRC.

The focus of China's international "going out" is to bring back energy and resources to build the Middle Kingdom's dream of the future. Glance at a map and count the countries that border the PRC: China has fourteen neighbors, more than any other nation in the world. If Yunnan's impoverished ethnic nationalities are to increase their standard of living and if the expanding middle class must own automobiles, then fossil fuels must flow into China as never before. The trouble is, a fuels transportation infrastructure barely exists, the ecological consequences of constructing it are unknown, and the

Upper Nujiang ("angry river") valley

Yuan dynasty jade urn, Tuancheng, Beihai Park, Beijing

Building modern China, Kunming

Village hearth, backcountry Yunnan

On the trail near Dimaluo village

Lily, Yi ethnic nationality, Xuehua village

Charcoal for sale, Lijiang

*One species from the "kingdom of Rhododendrons," Laojunshan,
which contains 10% of the world's rhododendrons*

Monkey station base camp, Laojunshan

Tibetan weaver, near Nizu village

Tibetan prayer flags and peaks, northwest Yunnan

Bingzhongluo town, upper Nujiang

Dayan, Lijiang old town

On the "road" to Mengyong village, southern Xishuangbanna

Rubber replaces rain forest, Xishuangbanna

political ramifications are unsettling. No matter; a cursory inventory of plans for pipelines, ports, and new political pacts reveals the power, scale, and sweep of China 2020.

Russia is China's northern neighbor; the Bear contains more oil, gas, coal, and timber than the United States, European Union, and the PRC combined. Russia can help China: over the next decade, the PRC is facing a burgeoning oil and natural gas deficit. Though the two countries have a convoluted history, Russia is building the 2,800-kilometer (1,740-mile) Altai gas pipeline from fields in Siberia to Xinjiang, from where the fuel can be sent directly to Shanghai by 2011. The pipeline is crossing the Altai Mountains World Heritage Site. No environmental impact statement has been made public even though the area is mostly roadless and provides habitat for snow leopards and many other endangered species. Russia and China are also discussing two other potential gas pipelines, one of which would transect Tunka National Park in Siberia.[18] And, on a route running through roadless taiga that is twice as long as the Alaska pipeline corridor, Transneft, Russia's pipeline monopoly, is finishing construction of China's second overland oil pipeline. This line runs through the largest intact forest on Earth after the Amazon, but no environmental impact report has been released.[19]

China's first overland oil pipeline opened in 2005, linking the PRC to Kazakhstan This connection enmeshes China in murky Central Asian petropolitics. Kazakhstan may have the world's largest untapped oil deposits, and Russia would like Kazakhstan oil to flow into Russia. The United States and the European Union want the oil to move south through Georgia and Turkey (or possibly Afghanistan). The PRC wants more of the crude to enter Xinjiang along a new Silk Road.[20]

Moving south to Pakistan, the complexity of China's long-term oil and gas import strategy deepens. One word sums it up: Gwadar. Spending close to a billion dollars, China is building a megaport here on Pakistan's far west coast. Complete with two oil terminuses,

Gwadar could become the focal point of land-based shipments of Middle Eastern and Central Asian oil to China.[21] This would help China reduce ocean transport of oil through the Strait of Malacca between Malaysia and Sumatra, where 50 percent of all global oil shipments, including the majority of China's and Japan's supplies, steam through a narrow passage. China leans heavily on the U.S. Navy for sea-lane security; the PRC would prefer to eliminate this dependency.

Still, most of China's oil comes from the Middle East. Like the United States, the PRC depends greatly on Saudi Arabia. After that, the two countries' sources differ in ways that will color China 2020 geopolitics.

Long before 2020 arrives, the entire Middle East/Asian energy market will have shifted into some new configuration. Iran is China's number three oil partner. U.S. politicians complain about this relationship, but Japan, a staunch American ally, buys more Iranian oil than any other country. In 2008, Iran applied for formal membership in the Shanghai Cooperative Organization, an increasingly powerful trade bloc that includes China and Russia. (Afghanistan and Pakistan have observer status.) Multiple future pipeline projects are under discussion between several sets of unlikely partners: India-Iran, Afghanistan-Pakistan, China-Iraq. Fuel and electricity needs are so high in all these countries that their leaders are willing to recalibrate old relationships if the result is energy security.[22]

How will China's new resource partnerships affect global energy supplies in 2020? World oil use in 2008 stood at 86 million barrels a day, with demand projected to decrease in the developed world while growing rapidly in countries like China and India. By 2020, the Energy Information Administration projects global demand to reach about 100 million barrels a day. Though this forecast is contentious, there is little debate about another trend over this period: Western oil companies' market domination will decline as their domestic oil fields play out and new sources in Russia, Iran, Iraq, and Nigeria are tapped. The amount of oil left in the ground to pump may be arguable, but the plain truth is that developed countries are running out of oil that is under their direct control.[23]

This fact belies much of the concern emanating from Washington, D.C., over China's energy activities. China is accused of burning through global oil stocks, driving up prices, and tightening demand. Yet the oil consumption of one Chinese is five times less than the average American. The U.S. castigates the PRC for striking fuel deals with unsavory regimes that show little regard for human rights. But American leaders look the other way when it comes to the human rights track records of major U.S. suppliers, including Saudi Arabia, Nigeria, and Equatorial Guinea.[24] In its quest for fossil fuels, the United States has always attempted to secure stable supplies of oil at their source. Now that China is wealthy enough to act on behalf of its own energy security, U.S. politicians scapegoat the PRC for doing what America has always done—directing oil homeward, subsidizing energy costs, and doing little to control domestic demand.

Political double standards aside, China shares one perspective with all global energy players: for every country, it remains easier to enjoy the benefits of burning coal and oil than it is to face the costs of mounting carbon dioxide emissions.

There is a good chance that China 2020 may change all this.

The Carbon Footprint of the Dream

In 2005, Chinese energy experts projected that by 2025 the PRC would replace the United States as the country emitting the most carbon dioxide into Earth's atmosphere. Two years later, Chinese experts suggested that the country would "likely" become number one in 2010.

In reality, 2008 was China's second year in a row as the world's carbon emissions leader. The PRC is already burning through as much energy today as its 2005 *National Energy Strategy* report projected the country would use in the worst-case scenario in 2020.[25] "No one really knew what was driving the economy, which is why the predictions were so wrong," said Yang Fuiqiang, one of the PRC energy planners who worked on the report.

We know now. The central government assumed that pushing economic growth before all else would create enough wealth to power China into an all-round well-off society. China's leaders expected that the resulting greenhouse gas emissions could somehow be accommodated. The truth is a different story. There isn't enough room for China's current or projected emissions, nor is there room for those emanating out of other industrialized countries.

The goals of the Kyoto Protocol provide clear evidence. Under Kyoto, participating countries committed to reducing greenhouse gasses to 5 percent below their 1990 levels by 2012. As of 2007, however, U.S. levels had increased 22 percent, Japan's had risen 16 percent, and EU emissions had grown as well. Both Chinese and Indian carbon emissions have gone up at least 100 percent.[26]

China should not be blamed for the world's runaway carbon emissions; the United States never even ratified the Kyoto Protocol. But global growth in carbon emissions has been *speeding up*. And China is responsible for two thirds of the current increases. So much carbon is wafting up out of China today that PRC scientists expect their country could double current releases again by 2030.

There are several driving wheels behind China's emissions trajectory through 2020 and beyond. The most important is also the easiest to grasp: nations burn fuel to power growth, and the economy of the largest human population in the world is exploding. In 2005 alone, the PRC added power capacity equal to the entire existing British energy grid. In 2006, 2007, and again in 2009, China brought online each year new power capacity equivalent to that in all of France. Most of these power plants continue to burn dirty coal because that is the least expensive fuel China has.

Beijing officials are unhappy with the country's dramatic expansion in energy use and carbon dioxide emissions. The pressure is on China to control its emissions growth. The PRC has always argued that its sterling track record in reducing energy intensity—the amount of energy burned per unit of GDP—is what counts; certainly, using this metric, the United States lags far behind China. But global warming is not driven by energy intensity. World temperatures are rising because of absolute emissions, the total parts per million of carbon dioxide in the atmosphere. Even if the European Union and the United States magically reduced their carbon emissions to zero while you are reading this sentence, China's current pace would keep global greenhouse gasses rising through 2020.[27]

What does humanity's ever-expanding carbon footprint portend? Some trends are more certain than others. Our best attempts at modeling climate change were published in 2007 by the United Nation's Intergovernmental Panel on Climate Change (IPCC). To deal with the uncertainties of emission rates over multiple decades, the IPCC created best, medium, and worst-case scenarios and assigned high, medium, and low levels of probability to all projected outcomes. There is solid consensus that humans are responsible for much of the 0.8° C (1.4° F) of warming that has occurred since the Industrial Revolution. Experts agree that another 0.6° C (1.08 ° F) of warming is "in the pipeline" due to the fact that carbon dioxide remains in the atmosphere for up to a century before it dissipates. So Earth is already certain to warm by a total 1.4° C (2.5° F) on average. For perspective, most scientists consider a 2° C (3.6° F) rise to be a potentially "dangerous" level of warming that could trigger the loss of most of the planet's ice, disastrous sea-level rise, and wholesale species extinctions, rendering Earth a challenging place for humans to live.[28]

China 2020 is not reducing these projections. Almost every empirical study published since 2007 indicates that IPCC worst-case scenarios are being exceeded: emissions are rising faster, ice is melting more rapidly, ecosystems are under greater duress.[29] These developments expose one of the central conceits of current climate discourse: that warming will occur in the indeterminate future, say, by 2050 or 2100. This timeline is a myth; complex, uncertain shiftings of wild species and ecosystems are already under way.

I don't want to live in a world that is two or three degrees warmer. Climate change science is difficult to digest, not only because of technical complexities, but also because of the emotional charge triggered by unsettling news. But I had to confront the data. So I went back to the 2007 IPCC report and recent updates from the literature to look more closely at worst-case temperature projections and their potential impacts.

By the 2020s and 2030s, the IPCC projects that temperatures will rise an additional 1.52° C (2.7° F) in central and eastern China, 1.84° C (3.3° F) in western China's Tibetan Plateau, and 0.86° C (1.5° F) throughout much of the Greater Mekong Subregion. All these regions show a "dangerous" 2° C (3.6° F) or (much) greater rise in temperatures well before the end of the twenty-first century.

Across Asia, these temperature increases are almost certain to wreak havoc with species and ecosystems, glacial ice, soil permafrost, and sea levels. For plants and animals, the IPCC states that "up to 50% of Asia's total biodiversity is at risk due to climate change." I understand why scientists use percentages to convey research projections, but ecology is not equivalent to a business balance sheet. Species inhabit ecosystems; without their constituent plants and animals, the structure and function of nature from nutrient cycles to pest control evolves toward some new "normal." As China warms up, many plants and animals will disappear; the rest will move in search of the environmental conditions they are suited for. At 2° C (3.6° F) and more, these shifts will begin to create "novel" ecosystems that humans have never encountered before.[30]

Think of your house—now remove "up to 50%" of its physical structure. Shift cinderblocks from the foundation to doorways, siding from exterior walls to indoor ceilings. Remove the roof, replace it with your furnace. In this "novel ecosystem," what do you have left to live in?

Some of the world's most rapid and steep temperature increases are projected to occur in the so-called Third Pole, the Greater Himalaya region. One and a half billion people are sustained by Asia's "water tower," the rivers that flow down from the world's highest mountains: the Mekong, Yangzi, Ganges, Indus, and others. A 2° C (3.6 ° F) rise in temperatures, almost a certainty by the early 2030s in highland Asia, will shrink Third Pole ice anywhere from 75 percent down to zero. These losses will at first be masked by greater river flows due to melting. They will become more pronounced as ice disappears, until there is little water left to drink and to sustain dry-season agriculture for 300 million Chinese, 410 million Indians, and almost every Pakistani.[31]

Rising temperatures melt glaciers; they also dissolve permafrost. Over half of the Tibetan Plateau consists of high-altitude steppes and alp lands underlain by soils that never thaw. These semifrozen ecosystems store as much as 25 percent of China's organic soil carbon, but plateau permafrost is going to melt, likely releasing much of its carbon load sometime after 2050.[32]

Melting ice, whether from Himalayan glaciers or Arctic and Antarctic ice caps, eventually ends up in the world's oceans. When I scan a map of China, I see three east coast urban areas: Tianjin, Shanghai, and Guangzhou all sprawl across low-lying river deltas. By 2020, with the influx of job-seeking migrants, these three deltas will be home to more people than currently live in the United States. But if sea levels rise by thirty-three centimeters, a little over a foot and well within IPCC projections for 2050, an average of 64 percent of these delta lands will be submerged.[33]

Such wholesale changes to ecosystems, glacial ice and snow, and sea levels will place water and food systems all over China and Asia at risk. Along with the world's largest rice crop, there are cornfields in southern China and wheat farms in the north that collectively produce much of the world's output of these agricultural staples. Recent reports project a 5–10 percent reduction in PRC food productivity by 2030, with losses deepening to 15–30 percent in high emissions scenarios. Also a factor is that Asian populations are rising; the United Nations expects that global increases in human numbers by 2050 will require us to grow at least 50 percent more food than is produced today. [34] "You are talking about hundreds of millions of additional people looking for food," said David Battisti, coauthor of an influential 2009 study of climate change impacts on agriculture, "because they won't be able to find it where they find it now."

Now I can comprehend the reasoning behind the Ministry of Agriculture's recent proposal to subsidize the purchase of overseas farmlands by Chinese companies.[35] I can understand why China is "going out" to invest in millions of acres of food plantations in Laos, oil palm in Indonesia, and soybeans in Brazil.

Just as wild species are already migrating due to the impacts of climate change, and governments are grappling with shifting food policies, so will humans move to find more favorable conditions. Several recent reports place the coming flood of global warming refugees in context. Craig Johnstone, the deputy commissioner with the UN High Commissioner for Refugees, said recently that because there are a potential 250 million to 1 billion people that may lose their homes by 2050, the world must prepare for a "global-scale emergency."[36] The 1951 Geneva Convention, however, has nothing to say about people fleeing environmental disasters such as droughts and famines. At a spring 2008 summit in Brussels, EU officials warned that the international "multi-lateral system is at risk . . . climate change impacts will fuel the politics of resentment between those most responsible for climate change and those most affected by it."[37] Refugees from climate change will certainly be angry if the international community follows the advice offered in *Towards a Grand Strategy for an Uncertain World*. Written by former defense chiefs from the United States and four EU countries, this document narrowly portrays climate change as a "security threat" to wealthy northern countries as refugee masses flee a destabilizing south. The solution? Keep these "others" out.

The Dissolution of the Dream?

"The nation is ruined / but mountains and rivers remain": China's great poet Du Fu penned these lines in 755 as the disastrous An Lu Shan Rebellion swept over the Tang dynasty capital of Chang'an, commencing eight years of bloody war. By the conflict's end, two-thirds of China's people were either dead or displaced and homeless. Du Fu himself became a wanderer, fleeing ongoing outbreaks of civil strife over the last decade of his life. He was not buried with his family until forty-two years after his death.[38]

The dream of a harmonious society has been elusive over the vast sweep of China's history. There have been periods of social unity and ease followed by disruption and decay. The economic growth of the handful of decades since 1978's Reform and Opening must be placed in perspective alongside the prospects for China 2020. Of course, China's dream is not a vision exclusive to the PRC. Beyond the Middle Kingdom, there are another 1.2 billion people around the world desiring cars, a decent house attached to a sewer system, clean water, and a measure of education and health care.[39]

But rising China is special. The PRC could shift the world toward sustainability or collapse. "Our country's development path cannot repeat the unconstrained emissions of developed countries' energy use," states the 2008 China energy report. But in early 2009, Land and Resource Ministry chief planner Hu Cunzhi announced that the central government expected to increase coal production some 30 percent by 2015, an amount greater than all coal currently burned in Europe, Eurasia, the Middle East, Africa, and South America.

Growing and building China's dream means distributing, fueling, and feeding it. While each of these tasks is daunting by itself, none are insurmountable. But until China, the United States, and the rest of the industrialized world recognize that under climate change even mountains and rivers have their limits, the dream cannot come true.

Chapter 9

Conservation with Chinese Characteristics

Knowing others is wisdom;
knowing the self is enlightenment.

LAO-TZU, sixth century BCE
(translation by G. Feng and J. English)

*I*N ALL OF THE MAJESTY of the Middle Kingdom, there is no place like Haleakala, the 3,000-plus-meter (10,023-foot) volcano whose Hawaiian name means "House of the Sun." There are numerous small volcanoes in China, but none that have formed a gaping black and red crater holding the sky, or built a Pacific Ocean island out of their viscous flows.

"Will you, please?" Ms. Yuan, director of wildlife conservation at the Beijing Greening Bureau, handed me a camera and I snapped her picture with the crater yawning behind. A mile below us, thin clouds shadowed a long, jagged lava ridge; otherwise, the day was perfectly clear in Maui's Haleakala National Park.

I was traveling with the twenty-five members of the Chinese Protected Areas Leadership Alliance, working as a consultant for this group of government managers from across China who were spending a month visiting American nature reserves from New York to Hawaii. Led by Ms. Guo Hongyan from the State Forestry Administration, the study tour's purpose was to build professional knowledge so that participants could spark a nationwide movement for more effective management of China's nature reserves. After two weeks with the group it was clear to me that, while the managers were learning much about American park management methods, they were quite ready to return to China and create something new.

Successful protected areas are just one component of a sustainable China, but they are linked to myriad other issues. They represent another step toward the dream of creating a future "harmonious society." But how will parks and protected areas do anything to solve the daunting issues facing China in a rapidly warming world?

In their search for a way forward, Chinese conservationists cannot look much to the recent past. After establishing the PRC's first protected areas, Mao left a legacy of little support for nature reserves. With Reform and Opening in the 1980s, the government focused on joining the global economic order and called it "capitalism with Chinese characteristics."

Now things are different. China can no longer ignore the environmental issues that are irrevocably tied to its economic and political future. Go West development and globalization are bringing "eastern China" to the frontier, and there are fewer forests left for tigers and elephants to hide in. Villagers in Yunnan cannot be integrated into the national economy without stable systems of land-use rights and responsibilities. International NGOs will not provide major portions of PRC conservation funding forever. Global warming is beginning to assert nonnegotiable demands.

From community-based ecotourism to new national parks and international energy policy, the PRC has the opportunity to create "conservation with Chinese characteristics" that can influence domestic environmental affairs as well as Earth's future. In its villages and provinces, China can forge a path toward sustainability. Here is a rough roadmap.

Village China

People are part of the landscape in China. Therefore, effective conservation must benefit villagers. Village-level conservation is traditionally based on respecting nature while using it; foreign conservation models adopted by the government are based on protecting nature from use.

But there is encouraging news from Yunnan. Researchers working in the south have discovered that if local people are allowed to participate in resource management, they become more motivated to maintain wildlife habitat. In Laojunshan, Mr. Zhang's ecotourism guide co-op seeks to open up the mountains to visitors within sustainable-use limits. Conservation activist Li Bo, working with villagers in northwest Yunnan, found that they accomplished more conservation work the less local officials interfered. At the village level, virtually every study concludes that successful community-based conservation "requires collaboration, transparency, and accountability so that a learning environment can be created."[1]

The problem in China is that authorities at all levels have a poor track record of sharing decision-making authority. Protected area designation, logging bans, reforestation, rubber plantations—most conservation programs have come down from the top. But times are changing. Since 1998, the central government has sponsored rural elections throughout the country, and though this voting is not often about conservation, corruption has been reduced. The state could expand village elections to include referendums on local environmental issues. To stimulate community-level conservation with Chinese characteristics, leaders could also support preferential hiring of local people for jobs in protected areas, priority access to villagers for business licenses to offer tourist services, and restructuring use rights for sustainable grazing and fuelwood gathering in newly declared reserves and corridors.

In light of China's continuing emphasis on economics, instituting payment for environmental services in rural areas would help extend conservation benefits to local people. These payments could provide cash to communities for the clean water and carbon banks that local rivers and forests provide to urban dwellers downstream. Such payments are already part of China's successful reforestation programs; they need to be expanded throughout the country's hinterlands.

Provincial China

"Protecting Yunnan's biodiversity is not only the responsibility of the government . . . it's our responsibility to the nation and the world": Yunnan provincial governor Qin Guangrong spoke these words with authority in February 2008 as he announced a bold new program to protect biodiversity in northwest Yunnan.

Governor Qin elaborated by saying that the goal was to complete a science-based biodiversity protection system by 2012, with a majority of endangered species and ecosystems under special protection by 2020. The plan was to protect 13 percent of the northwest as nature reserves and national parks, with corridor linkages between protected areas to knit the system together. Promising RMB 7 billion (USD 1 billion) for the ten-year program, the province's highest official was going to lead Yunnan into the future as a conservation role model for the rest of China.

Governor Qin wanted to do more than increase the total number of reserves. He also wanted to marry environmental protection with provincial development; no more would Yunnan segregate blueprints for roads and tourism from plans for parks and forests. Governor Qin knew that his mandate would require changes in the way provincial officials' job performances were evaluated within China's target-based, quantitative promotion system so that conservation incentives would become part of the new strategy.

What happens next with Governor Qin's plan in Yunnan will tell much about the future of environmental action across China. The plan addresses head-on the weak relationship between environmental science and conservation action. This traditional disconnect has less to do with science, a field that has great status in the PRC, and more to do with spotty management.[2] Chinese bureaucracies are competitive; agencies often work at cross-purposes. Notions of "success" and *zhengji*, "political achievement," are predicated on workers gaining approval from their supervisors in the hierarchy. If Governor Qin's plan can join conservation targets to job promotion, and can begin to stimulate a different kind of *zhengji* in the Chinese system, there is hope for success.

Another strategy is to restructure the Chinese bureaucracy. Along with revamped job incentives, Yunnan's leaders are adding a new National Park Management Office to the provincial forestry department. Breaking with the past, officials are allowing an outside steering committee to provide input. Laojunshan and the area around Kawagebo, a sacred mountain to Tibetans and the tallest peak in Yunnan, are being studied as the next national parks after Pudacuo.

The Yunnan national parks are the latest attempt to address the bedrock conundrum in conservation everywhere in the world: the balance between using nature and protecting it. With 13 percent of northwest Yunnan in protected areas, what will happen to the other 87 percent of the province? The strongest attribute of Governor Qin's "science-based biodiversity protection" vision is that it explicitly links conservation *and* development. Protected areas in northwest Yunnan do not exist in a vacuum; they are the "upstream" of the three parallel rivers' watersheds that flow downstream into Southeast Asia. The challenge is to expand conservation from northwest Yunnan to the province as a whole, the PRC, and beyond.

Yunnan is attracting attention from Beijing for its visionary conservation plan. But the central government is also intent on increasing hydroelectric production in China. Leaders are aware of the tight corner they are hemmed into: biodiversity protection versus replacing coal burning with dams. In May 2009, Premier Wen Jiabao once again extended the Nujiang dams moratorium—"for a while." Much depends on how the dragon meets the Angry River. The world awaits future government decisions over the proposed Nu, Lancang, and Jinsha dams.

China the Country

Building *hexie shehui*, a "harmonious society," has been an official PRC goal promoted by President Hu Jintao and Premier Wen Jiabao since 2004. Hu and Wen have given numerous speeches claiming that a "scientific concept of development" underpins *hexie shehui*. China's top leaders highlight energy efficiency, "environment-friendly society," and increased political participation as the means to harmonious ends.[3] But aside from renewable energy, is ecological health really part of the vision?

So far, *hexie shehui* has had little to do with inventing a country-wide conservation with Chinese characteristics. It has instead been about creating national unity for a diverse citizenry that is bumping up against the ecological and social limitations of past Communist Party policies. PRC leaders are just beginning to come to terms with fundamental environmental constraints: *Wu xing*, the "Five Elements"—energy, land, wood, water, and metal—are dwindling relative to peoples' demands and expectations. If the Party wants to maintain social stability and build an "environment-friendly" nation, it must support a stronger rule of law, fine-tune decentralized authority, work closely with NGOs, and respond more directly to the desires of the Chinese people.

No one has ever voted for national leaders in China; through emperors, warlords, and Party authorities, the country has employed the rule of man for thousands of years. The PRC has only begun to build a rule of law since 1979. The United States took the greater part of the twentieth century to craft robust environmental legislation; in China, great progress has been made in thirty years. The number of practicing lawyers has quintupled since 1990. Until recently, citizens had no standing to sue the government in the public interest, but in July 2009 the first lawsuit by a Chinese environmental NGO was accepted in a municipal court.[4]

Legal reform remains a work in progress. A draft of China's first protected area law is in its sixth year of debate with little sign of closure. The PRC does not require environmental impact assessments to analyze alternatives to development, say, of the Nu dams. Social impacts are not addressed. And it is easy to see why local corruption and cronyism undermine environmental policies: judges are hired, paid, and fired by local government officials.[5]

Judges interpret environmental law; they don't enforce the rules. That is the job of the Party, the largest bureaucracy in the world. The PRC has not, however, developed a sizeable environmental bureaucracy. The Ministry of Environmental Protection has less than three thousand employees while the U.S. Environmental Protection Agency (EPA) has seventeen thousand to serve a population that is four times smaller. China still doesn't have a separate ministry for energy policy.[6]

In China, administrative size is not always equivalent with power. But since the 1980s, when Beijing delegated a great deal of decision making to local authorities, it is not easy to comprehend who is responsible for any given ruling. To foreigners, the Chinese system is opaque: remember that there are nine different ministries that control nature reserves and no binding national law. Instead, there is a culture of *guanxi* based on cultivating personal relationships. Bringing order to conservation management will remain a challenge in China because things don't always operate according to procedural rules.

Outsiders are often confused about "the rules" in China, yet international NGOs operate under plenty of regulations. The central government originally encouraged foreign organizations to import skills, strategies, and funding to help China gain the capacity to untangle its own environmental problems. Foreign groups have been joined by some 350,000 domestic NGOs working on every imaginable issue. But the PRC maintains control. The government used to restrict charitable foundations, corporate giving, and private donations; hence, there is almost no Chinese philanthropic tradition.[7] International groups still cannot raise money in China. Imagine how effective the Sierra Club or Greenpeace would be if the U.S. government only allowed such groups to use money raised *outside* the United States.

Conservation would be better served if regulations were relaxed, but the government is concerned about political organizing. Most environmental NGOs are only allowed to have a few offices. These barriers may satisfy the state, but they also narrow the effectiveness of NGOs. This, in turn, reduces the likelihood of resolving complex issues that demand coordinated action from multiple players, the very kinds of conservation problems that exist across China.[8]

Despite ongoing restrictions, the Party has made some efforts to accommodate its citizens. In the past few years, Beijing has dramatically increased funding to rural Chinese, sponsored more liberal land and labor laws, and has passed legislation that allows the public more open access to environmental information.[9]

Yet it remains difficult to know what Chinese people want for their future. A 2008 poll showed that Chinese citizens overwhelmingly support their government; another found that more than 86 percent of Chinese believe that they have no "important" role to play in environmental protection.[10] These attitudes reflect traditional values that place great faith in leaders, mixed with sixty years of Party rule, and so there is little history of citizen input into national discourse and decision making. But China is changing. Two groups will greatly influence how conservation with Chinese characteristics evolves: the expanding middle class and the initial one-child generation.

When it comes to environmental awareness, it is challenging to characterize the Chinese middle class. These are people who lived through the transition from Mao to markets, from being have-nots to home owners. They are full-fledged consumer capitalists, the first generation to experience Deng Xiaoping's promise that "to get rich is glorious," and they purchase apartments, the latest fashions, and

SUVs. They also have the leisure time to go bird watching and visit Pudacuo National Park. Global recession may slow down these new consumers, but it won't stop them from multiplying. By 2020, China's middle class may reach five hundred million people.[11] Experts are less certain about whether their connection to nature will grow as well.

The six hundred million adolescents and young adults of the one-child generation form the fastest-growing cohort in the country. With few or no siblings, these "Little Emperors" continue to be subject to great pressures to succeed in school and to gain employment; yet, even before the global economic slowdown in 2007, recent college graduates were having trouble finding work. Young Chinese appear even less interested in conservation than their parents are.[12] I have met a handful of young people dedicated to environmental issues, but the majority seem more concerned with constructing online social networks than conservation corridors. They still don't have a clearly defined pathway to public participation in environmental affairs.

The environmental future of China depends on opening a voice for citizens much as opening the economy boosted the country into the modern world. NGOs and the exposure to international news and environmental norms through the Internet is slowly shaping this process; I would prefer that these changes were blocked less by the central government. Then I remember that even in democratic America direct citizen participation in environmental law and policy took some seventy-five years to evolve.

Call it "conservation with Chinese characteristics," "harmonious society," enlightened self-interest, or common sense—people and nature in China (and in all societies) are mutually interdependent. Twenty-six hundred years ago, Old Master Lao looked inward and remarked, "Knowing others is wisdom; knowing the self is enlightenment." Confucius also illuminated abiding links between humans and *tian* (heaven): "when personal lives are cultivated, states are governed; only when states are governed is there peace all under Heaven."[13] Conservation in the PRC today must reclaim some of its traditional Chinese roots, without neglecting modern ecological insights. A strength of the Confucian system was that it envisioned human behavior operating within the bounds of Heaven and Earth. Contemporary concepts such as biodiversity protection, sustainable livelihoods, ecosystem management, and payments for environmental services fit neatly into this ancient framework as healthy social norms.

Today, traditional Chinese philosophy barely influences management despite its parallels with modern conservation principles. Yet the fundamental embeddedness of people in nature is reflected in China's embrace of bold national experiments to quantify environmental services. The world's most populous country is revamping the international national park ideal in an attempt to ensure that both biodiversity and human livelihoods are maintained. These Chinese experiments in backcountry villages and protected areas won't directly solve global problems like climate change. But safekeeping national parks goes far beyond protecting nature. Reserves can bolster local people's participation in management and provide an alternative platform to economic growth on which to build national pride. And protected ecosystems sequester carbon from an atmosphere under increasing assault.

China in the World

In 1793, after expelling the British trade envoy Lord MacCartney from his kingdom, Emperor Qianlong sent a letter to King George III: "our celestial empire possesses all things in prolific abundance and lacks no product within its borders." The emperor was wrong; China lacked silver for currency and needed trading partners to purchase its tea, silks, and ceramics. The country was already in decline; a short time later, 2000 years of dynastic rule was over.

Despite evidence to the contrary, Emperor Qianlong believed that the unitary power of the Middle Kingdom was insurmountable. He did not feel any special need to project power beyond bordering realms. Even in the 1600s and 1700s, when China dominated the world economically, rulers did not attempt far-reaching political hegemony.[14] The dominant Chinese storyline of collective cultural solidarity continues to guide Party leaders. The Chinese see themselves as providing an alternative to the West, even as the PRC assumes a greater role in global affairs. But thirty years ago, when the PRC decided to hitch itself to the developed world's economic model, nobody told China that there wouldn't be enough room at the table.

The fundamental problem has nothing to do with politics. It's about numbers and behavior. China has 1.3 billion people; if the PRC consumed steel and paper at U.S. per capita rates, the country would require every bit of steel and twice as much paper as are produced today. In terms of oil and coal, China would burn more of these fuels than are extracted worldwide.

In 2008, Jared Diamond distilled reams of data into one simple ratio: 32 to 1.[15] That's the average annual amount of oil, electricity, and just plain stuff that an advertising executive in Los Angeles or a postal clerk in Sydney consumes compared to a dryland farmer in Algeria or a Tibetan guesthouse manager in northwest Yunnan. When Diamond assigned the developed-world rate to everyone living in China and the United States, he found that this level of consumption was equivalent to a total human population of 13 billion. Then Diamond added in all Indians; this bumped humanity's ecological footprint up to 19.5 billion. When Diamond included every poor person on Earth as if they ate steak, drove sedans, and used electricity to read at night like Americans, Japanese, and Germans, he discovered that the planet would need to support 72 billion humans.

Which planet do we want to live on? I am aware that most people today don't own cars or credit cards or have indoor flush toilets, yet I can't conceive of Earth supporting Diamond's low-end 13 billion people, two times the current population.

The most profound conservation problem confronting China and the world is this: if it's true that there isn't enough Earth to share at the levels that politicians promise and people desire, then who is going to initiate change? Facing greater energy scarcity, will global leaders begin to act more cooperatively, or will they set off an end-game scramble for the remaining stocks of fossil fuels? In fact, the place where Long is meeting the Angry River is not located in the PRC at all; the real dragon is the fossil-fuel-dependent world of wealth and the river is Earth's atmosphere.

The Middle Kingdom's deep dynastic pattern of sovereign self-sufficiency, the Party's decades-long role as adversarial "other," and the current leadership's commitment to economic growth appear to make China an unlikely catalyst for promoting sustainable alternatives to business as usual. But China is different from other countries: it is both inside and outside the international system. Its leaders have bought the economic but not the political vision of the developed world, and it remains challenging to forecast whether China will become a "responsible stakeholder" as defined by the current geopolitical system.[16]

The PRC is poised to assume a leadership role in international affairs. But it is difficult to tell whether Beijing is ready for this responsibility. In the Greater Mekong, for example, China could fully partner with downstream countries to create a sustainable hydropower system that would not deplete the three parallel rivers. Of all the lands in the Greater Himalaya, some 75 percent are within the PRC, and Chinese scientists have done the best work defining regional water issues. Hundreds of millions of Chinese will be deeply affected by impending water losses, yet Beijing so far has done little to convene Himalayan nations to deal with this issue.[17] If powerful China doesn't lead the way, who will?

China is certainly crafting an energy conservation with Chinese characteristics.[18] Yes, the PRC adds far too many coal-burning power plants to its energy grid, but it is on track to build its first "clean coal" emissions-free plant by 2015. Beijing is pushing the world's most aggressive increases in all forms of renewable energy. The Party has committed to a national target of getting 20 percent of the country's energy from non-fossil-fuel sources by 2020. China already has under construction or approval enough nuclear power plants to double this source of energy from current levels. As for other emissions reduction strategies, the PRC has the world's most rapidly expanding mass transit system and leads the world (or is among top producers) in making wind turbines, solar water heaters, compact fluorescent bulbs, rechargeable batteries, and photovoltaic panels. The six largest Chinese companies in this last sector didn't even exist ten years ago.[19]

Though it may appear unlikely, Beijing could project *hexie shehui,* the "harmonious society," out beyond the PRC, offering it as a template for cooperation on global environmental problems. China could combine its traditional version of *tuanji,* "unity," with its insistence on an international order influenced by multiple countries, not just a few. This brand of politics could spark multilateral collaboration to reduce CO_2 emissions; after all, even conservative Chinese policy analysts can see that "a Harmonious Society cannot be built in just one country."

There is little time to act. The International Energy Agency's 2009 business as usual projection estimated that worldwide emissions will rise 40 percent by 2030. Over the twenty-first century, Intergovernmental Panel on Climate Change models suggest that to keep atmospheric CO_2 at 450 parts per million (therefore limiting average temperature increases to about 2° C, or 3.6° F), cumulative annual emissions would have to be limited to no more than 5 billion metric tonnes of carbon per year for the rest of the century. In 2008, cumulative carbon releases stood at more than 8.5 billion metric tonnes per year.[20]

Stabilizing CO_2 at 450 parts per million means that global emissions must peak by 2015–2020 and then fall sharply, with the world becoming carbon neutral around 2050. This difficult regimen only yields a fifty-fifty chance that temperature increases will remain around 2° C (3.6° F). The alternative? MIT and Hadley Centre scientists project that with no action taken, rising emissions will result in a catastrophic and irreversible 5.5–7.1° C (9.9–12.8° F) increase in average temperatures by 2100.[21] Unhitching the massing of material wealth from the atmospheric accumulation of greenhouse gasses is the most intractable problem in history. But it's not just about the developed world's addiction to fossil fuels; it's about everyone's dependence on unrestrained economic growth.

Throughout 2009, as a run up to the UN climate meetings in Copenhagen in December, Chinese negotiators floated a proposal for wealthy nations to divert 1 percent of their GDP to poor countries to help finance clean energy technology and the coming costs of global warming disruptions. The dragon was displeased—since 1850, wealthy nations have been responsible for some 75 percent of all greenhouse gas emissions; poorer countries have released 24 percent. China's cumulative emissions load is 8 percent, the European Union's is 26 percent, and the U.S. contribution is around 29 percent of the total.[22] Even China's recent rise to become the number one emitter has numerous strings attached to consumption in the developed world. A TV or toy made in China bound for a mall in Minneapolis leaves its carbon footprint in the PRC. This is "carbon leakage"; the Tyndall Centre for Climate Change Research, in the United Kingdom, estimates that some 23 percent of China's total emissions result from exporting products to shoppers in the developed world.[23]

In climate negotiations, the diplomatic code for referring to the overwhelming carbon footprint of the wealthy world is "differential responsibilities." To Americans who have enjoyed a middle-class existence for generations, these distinctions appear easy to resolve; it just comes down to supporting renewable energy and limiting growth. But to China, India, Brazil, and the bloc of other countries whose people have never experienced a decent standard of living, "differentials" are disparities.[24] These countries will not limit their emissions until the "responsible" parties act first.

But Earth's atmosphere bears a message: we are all in this together.

Already, by 2005, total greenhouse gas emissions from the less developed world were 7 percent greater each year than those from the developed world. By 2030, this disparity is expected to have grown so rapidly that energy consumers in the "less developed world" will be releasing sufficient gases to trigger dangerous climate change *without any historical or future contributions from developed nations.*[25]

In the United States in 2009, President Barack Obama took office as a candidate of change—global warming will see to that. Acting to stabilize the faltering American economy while pushing hard for health-care reform, the Obama administration had a difficult time convincing Congress to pass new energy legislation that limited U.S. emissions. In November 2009, President Obama visited President Hu in China to jumpstart what will no doubt be the most important negotiations of the American president's term.[26]

At the Copenhagen climate conference in December 2009, President Obama played a key role on the final day of the talks. But even as the world's political leaders accepted for the first time consideration of the goal of keeping the average global temperature increase to 1.5° C (2.7° F), they produced no hard deadline for legally binding action. What had originally been intended as a conference that would yield such an outcome devolved into a meeting where an acceptable political framework might be reached. What was finally produced, however, was a statement of intention, an "accord" bereft of any overt recognition that this delay into 2010 and beyond had any carbon consequences.

The economic recession that began in 2007 has made none of these steps easy. But maybe the global slowdown has had a silver lining— world leaders can shape a response that builds a carbon-neutral society out of the shell of the old. After all, when the recession recedes, we can't return to pumping CO_2 out of tailpipes and smokestacks.

China and climate change are collapsing "us" and "them" into "we": Alou grew up planting corn and herding; now he guides visitors from all over the world into the forests around Dimaluo. Dr. Zhou struggles to bring collaborative planning into the Lijiang County bureaucracy. In Laojunshan, Mr. Zhang offers a villager's voice to an international NGO. Ainipa leaves Manmai village in upland Xishuangbanna and becomes a student in the world.

Hovering over northwest Yunnan, sacred Kawagebo, the highest mountain in the province, has built ice for thousands of years. Today, its glaciers melt into a warming world. The Lancang morphs into the politicians' Greater Mekong Subregion, all the while posing a question; what is a river supposed to provide? The Nujiang, the Angry River, bends downstream, hits a dam in Myanmar, and lights go on in Bangkok.

Looking from the inside out, I see the people, rivers, and ecosystems of Yunnan and imagine what is happening there taking place on a nationwide scale, trying to picture a conservation with Chinese characteristics. From the world outside China gazing in, I recognize so many disparate points of view that I wonder if they can be reconciled. Then I hear Tsering telling me a Tibetan adage on the trek to Nizu village: "Nature does as it pleases. There is never a thunderstorm to announce the beginning of a new year. Even when a new century begins, it is only we mortals who ring bells and fire off pistols."

The world, of course, is full of surprises. The dragon Long remains complex, multifaceted, subtle, hidden. The Chinese dragon is catalyzing a great transformation, pushing the world toward an imminent environmental reckoning.

And the dragon is magical. It can shrink to the size of a silkworm or swell up to embrace all of Heaven and Earth. In the Middle Kingdom, Long is, finally, a sign of luck, a good omen. The dragon stands in the East, the sun's home, and by its power the Earth is renewed.

Notes

Introduction

1. For the most part, I use the modern Pinyin transliteration system to render Mandarin into English (i.e., *Yangzi = Yangtze*). Though older systems may be more familiar to readers, the Pinyin is preferred. So *Taoism* becomes *Daoism*, *tofu* becomes *dofu*, *Peking* becomes *Beijing*, *Szechuan* becomes *Sichuan*, and so on.

Chapter 1. The Highest Good

1. For a summary of Yunnan's biodiversity, see studies by Yang et al. (2004) and Xu and Wilkes (2004). For comparison, the United States has less than half as many plants and about a third fewer mammals and birds. Mittermeier et al. (2004: 159–164) describe the mountains of southwest China as a biodiversity hotspot. MacKinnon and Wang's report (2008) is a general reference on biodiversity across China. Stein et al. (2000) are a good source for comparative global biodiversity data.

2. Income figures are from a report by Young and Yang (2005). Life expectancy and literacy rates for Yunnan are from the China Statistical Yearbook (2006).

3. TNC China's Web site is www.nature.org/china.

4. D. Wang (2000) gives an account of this transition along with population data. In the Nu, about 22 percent of all farmland lies on steep slopes greater than twenty-five degrees (Xu and Wilkes 2002: 6).

5. This *I Jing* quote is from hexagram 4 in the translation by Wilhelm and Baynes (1950: 20–24). The *Daodejing* quote is from the translation by Feng and English (1972); this translation does not have numbered pages. See Porter's book (1996) on the text for a scholarly translation with valuable commentary.

6. The Go West policy is treated thoroughly in chapter 2.

7. Wilkes (2005) provides background information on Dimaluo.

8. The Chinese currency is the renminbi (RMB) or yuan. The vernacular for both is *kuai*. During the writing of this book, the exchange rate with the U.S. dollar was 6.8 to 1; to simplify conversions, I have rounded this ratio up to 7 to 1 throughout the text.

9. Wilkes (2003) gives a detailed treatment of villager issues.
10. The number of organizations petitioning the PRC grew eventually to ninety (Y. Wang 2007).

Chapter 2. The Frontier and the Middle Kingdom

1. Fortey (2004) provides an overview of the region's geological evolution. For details, see work by Shi et al. (1999).
2. Yang et al. (2004) summarize Yunnan's biodiversity across many taxa.
3. Elvin has written the definitive environmental history of China from its earliest beginnings up to the twentieth century.
4. Needham and Ling (1954: 242) provide a fascinating table cataloging Chinese mechanical inventions and the lag time (in centuries) before these technologies were transported to ("discovered by") the West. Paper, for example, took ten centuries to be transmitted; the magnetic compass took four centuries. Winchester (2008) writes a compelling biography of Needham.
5. J. Goodman (2000) provides a summary of Yunnan's prehistory. Scott (2009: 120–121) shows how the ancient Han used their own cultural markers (irrigated agriculture, use of plows, fixed settlements, etc.) to label ethnic minorities as barbarians (*sheng*, "raw") compared to the Han (*shu*, "cooked"). For details on how Han expansion affected local peoples' migrations throughout southern China, see studies by Wiens (1954), Fitzgerald (1972), and Fiskesjo (2006). See also Sturgeon's work (2007).
6. For a concise history of Beijing, see Haw's account (2007).
7. Donald and Benewick (2005) offer a wealth of data for each province in an easy-to-read format. Young and Yang (2005:18) break down Yunnan's ethnic nationalities by percentage of total population and by geographic distribution.
8. However, people living on Yunnan's border *were* severely affected by the Cultural Revolution. At least 17,000–37,000 ethnic nationality people were killed and a minimum of 50,000 people fled west out of China to escape persecution (Schoenhals 2004).
9. Young (2007b) is an excellent analysis using PRC data.
10. Wilkes (2005) has provided the most cogent analysis of multiple points of view concerning the social construction of ethnic nationality identity in Yunnan. He has not published this material; it is only available in dissertation format (copy in author's files).
11. Weller (2006: 20–23) discusses Chinese terms for *nature*; I have based much of my treatment on his work.

12. For coverage of Daoism and Buddhism as sources of environmental values in China, see the work of Girardot et al. (2001) and Tucker and Williams (1997), respectively. Porter (1993) provides a first-person account of Daoist monks in modern China.

13. M. Elvin (2004: 323) uses China's famous *shanshui*, "mountains and rivers," poetic tradition to accent this paradox. This tradition blossomed in the fourth century CE when nature in China remained largely intact. Six hundred years later, "this would begin to be doubtful. A thousand years later it would be untrue" (368). Elvin is saying that at the beginning of the classical nature poetry tradition in China, there was little contradiction between what people wrote and what they experienced (i.e., healthy ecosystems). The gap between poetic perception and biological reality widened over time, yet the chasm was not reflected in the writing.

14. W. Chan (1963) translates Wang Yangming's sixteenth-century Confucian interpretation, "Inquiry on the Great Learning." Sources related to environmental values in Confucianism are found in work by Adler et al. (1998). Tu (2001) makes a case for an ecological neo-Confucianism; in my Chinese experience, I have not seen this trend. Overall, however, Confucianism is increasingly influential in modern China (see Bell 2008).

15. The quote is from R. Harris's book (2008: 59) on wildlife conservation, from his excellent material on the subject of wildness. Gary Snyder (2003: 203–208) also makes important observations on this point: nature in China is "not a 'wilderness' but a habitat . . . a model for a better way of life." Snyder goes on to point out that in a country as large as China with a mobile population, "a 'sense of place' would be hard to maintain. Humanistic concerns can be cultivated anywhere, but certain kinds of understanding and information about the natural world are only available to those who stay put and keep looking" (208). I would add that the natural world has to "stay put" too; the Chinese, due to a variety of pressures, continue to transform wild nature.

16. Scott (2009) lays out a strong case that across mainland upland Asia (including Yunnan) state-centered powers have always attempted to control ethnic nationality peoples who choose to live on borders, a choice these peoples make precisely because they want to *avoid* the state.

17. Dams in Yunnan are covered in detail in chapter 7.

18. R. Harris (2008: 55, 250–251) discusses in detail the difficulties in understanding the meaning of *shengtai jianshe*.

19. McBeath and McBeath (2006) describe issues related to linking Chinese biodiversity conservation policies with management practices. H. Xu et al. (2009) quantify the mixed results from recent Chinese efforts to lower rates of biodiversity loss.

Chapter 3. Under the Jade Dragon

1. Sicroff et al. (2003: 536) describe Lijiang as a "tourist ghetto." McKhann (2001: 150) labeled it "totally out of control." And these comments do not reflect the spectacular growth over recent years. Oakes (1997) and Ruch (2006) provide insightful analyses of authenticity in Chinese tourism.

2. During the 2008 spring festival, "Golden Week," Xinhua News Agency (2008b) reported that Chinese railroads would carry 178.6 million passengers. For perspective, 41 million Americans traveled over Thanksgiving weekend in 2007. Tourism in China is growing rapidly; the prediction is for the PRC to be second only to the United States by 2017 (Z. Li 2006a).

3. For insights into Chinese tourist values, see the work of Wu et al. (2000) and Sofield and Li (1998).

4. Sicroff et al. (2003) describe this project.

5. This is the beginning couplet of "River Snow," a poem by Liu Tsung-yuan from the Tang dynasty. Hinton (2005: 154) is the translator.

6. This is the Chinese story/myth of Peach Blossom Spring, well-known to many Han Chinese and written by the famous poet T'ao Ch'ien in the fourth century CE. The translation is Hinton's (1993: 70).

7. Swope et al. (1997) and Zackey (2007) provide detailed accounts of these events in Wenhai. Land tenure throughout the PRC is a contentious matter, one that most observers agree will have to be resolved before conservation (and the market economy) can evolve much further. Ho (2001) makes the point that the Party believes that current policies provide an ideological alternative to Western-style private property. A basic reference on these matters is by Oi and Walden (1999). Recent changes in Chinese law are "privatizing" the management of collective forests (Stone 2009).

8. The following data come from bulletin-board displays in the dining room at the eco-lodge.

9. Bullock (2003) was the lead TNC staff person working on the eco-lodge project.

10. See the report by The Nature Conservancy and Yunnan Provincial

Government (2001). The provincial government also contracted with the World Tourism Organization (2001) to build a province-wide plan at the time.

11. The International Union for the Conservation of Nature (IUCN) defines *ecotourism* as "environmentally responsible travel and visitation to relatively undisturbed natural areas in order to enjoy and appreciate nature . . . that promotes conservation, has low negative visitor impact, and provides for beneficially active socio-economic involvement of local populations" (quoted in Wood 2002). There are many other definitions (e.g., see Honey 2008). For work in Wenhai, Bullock (2003: 568) used "small-scale green tourism that provides an opportunity to directly experience the unique natural and cultural resources of pristine areas in a small group environment." This definition has many problems; for example, the land in and around the eco-lodge hasn't been "pristine" for a very long time.

12. An overview of environmental NGOs in China is provided by Lu (2005). TNC protects about 117 million acres of land worldwide. Its operating budget is close to one billion dollars.

13. Visitor data from the eco-lodge is courtesy of Cun Xuerong, the manager, in an e-mail received February 16, 2008. Lijiang income figures are from Donaldson's work (2007: 346); he does not provide a specific year for the data.

14. This government pronouncement is quoted by Donaldson (2007: 342). See also the report by the Yunnan Province Department of Commerce (2006). Holz (2007: 38) shows that cadres in the Party have benefited greatly from their position. Of the 3,220 wealthiest Chinese, 2,932 are children of high-level Party members.

15. The group claims that their project's "ultimate goal is to achieve ecological conservation and sustainable development" (Shui On Group 2007: 1).

16. This is a couplet from the Tang dynasty poem by Chia Tao, "Farewell to Scholar Keng," from a translation by O'Connor (2000: 80).

17. Donaldson (2007) and Nyaupane et al. (2006) make a strong case for government policy being a critical factor in how much money actually reaches villagers. In neighboring Guizhou Province, officials have explicitly tied development to poverty reduction, and rural incomes in poor counties have risen faster there than in Yunnan.

18. This image of the sand gull comes from Du Fu's famous Tang dynasty poem, "Thoughts in Travel." The translation is by X. Qiu (2005).

Chapter 4. Old Mountains, Young Parks

1. See also the description of Three Parallel Rivers at the UN Environmental Programme Web site, http://www.unep-wcm.org.

2. The situation still hasn't changed much—John MacKinnon, a protected area specialist with a long history in China, said recently that "there aren't any real rules. Every agency can set up whatever they like and call it a nature reserve and then do whatever they like in it" (quoted in Mozur 2008: 77). Since 2004, there has been a central-government movement to craft protected area legislation. For perspective, it took the U.S. Congress forty-four years after the designation of Yellowstone to create a national parks act in 1916.

3. Jim and Xu (2003: 41) provide a description of the evolution of China's nature reserve policies.

4. Jim and Xu (2003: 48) reveal that competition "feeds the parochial tendencies of local government units and works against joint endeavors . . . lack of cooperation [is] . . . a long-standing legacy of the competitive and hierarchical structure."

5. L. Buckley (2006) describes the brief history of the co-op.

6. Surveys from the late 1990s comparing nature reserve funding between developing countries showed that China was 28 percent below the average for poor countries (see James 1999). Lindberg et al. (2003: 115) cite a survey of Chinese nature reserves that found 22 percent of reserves were "so damaged that they failed to meet conservation targets." Han and Ren (2001) found that seven of fifteen of the reserves they studied spent only 5 percent of income on conservation management (see also D. Xu 2000). Recent progress has been made with protected area management in China, though this is not yet reflected in the academic literature (see chapter 9).

7. Over the same period, forests in western Sichuan were reduced by 76 percent. Because the forestry sector was not well regulated, it is difficult to assess the accuracy of government figures, especially prior to 2000. For a revealing vignette about how one village in northwest Yunnan was impacted by state-sponsored logging, see the study by Melick et al. (2007: 18–20).

8. R. Harris (2008: 112–115) discusses Chinese regulations for core, buffer, and experimental zones. He describes the overall situation as "an incomprehensible mush" (119).

9. Data on people living in and around nature reserves are estimates. Jiang (2005) says 1.25 to 2.85 million people live in cores. Jim and Xu (2003:

223) suggest that 60 million live "in and around" reserves. Harkness (1998) puts that number at around 30 million people.

10. Harris (2008: 114) makes this line of authority clear: "prohibitions contained in the [nature reserve] regulations sit uncomfortably atop whatever other activities are already legal and ongoing on the land at the time of designation, as provided for by local, regional, or provincial *economic imperatives*" (emphasis added).

11. Recent research has revealed that the snub-nosed monkey is not 100 percent dependent on old-growth fir forests (see D. Li et al. 2008 and Grueter et al. 2008).

12. Ma et al. (2006: 761) state that "population viability data are lacking for all species in the Yunnan Great Rivers Project." In a position paper outlining major policy issues in Asia, written for the Society of Conservation Biology, McNeely et al. (2009: 806) describe the impact of conservation biology as "depressingly minimal." Vina et al. (2007) summarize changes in giant panda habitat over recent years from a landscape perspective. See also the giant panda report by W. Xu et al. (2009).

13. See L. Buckley's report (2006) for details about GEI's work in Laojunshan. GEI's mission is to "make conservation profitable and economic development ecologically sound by supporting conservation efforts with market-oriented solutions" (1).

14. Similar results are described by Li and Han (2001) and Han and Ren (2001). Lindberg et al. (2003: 117–118) make the important point that reserve staff who do have scientific professional training often have difficulty working with social management issues, including ecotourism and local community concerns. Similar problems have also been noted in the U.S.

15. The internationalization of protected areas is a complex and contentious topic. In the early 1990s, the International Union for the Conservation of Nature (IUCN) added two new categories to their global framework, saying it was time for a "new conservation paradigm." (Phillips 2003: 20-21; IUCN 2003). The idea was to link poverty alleviation with biodiversity protection, but the new categories allow significant human use *within* reserves. Over the last decade, 50 percent of all new reserves are in these categories, leading some scientists to charge that protected areas no longer do their job (see Locke and Dearden 2005; Lapham and Livermore 2003). There are many sources of information on the questions surrounding people and protected areas. West and Brockington

(2006) and West et al. (2006) give excellent summaries. Agrawal (2005) offers a political ecology framework that he calls "environmentality" to understand these issues.

16. For another perspective, see an article by Young (2007a: 27).

17. In 2001, the PRC allowed both Zhongdian town and county to change their names to Xiangri-la, a fascinating political move that has been documented by Hillman (2003). It is difficult to reconcile this change with the fact that the well-known fictional Shangri-la, the setting of James Hilton's 1933 novel *Lost Horizon*, is a product of the imagination. Investment capital is pouring into Zhongdian; one recent estimate is 500 million yuan (USD 67 million). If this figure is correct, these monies could support more than four hundred thousand villagers for a year at current local per capita incomes.

18. The park officially opened in June 2007, one month after our visit.

19. Americans are not the only people to romanticize ethnic peoples; Huber (1997) shows how Tibetans have created a green image of themselves.

20. This three-part framework is from a report by Agrawal (1999). Village development is complex; Litzinger (2007: 286) confirms this general view in northwest Yunnan: "most mountain residents are tired of isolation, eager for development, and ready for change."

21. See also studies by Jagerskog and Zeitoun (2009) and Barrett et al. (2001). These authors suggest that it takes roughly ten years to build community-based conservation.

22. Then there are the attitudes of specific ethnic nationalities to consider. Salick et al. (2005, 2006) provide details on how Tibetans manage sacred landscapes. Studley (2007: 36, 34–38) gives a general overview on Khamba Tibetan attitudes toward land: "Khamba . . . aren't deliberately conservationists . . . they manifest an ethical attitude because Nature has intrinsic value having been created by or presided over by a deity." Many indigenous people around the world have similar views (see Krech 2005). There is a growing literature on changes in agropastoralist livelihoods in Yunnan (see Buntaine et al. 2006; Byg and Salick 2009; Willson 2006; Yi et al. 2007).

Chapter 5. In the Land of Twelve Thousand Rice Fields

1. Zhu et al. (2006) provide a description of Xishuangbanna's vegetation history and biogeographical affinities.

2. The Dai, with five subgroups, and the Hani, with at least thirty, are complex. Both are part of larger cultures whose territories extend well

beyond China. Quenemoen (2004: 201–205) discusses Dai history. For a cultural description of the Dai, see work by J. Goodman (2000: 292–300). Michaud (2006) offers an accessible overview of the ethnic nationality peoples of mainland Southeast Asia.

3. Shapiro (2001: 169–193) gives a nuanced account of the Communist Party origins of the rubber industry in Yunnan. See also work by J. Goodman (2000: 211–216) and J. Xu (2006). June 2009 was the first period that any country (China) surpassed the United States in monthly auto sales.

4. J. Qiu (2009) and Zhu (2008) provide overviews of this dramatic transition.

5. *Eucalyptus* spp. and other widely planted nonnative trees in Yunnan (and China) are also counted as "forest" in official statistics. In fact, the UN Food and Agriculture Organization's definition of forest only requires 10 percent cover, "a criterion that would satisfy few forest-dwelling species" (Chazdon 2008: 1458). Research from Yunnan (Tang et al. 2007) bears this out.

6. For villager income data, see studies by Manivong and Cramb (2008) and W. Liu et al. (2006). China uses 50 percent of its rubber to produce auto tires for export. The global price of rubber has tripled since 1998 (Shen 2008).

7. See the studies by H. Liu et al. (2002: 707–708). Pei (1991) and J. Xu et al. (2005) describe traditional conservation practices of ethnic nationalities in Xishuangbanna. Maneeratana and Hoare (2007) track regional trends in swidden agriculture throughout the upper Mekong watershed.

8. J. Goodman (2000: 324–325) briefly describes the Bulang.

9. Production statistics are from 2003 and are found in a study by Weng (2006: 104); this number has since risen. Tea in China is a vast subject; though I have not found a definitive treatment, the works by Chow and Kramer (1990) and, especially, by T. Liu (2005) stand out.

10. These were prices in 2005. Harney's discussion (2008) is thorough and contains various wage comparisons across employment sectors in China.

11. Scott (2009: 5) offers a powerful argument that the state's objective has been less to make hill peoples productive than to ensure that their economic activities are legible, tax assessable, and confiscatorial. Note that Yin (2001) portrays swiddens as ecologically adapted, not some "primitive" system; see also Ediger and Chen (2006). Regarding food security, Fu et al. (2006) have shown that village households with more off-farm

income tend to prefer monocultural crops due to labor limitations. At the regional scale in the Mekong, food security is predicted to become much more tenuous. Maneeratana and Hoare (2007: 798) suggest that a 2 percent annual increase in food production out to 2025 will be necessary, accounting only for population growth. They point out that such yields would be unprecedented and therefore declare that more cash crops are inevitable. Shen (2008) captures the expanding rubber market in Yunnan and its neighboring countries, while J. Xu et al. (2009b) give a current overview of land-use changes and their implications.

Chapter 6. Into the Great Green Triangle

1. The higher 2008 figure of 334,000 hectares (825,330 acres) is from Shen (2008). The 2005 official government data is in a report by W. Shi (2008: 57). Qiu (2009) estimates that about 20 percent of Xishuangbanna is now in rubber. For regional perspective, Bradshaw et al. (2009) point out that the highest rate of rain forest loss is occurring in Asia.

2. Dave Smith, e-mail to author, June 21, 2008. The photo of the female tiger appeared in an article by Morell (2008: 1314).

3. Species at risk in Nam Ha are outlined by Hedemark and Vongsak (2003). The endangered status of the various species mentioned here can be found in a guide by Smith and Xie (2008).

4. For details on Corridor E and its current management, see work by Hu (2008) and the Asian Development Bank (2008a).

5. Designing corridors is complex; a general reference is one by Hilty et al. (2006). Recent innovations are summed up by Beier et al. (2008).

6. Alton et al. (2005) give a thorough account of rubber's environmental impacts in the region. See also work by Qiu (2009).

7. On tiger conservation, see studies by the IUCN (2008), Morell (2007), and Dinerstein et al. (2007). Terhune (2008) describes a new World Bank tiger initiative that offers some hope. Current events lead me to be cautious about the trajectory of heretofore "stable" tiger populations; in 2008, the Nepalese population was shown to be 40 percent less than expected because of poaching.

8. Major tiger prey species are sambar, wild boar, gaur and red muntjac. IUCN listing statuses for these species are in work by Smith and Xie (2008).

9. For perspective, in an area about equivalent to the size of the San Francisco Bay Area, Nam Ha harbors roughly 30 percent of the total number of birds found throughout North America. For a survey of wildlife in Nam Ha, see work by Hedemark and Vongsak (2003).

10. Laos is the least developed country in Southeast Asia, and Luang Namtha Province is one of the poorest regions: as of 2002, 93 percent of villages had no electricity, 73 percent had no piped water, and 25 percent of all infants died before the age of one year. Adult literacy in Luang Namtha is the lowest in Laos.

11. W. Shi (2008) provides the most detailed report on rubber in northern Laos.

12. For examples, see works by W. Shi (2008: 28) and McCartan (2008, 2007) and an article in the *Nation* (2007).

13. Anonymous e-mail to author about plantations inside Nam Ha, September 29, 2008.

14. Rubber contract information is in a report by W. Shi (2008: 16). The Luang Namtha provincial government has designated some 240,000 hectares (593,050 acres) as suitable for tree plantations and cash crops. As in Xishuangbanna, smallholders are benefiting from rubber (see Manivong and Cramb 2008).

15. Food plantation data are from McCartan (2008: 2).

16. This transition is examined by W. Shi (2008: 23–28). An estimate of the amount of rubber plantation in Myanmar is 243,000 hectares (600,470 acres) (McCartan 2008: 3); due to lack of transparency, this figure is impossible to verify. Hanssen (2007: 3–6) argues that Lao PDR government policy supports awarding large contracts to China to further control ethnic nationality hill peoples. He labels these land-use transitions "historically significant" in Laos. See also a summary by Rowcroft (2008).

17. Butler (2009) describes current threats caused by economic development in northern Laos. The Asian Development Bank's *2007 Biodiversity Corridors Status Report* portrays serious threats to every pilot program. In Cambodia, five dams are proposed inside the national protected area that corridor work has focused on. Another project in Cambodia is subject to government-sponsored mining and plantation concessions along with several hydropower proposals. The Xe Pian Corridor in Laos and the Tenasserim pilot in Thailand both are threatened with large plantations that have already secured government permits. The test corridor in Vietnam faces habitat fragmentation from Asian Development Bank–funded highways as well as from dams that would resettle villagers into areas "not always suitable for providing a sound basis for their livelihoods" (Asian Development Bank 2007: 47).

18. The baseline year for this goal is 2007; see the Greater Mekong Subregion Economic Cooperation Program report (2009) for current

economic policy. Data on trade between China and Laos is from an Intellasia report (2008); on China and Myanmar, from the Xinhua News Agency (2008a); on China and Vietnam, from a VietNamNet Bridge article (2008). Overall, China is working within the Association of South East Asian Nations (ASEAN) to create by 2010 the world's largest free-trade area encompassing 1.8 billion people (China Briefing News 2008b). China-ASEAN trade has a good chance of surpassing China–United States trade before 2015 (People's Daily Online 2008).

Chapter 7. The Dragon Meets the Angry River

1. For comparison, as of 2008, total U.S. hydropower capacity was 95,000 megawatts (U.S. DOE 2008).

2. Molle et al. (2009) state that some 17 percent of global inland fisheries come from the Mekong Basin. Depending on the country, people get anywhere from 27 to 78 percent of their animal protein from the river.

3. MRC (2007) and Baran et al. (2007) characterize flow dynamics of the Mekong.

4. The term *powershed* was coined by Magee (2006: 26) to signify a space where "a potable resource is collected and concentrated for use, with use … occurring far from the site of collection." Dore et al. (2007) provide the data for the following discussion that fleshes out the powershed concept.

5. Li and He (2008) see things differently, finding little significance in these changes. For downstream perspectives on dams, see work by Mehtonen (2008) and Menniken (2007).

6. International Rivers staff e-mail to author, December 15, 2008. These numbers include only Chinese-financed dams in the GMS.

7. Sunchindah (2005: 6–8) gives a balanced view of the MRC.

8. For details on integrated basin flow management, see studies by Guttman (2006) and the MRC (2006). On stakeholder forums, see an article on Mekong development by the MaximsNews Network (2008).

9. These prevailing views are emblematic of globalization in general and neoliberalism in particular. The logic is this: Building economic corridors stimulates transboundary flows of goods and services; competition grows, prices fall, efficiency increases; the resulting growth creates jobs and increases personal income, with poverty thereby reduced. The flow of goods is paramount; there is little need to address what kinds of goods are produced, who does the work, how goods are made, and who benefits. Institution building is also secondary. Phillips and Ilcan

(2004) and Harvey (2005) give accessible critiques of neoliberalism. Bush (2008), Oehlers (2006), and Clake (2007) critique neoliberal assumptions as they apply to the GMS. Igoe and Sullivan (2008) do the same as applied to biodiversity conservation. Leichenko and O'Brien (2008) describe how globalization influences environmental change.

10. Each of China's five largest hydropower corporations, the "Five Brothers," is majority owned by the PRC, so it is difficult to call these corporations either public or private. Authors that attempt to untangle the murky politics of China's public/private hydropower corporations are Molle et al. (2009), Mertha (2008: 45–48), and Magee (2006: 35–40).

11. See reports by Brewer (2008: 14–17) and Middleton (2007). This data was already out of date in December 2008. I use the unpublished December data here, which continues to be updated by International Rivers (see http://www.internationalrivers.org).

12. See Bosshard's study (2008) for China's role as global financier of dams.

13. Population projections are from the country-by-country poverty data in an Asian Development Bank report (2007: 15–24).

14. Asian climate trends are from work by Cruz et al. (2007). For data on the Greater Himalaya, see the study by J. Xu et al. (2009a); see the WWF's report (2009) for the Greater Mekong.

15. See studies by Goh (2004), Molle et al. (2009), Baran et al. (2007: 18), and Oehlers (2006). The authors of all of these studies have many good suggestions on Mekong Basin issues. Brooks and Liu (2006) suggest that China help create a transboundary river commission modeled after the International Joint Commission between the United States and Canada.

16. The lines are from the poem "Hundred Pace Rapids" translated by B. Watson (1994: 75).

17. A detailed account of Nu dam politics through 2006 is in a study by Mertha (2008: 110–142).

18. Fan is quoted by Zhang (2008: 1); see also Bezlova (2008). See an article by LaFraniere (2009) for links between dams and earthquakes in southwest China.

19. In China, relocation and compensation of villagers resulting from dam building is contentious. Larson (2009: 1) estimates that some twelve million Chinese have been relocated because of dam construction, with 50 percent now living in "abject poverty." Brown and Xu (in press), McDonald (2007), and J. Liu (2007) provide insightful accounts of these issues as they relate to the Nujiang, as does Mertha (2008).

20. Mertha (2008: 116) claims that drawing pro-dam boundary lines is an "open secret" in Yunnan, since the government official who negotiated with the United Nations still holds a high-profile political office.

Chapter 8. China 2020

1. As one executive in the U.S. solar industry said, "Here [in the United States], we're way behind. We're still messing around with energy bills. We need to get serious" (Climate Progress 2009d). For a comparison of Chinese and U.S. renewable energy efforts, see the report by Wong and Light (2009).

2. As to the pitfalls of long-term economic forecasts, even Wilson and Purushothaman (2003) (who coined the acronym BRIC to stand for Brazil, Russia, India, and China as paradigms of the emerging influence of the developing world) greatly underestimated China's GDP growth.

3. Bergsten et al. (2006: 18–39, 73–117) and Holz (2005) give excellent overviews of China's projected growth.

4. The GDP projection is from an Asian Development Bank study (2008b: 13). McMillion (2007) provides financial data to support this statement and Mahbubani (2008) offers an overview of this trend. For a dissenting view on Asia's rise, see the work of Pei and Anderson (2009).

5. I emphasize this point in an article for *BioScience* (Grumbine 2007). Flavin and Gardner (2006) provide another view.

6. The 2009 sales figures are from Reuters (2009). There are many projections on Chinese vehicle ownership out to 2020; studies by Economy (2007) and Fairclough and Oster (2006) are two examples. Despite the 2007–2009 world recession, by the second half of 2009 Beijing was experiencing record auto sales (Cui 2009). The Asian Development Bank (2008b: 48) suggests that stabilization of the (Asian) "private vehicle fleet . . . appears out of reach. It should be noted that just as GMC, Ford, and other American carmakers are losing tens of billions of dollars, most Chinese manufacturers are experiencing record sales. An additional irony is that American companies would be in worse financial straits if their China divisions were not making profits.

7. Details on China's highway system are in the *Economist* (2008d). Bradsher (2009a) surveys China's transportation infrastructure.

8. Economy (2007: 40) puts the number at four hundred million people.

9. Z. Li (2006b) quotes planners as expecting another 10 million hectares

(24.7 million acres) of arable land to be available for construction by 2030. This is despite the Chinese government's policy to offset losses of farmland (Bradsher 2009a). Studies from Beijing and Tianjin show that 75 percent of urban construction occurs on arable lands (M. Tan et al. 2005). Zhao et al. (2006), though they show Shanghai losing 21 percent of surrounding arable land from 1975 to 2005, have a somewhat more positive view of urbanization trends. See also work by Woetzel et al. (2008: 20).

10. Larson (2008) describes serious problems with the plan to move Yangzi water north.

11. Woetzel et al. (2008: 21) project that urban water pollution will increase by a factor of five by 2020.

12. China has less stringent air quality standards than the European Union or the United States, and there is also debate about whether Beijing air pollution data has been manipulated by the government. Air pollution will remain a problem in China. Mercury is released through coal combustion. It is borne aloft on global westerlies and a great deal ends up in California and the Pacific Northwest, a toxic reminder to Americans that inexpensive DVD players, baby clothes, and running shoes bear an additional price tag. Nitrogen has a different story. It is both air and waterborne, and it is on the loose because of vehicle exhaust fumes and the fact that Chinese agriculture uses twice as much nitrogenous fertilizer as any other country. Scientists still don't have a firm handle on what happens to wild ecosystems as nitrogen loads rise. Loss of forest soil productivity is one concern. Nevertheless, more nitrogen pollution is almost guaranteed in China—in the quest to grow more food, PRC fertilizer use is expected to double over the next several decades.

13. No one knows exactly how many migrants there are; government definitions of migrants are complex, and many people do not register as temporary workers once they arrive in a city. In fact, China's overall population census is lacking critical data and may not be particularly accurate.

14. Fan (2008) gives an account of migrants and the *hukou* system. For an overview of *hukou*, see F. Wang (2003). Woetzel et al. (2008: 22) project that social services for migrants from 2020 to 2025 will cost about 2.5 percent of urban GDP across China. Shenzhen population figures are from a study by K. Chan (2007: 390).

15. China's inequalities, already profound, are projected to worsen through 2020. A major problem is the wealth gap: not only are incomes skewed

between rural and urban areas, but the rate of income growth is twice as high in cities as in the countryside. Some background follows. Jobs: Given the numbers of new migrants and college graduates attempting to enter the workforce, and despite recent double-digit economic growth, job creation is lagging by the millions (Shirk 2007: 29–30). Health care: In 1978, 85 percent of China's citizens had state-subsidized health care; in 2005, 80 percent had none. In rural Yunnan, the number of hospital beds has declined by about 25 percent since 1985 (Young and Yang 2005: 61). The PRC recently promised to revitalize national health care (Valdez 2009). Social security: As in the United States, China's population is aging while its working population is shrinking, and by 2020 this trend will be affecting how younger workers can support retirees. Unlike the United States, China is getting old before becoming rich enough to pay for social security (Nowak 2007). There is also a growing gender gap that will become serious around 2030 (Hudson and den Boer 2004). These problems are compounded by the fact that less than 20 percent of the population (which doesn't count migrant workers) has benefits (Jackson and Howe 2004). Since the 1990s, Beijing has allowed provincial governments to borrow from state-funded personal retirement accounts to use as loans to finance local budgets, and these have yet to be repaid. These loans now equal USD 1.5 trillion (Pozen 2006; Frazier 2006). Overall, China's GINI coefficient, the international standard for measuring social inequalities, continues to grow (Fu 2008; Shirk 2007: 30).

16. Liu et al. (2009) describe the results of misused and/or inefficient management in the wastewater treatment sector, where over half of all plants do not run at optimal levels. For an overview of corruption, see the report by Bergsten et al. (2008: 94–100).

17. For data on demonstrations, see studies by Lum (2006) and O'Brien and Li (2005). The PRC no longer releases annual counts of demonstrations. On Beijing's push to allocate financial resources to the countryside, see the work of J. Fu (2008). On the 2008 land law, see reports by Batson (2009) and E. Wong (2008a). Absent a stronger *rule* of law as well as documentation of land leases, it remains to be seen whether the 2008 land law will benefit farmers.

18. Kylychbekova (2007) asserts that Russian authorities prevented NGOs from critiquing the Altai pipeline's environmental impacts during a visit to the World Heritage Site. The Altai project is described by Mosolova (2008), Helmer (2008), and Tomberg (2006).

19. For China 2020, the political consequences of Sino-Russian energy projects are complex (see Cooley 2009; Ahn and Jones 2008; Kandiyoti 2007; Kuchins 2007; Menon and Motyl 2007; Pan 2006). Both countries are founding members of the Shanghai Cooperative Organization (SCO), which could grow into a political counterweight to NATO and the European Union as Asian economic strength expands. This would fit the two countries' distaste for U.S. unipolar power and influence. (In March 2008, Iran formally applied for SCO membership.) But China's rise also worries Russia. Even as trade between the two countries grows by leaps and bounds, Russians are leaving Siberia for Moscow and Leningrad; the regional population has fallen to 5 million people. There are 107 million Chinese who live across the Sino-Russian border, and Chinese traders are exerting tremendous economic influence, leading to the question of whether China will "own" Siberia in the future.

20. Roque (2007) and Pan (2006) chronicle the developing energy ties between Kazakhstan, China, and their Central Asian neighbors. In addition to fossil fuels, China is investing in highways and special trade zones and is also aware that Kazakhstan holds the world's largest undeveloped deposits of uranium, lead, and tungsten.

21. The path to an operational port at Gwadar will not be straightforward. In August 2009, China pulled the plug on funding because of economic recession and security concerns (Fazl-e-Haider 2009). China is also negotiating with Myanmar to build another port and pipeline for oil from the Bay of Bengal to Kunming (Storey 2009).

22. Leverett and Bader (2005–2006) provide a portrait of evolving Sino-Arab-American energy relationships. For example, they note that the Saudis may be interested in moving away from using U.S. dollars as the exclusive currency for oil purchases (see also Siddiqi 2007). Engdahl (2006) gives a fascinating overview of this changing of the guard in Central Asia (see also Bustelo 2005). Given their huge populations and rapidly growing economies, China and India are often compared. In 2003, trade between India and China was less than USD 8 billion; it will likely reach USD 60 billion in 2010. But focusing on GDP numbers alone hides major differences in poverty, literacy rates, government infrastructure, development policies, and projected impacts of climate change, all of which greatly favor China (see Sharma 2006; Khanna 2008: 277). One example: during the next five years, India plans to spend USD 500 billion on infrastructure; during the same period, China plans to spend somewhat less than half that amount on *railroads alone*

(Economist 2008d). For background on trade issues between India and Yunnan see a working paper by Bhattacharyay and De (2005). Note, too, that similar trade trends are occurring between China and Africa (Sun 2006) and between China and Latin America (see Romero and Barrianuevo 2009; Oppenheimer 2008; Dominguez 2006).

23. A report by the International Energy Agency (IEA 2008: 41) says that "non-OPEC conventional oil production is already at plateau and is projected to start to decline by around the middle of the next decade." Crooks (2008) notes that in 2000, developed-world countries directly controlled 19 percent of global oil; by 2010, this number will decrease to 12 percent. For oil projections, see also studies by Beddor et al. (2009) and EIA (2008). Noreng (2004) analyzes the shifting oil production impact on the U.S. dollar.

24. Crooks (2008) points out that if China didn't purchase oil from Iran and Sudan, there would be even greater competition for global supplies; if China was not a willing buyer, some other country would step in. Similar logic applies to extracting oil from Canadian tar sands, a process that is extremely destructive to the environment. Canada is rapidly developing these fields, with the United States and China as major purchasers. Maass (2009) provides an accessible account of global oil issues.

25. Buckley (2008) and Levine and Aden (2008) cover recent Chinese projections.

26. M. Li (2008: 11–12) provides a summary of rising emissions.

27. Buckley (2008) suggests that by 2050 China by itself could potentially emit about 50 percent of all carbon dioxide released globally in 2007. For context, see the 2009 World Energy Outlook (IEA 2009) and the climate change study by Zeng et al. (2008).

28. Hare (2009:18–19) discusses clearly what "dangerous" warming means.

29. Meyer et al. (2009) survey climate science studies since 2007. For critical post-IPCC studies, see those by Parry et al. (2009), Solomon et al. (2009), NSIDC (2008), Global Carbon Project (2008), Anderson and Bows (2008), and Hansen et al. (2008). For data on more-rapid glacial melt, see a study by the UNEP (2008). The 2007 IPCC work was conservative in its treatment of carbon-cycle feedbacks, including sea level rise (Rahmstorf 2007), ocean acidification (McKie 2009), and melting permafrost (Schiermeier 2007). The IPCC also did not include carbon emissions from aviation and shipping, which together account for at least 5 percent of all global emissions (Adam 2008). Methane (another

global warming gas) from reservoirs was also not included, given lack of data and political pressure from Brazil and India (see Mascarelli 2009). Huge methane releases from the Arctic Ocean's continental shelf may be the most troubling source of all (Kennedy et al. 2008; Shakhova et al. 2008). And, of course, IPCC modelers did not capture China's rapid emissions growth (Aufhammer and Carson 2008). Hulme (2009) and Biello (2007) describe the complex politics of IPCC science.

30. Williams et al. (2007) project that by 2100, depending on what IPCC climate scenario is used, anywhere from 4 to 39 percent of Earth's terrestrial lands will shift into ecosystems that do not currently exist. Fox (2007) provides context on this research.

31. J. Xu et al. (2009a) provide the best summary of the region's water future. The IPCC (2007: 484) projects water stress for up to 1.2 billion Asians by the 2020s (see also UNESCO 2009). Zemp et al. (2008) cover global glacial ice loss. See also reports by Pomerance (2009) and Bates et al. (2008). There is, however, some disagreement on Himalaya glacial loss trends (Bagla 2009).

32. Cui and Graf (2009) and Wilkes (2008) survey global warming impacts on the Tibetan Plateau. For data on melting permafrost in China, see reports by the Xinhua News Agency (2009); for the Arctic and the globe, see those of Climate Progress (2009a), Zimou et al. (2006), and Connor (2008).

33. Lawrence et al. (2008) and Shakhova et al (2008) show that loss of Arctic Ocean ice may be speeding up Arctic permafrost melting. Because of this and other factors, in 2009 sea-level rise estimates were increased from 59 centimeters (23 inches) (IPCC 2007) to 90–120 centimeters (35–47 inches) (Pffefer, Harper, and O'Neel 2008).

34. Battisti and Naylor (2009) reviewed twenty-three climate models to show a high probability (90 percent) that growing season temperatures in the tropics and subtropics by 2100 will exceed the most extreme seasonal temperatures recorded over the last 100 years. Yet these scientists based their work on the median emission scenarios of the 2007 IPCC report; despite its dire forecast, this study is too conservative. See also work by Lobell (2008). The IPCC (2007: 471) also makes projections about worldwide hunger. Data on hunger in the GMS are from a UNEP study (2007: 11). Wang et al. (2008) suggest that China can continue to feed itself despite climate change impacts. However, they do not consider impacts of water loss in their study. A more recent study (Asia Society 2009) connects China's water issues, food security,

and climate change; for example, this report shows that if China's rice production is reduced by 10 percent because of climate change, that amount will equal about 50 percent of all rice traded globally.

35. Von Braun and Meinzen-Dick (2009) and McCartan (2008) discuss China's "going out" for agricultural lands. One concern expressed by the United Nations is that countries buying overseas agricultural lands will trigger a food "neo-colonialism" (Blas 2008). Anderlini (2008) describes PRC policy on overseas land acquisitions.

36. The refugee number is reported by Lewis (2008: 30). See also the IPCC study (2007: 488). Friedman (2009) reports that if you total all mass migrations since the African slave trade, the number of people involved is about 65 million. Stal and Warner (2009), Koser (2009), and Biermann and Boas (2008) discuss the need for a new global protocol for refugees.

37. Climate justice is little addressed by wealthy nations (see Adams and Luchsinger 2009). As a vice chair of the IPCC put it recently, "with climate change, as with other important problems, unless the poor help themselves nobody else will. Otherwise, governments will not move, because governments tend to be dominated by elites who are less directly affected" (Hilton 2009: 3). Meyerson et al. (2007) and Schellnhuber et al. (2007) discuss climate change and security; Morton (2008) focuses specifically on China.

38. The translation is by Gary Snyder from Du Fu's poem "Spring View"; it is found in the collection by Weinberger (2003: 100). For a biography of Du Fu, see Hung's book (1952).

39. Myers and Kent (2003) first brought attention to the sheer numbers of "new consumers," those who are about to join the ranks of the already affluent. Since their study was published, at least 93 million more people have become relatively wealthy—the number 1.2 billion used here reflects this growth through 2009.

Chapter 9. Conservation with Chinese Characteristics

1. There is a rich literature on the barriers and bridges to community-based conservation (see Acheson 2006; Agrawal 1999; Barrett et al 2001; Blakie and Muldavin 2004; Brechin et al. 2002; Larson and Soto 2008; Menzies 2007; Plummer and Taylor 2004). Sanderson (2005) and Redford et al. (2008) go into specifics on poverty and conservation.

2. Chinese science is not without its faults. R. Harris (2008: 192–208) develops a lengthy critique of wildlife science in the PRC; see also the work of H. Xin (2008).

3. The quotes from President Hu and Premier Wen on *hexie shehui* are reported by the Xinhua News Agency (2007c, 2005b). For insightful Chinese analysis of this concept, see the work of Lau (2006).

4. A. Wang (2007) gives many insights into Chinese environmental law. Problems still run deep in the PRC's evolving legal system; for example, witnesses are not required to appear in person at hearings, coerced confessions are not illegal, and legal standing remains fuzzy; courts can and often do refuse cases without explanation. In addition, lawyers are not well-distributed around the country. In Beijing the per capita ratio is 944 to 1; in rural Gansu Province, the ratio is 14,500 to 1 (J. Wang 2009). Xie (2009) details the first environmental lawsuit.

5. Van Rooij (2006) assesses implementation of laws in China. McElwee (2009) provides excellent suggestions on how to improve impact analyses in China.

6. These numbers do not include China's fifty-three thousand Environmental Protection Bureau staff at provincial and local levels.

7. At the end of 2010, a USD 30 billion conservation grant between China and the European Union will expire; it is unlikely that the PRC will pick up the next tab (EU-China Biodiversity Programme 2009).

8. Tang (2008) gives an overview of this situation. Weller (2006: 123) is more blunt: "NGOs either accommodate to the state or find themselves dismantled." Many foreigners see NGO activity as a window for opening to liberal democracy; increased citizen *participation*, however, is but one aspect of political *freedom*.

9. French (2008) and Parenti (2008) discuss these trends in general. Fu (2008) shows that rural funding increased 30 percent between 2007 and 2008. In 2009, Go West development monies reached a level of USD 6.8 billion (Ministry of Water Resources 2009). E. Wong (2008a) covers the recent land reform law. Qie (2009), Friends of Nature (2008), and Ma (2008) describe new PRC policies on information access. Klein (2008), however, shows that the Party remains interested in controlling information through surveillance (the domestic market for surveillance cameras and face-recognition software is booming). Despite its efforts, the PRC has a long way to go to address social issues. Investment in education, health, and social services was less than 2.5 percent of GDP in 2008 (Klein 2008), significantly less than the global average in the less developed world. China's GINI coefficient continues to rise (Fu 2008).

10. The Pew Global Attitudes Project found that 86 percent of Chinese were content with their country's direction (Friends of Nature 2008);

only 23 percent of Americans answered in this manner (French 2008). Wright (2007) provides several perspectives on why Chinese support their government: whether you are inside or outside the Party, it is easier to gain economic and social benefits by adhering to the political status quo. Leonard (2008) and Martens (2006) both give background on this subject.

11. Projections on the growth of China's middle class are from Farrell et al. (2006). For descriptions of the consumer tendencies of China's middle class, see the work of P. Harris (2004) and Hanser (2005). Hanser notes a growing sense that wealth is a "key indicator of social worth" and suggests that market consumerism provides a "depoliticized space" that increases individuals' feelings of power "in a society so lacking in political freedoms" (277).

12. Yan (2006), Osnos (2008), and Young (2008) provide general background on China's Little Emperors generation as well as data on the size of this group (see also Rosen 2009; Hanser 2005). In a survey of Chinese wildlife consumption and conservation awareness, Z. Li et al. (2008) found that wealthy young people ate the most wildlife from markets and were less aware of their environmental impacts. Education and employment for young people in China are complex subjects that go beyond the scope of this book. In general, rote learning styles, pressures to pass examinations, and quality disparities between urban and rural schools are problems (Chang 2008; Mooney 2006). As for employment prospects for the Little Emperors, the basic issue is that the number of Chinese college graduates has grown from 3.4 million in 1998 to some 18 million today; there are simply more graduates than jobs, even before the global recession tightened the market (E. Wong 2009).

13. Recent conservation biology research on the long-term cascade of effects precipitated by losing large predators from ecosystems provides interesting analogies with Confucian ethics. Remove mountain lions or wolves from ecosystems, and the losses over time ripple out to other community members such as elk, beavers, and aspen trees (Ripple and Beschta 2009; Soule et al. 2005). Remove an effective ruler from a kingdom or an ethical parent from a family, and harmony, too, is lost.

14. The expansionist Mongols of the Yuan dynasty colonized the Han as well as much of the rest of Asia and Europe. Lynch (2006: 114) notes that 64 percent of the PRC is officially designated ethnic nationality "autonomous" regions that the Han brought into China. He's right,

but this same logic applied to the United States shows that much of America's territory has been colonized too. There is extensive literature on China's rise and its geopolitical implications. Recently published sources I have benefited from include those of Jacques (2009), Bergsten et al. (2008), Fravel (2008), Lampton (2008), Leonard (2008), Overholt (2008), Kang (2007), and Shambaugh (2006). Two short, provocative papers on this theme are by Layne (2008) and Barma et al. (2007). For contemporary context, see the general references by Mahbubani (2008) and Khanna (2008).

15. In 2008, the World Wide Fund for Nature updated their *Living Planet Report*: they found that humans would be consuming resources the equivalent of two Earths by the 2030s. Their previous report from 2002 projected that the same level of resource use would occur by the 2050s.

16. Bergsten et al. (2008: 26) suggest that China must be seen as a full partner in global leadership, a "rule-maker and not simply a rule-taker." See also work by Kurlantzick (2008).

17. In July 2009, China and India held their first meeting to discuss Himalayan environmental issues (Lamont 2009); talks were still stalled in early 2010. Medeiros (2009) discusses Chinese global leadership.

18. Bradsher (2009b), Fenn (2009), and Graham-Harrison (2008) describe China's "clean coal" program. While China (and India, Germany, Britain, etc.) commit to new coal-fired power plants that are *not* clean, the situation in the United States is a bit murky. Fifty-two plants are under construction or permitted, while another fifty-eight have been "announced" (Shuster 2008). It is not clear how many of these will actually be constructed. What is known is that the average life of a U.S. coal-fired power plant is thirty-five years, and it is prohibitively expensive to retrofit them to reduce emissions. New plants represent industrial capital that cannot be spent on clean-coal technology; they represent a huge bet against a carbon-neutral future. An MIT study helps explain why "CO_2 capture and sequestration is the critical enabling technology that would reduce CO_2 emissions significantly while also allowing coal to meet the world's pressing energy needs" (MIT 2007: x). There are, however, several problems beyond the fact that we are quite tardy in testing these technologies. First (assuming technical problems are solved), transporting captured CO_2 would require a massive new pipeline infrastructure to carry the volume of material needed to be moved to underground storage—just 60 percent of U.S. coal-produced CO_2

emissions, compressed to liquid form for transport, would equal about the volume of oil currently used each day in the country (p. ix). Second, sequestering 60 percent of the total *world* production of carbon emissions released in 2008 would be equivalent to moving 240 million barrels of oil a day; total 2008 world consumption of oil was 86 million barrels a day. Finding a sufficient number of appropriate storage sites for this volume of CO_2 is another problem, and most sites will not be near points of production. There is a low likelihood of widespread carbon capture and storage technologies coming online before ten to fifteen years from now.

19. For China's impressive "green" energy targets, see the studies by Wong and Light (2009) and the Energy Foundation (2008). The PRC is still struggling with passing a national energy law (Wardell 2008). Liu and Diamond (2008) provide context.

20. Meinshausen et al. (2009) and Climate Progress (2008a) discuss global amounts of carbon emissions. Note, too, as mentioned before, that the IPCC (2007) projections are certainly conservative when it comes to the action of global carbon-cycle feedbacks.

21. The IEA (2008: 48) doubts that the 450 parts per million target is "technically feasible." The 2009 IEA report implies that this target is achievable but states explicitly that "a delay of just a few years would probably render that goal completely out of reach" (IEA 2009: 14). After reviewing national emissions reduction commitments in summer 2009, Rogelj et al. (2009: 4) stated that "unless there is major improvement, we see virtually no chance of staying below 2.0 or 1.5 C [rise in average global temperatures]." M. Li (2008), an economist at the University of Utah, links worldwide emissions targets to negative growth and economic depression. Attempting to match what scientists are suggesting about emission targets with the international political discourse is an exercise in frustration. The problem is that no leader will admit that there is very likely no way to meet the "dangerous" 450 parts per million/2° C (3.6° F) warming target. Scientists, too, can be prone to this way of thinking. For example, Wang and Watson (2007: 7), working on emissions scenarios for China, write that "the problem with these lower budgets [i.e., 450 parts per million] is that they make it more difficult to develop a plausible global emissions pathway. For this reason, we have chosen a larger budget that has a higher chance of causing severe impacts."

22. There are a number of ways to portray differences in energy consump-

tion between China and the United States—the average Chinese person produces five times less CO_2 than an American and uses seven times less overall energy (Chandler 2008). In global terms, the poorest countries have historically emitted less than 1 percent of all greenhouse gases (Global Carbon Project 2008). Biel and Muffett (2009) analyze America's cumulative greenhouse gas emissions.

23. Wang and Watson (2007) used 2004 data in their Tyndall Centre report; carbon leakage since then is certainly higher. For context, this 23 percent figure is about equivalent to recent annual emissions from Japan. Chatterjee (2007) also writes about this issue. There are numerous ways beyond emissions in which China and the United States are linked. As American consumption dropped in 2007–2008 because of global recession, factories closed in China (E. Wong 2008b).

24. The issue of transferring wealth from the developed world to less developed countries has been and continues to be a major sticking point. Eight years ago, wealthier nations committed to USD 18 billion in climate adaptation aid to poor countries; by the end of 2008, less than USD 1 billion had been distributed (Vidal 2009). This is true for many aid sectors where the promise of funds does not match the amounts actually given (see Brainard et al. 2009; UNESCO 2009). This issue is one where the ethical *values* of wealthy countries conflict with their (narrowly defined) political *interests*. Mahbubani (2008: 104) takes a global perspective: "the 900 million people who live in Western countries elect governments that in turn control a world order determining the fate of the remaining 5.6 billion people on the planet." Lewis (2007–2008) and Tan (2008) describe tensions in climate negotiations that result from North-South differences. Due to a host of issues, including climate change, world government structures are under great pressure (see, in general, Traub 2009). The United States has asked that China join the International Energy Agency, but membership rules would have to be revised (Oster 2008). Nevertheless, while China continues its economic and political rise, the country is still poor: the 2008 per capita income was USD 6,000 (CIA 2009), less than Albania or El Salvador. For rural Yunnan in 2007, the average per capita income was USD 377 (Simpson 2009). Compare this with the average American teenager's annual discretionary income of USD 2,600 (Hoffman 2008).

25. Problems exist *within* the less developed world as well. India, with per capita greenhouse gas emissions seventeen times less than the United States, is a case in point. Despite projections that show its agricultural

production dropping up to 40 percent (with the conservative IPCC scenarios), the country remains committed to boosting coal production (Mukherjee 2008; Mufson and Harden 2008; Economist 2008c).

26. On current U.S. climate politics and policymaking, see the studies by Jinnah et al. (2009), Asia Society/Pew Center on Global Climate Change (2009), Lieberthal and Sandalow (2009), Seligsohn et al. (2009), and Climate Progress (2008b).

Quotation References

Introduction

Page 9: For Daoists, the power of water is predominant: "against the hard and strong / nothing excels it" (Porter 1996: 64,156).

Chapter 2. The Frontier and the Middle Kingdom

Page 26: Geologists understand that "the remodeling of the face of the world that happens when crustal plates move is . . . a consequence of the power residing in the mantle" (Fortey 2004: 351).

Page 27: This toil formed the daily reality for Chinese peasants and had its consequences; historian Mark Elvin (2004: 87) notes that large-scale grain growing and the brute labor of construction work were tasks that people chafed at: "Fields end freedom."

Page 31: "Let culture merge with economics . . . to build Yunnan into an economically prosperous, culturally developed, ethnically united . . . province" (quoted in Wilkes 2005: 28).

Page 35: Then-premier Xu Rongji summed up the plan: it would "strengthen national unity," "safeguard social stability," and "control border defense" (D. Xin 2006: 3).

Page 37: How can conservationists support people and nature in Yunnan when Go West development is "reinventing another China" (Tian 2004: 636)?

Page 38: What Elvin (2004: 86) does discover is that the impetus to compete for scarce resources is common throughout human history and that, in China as elsewhere, "what might have been more viable long-term patterns counted for little or nothing faced with short-term choices for power."

Chapter 3. Under the Jade Dragon

Page 45: "Tourists arrive in large groups, overwhelm the town, commoditize everything in sight, and depart" (Sicroff et al. 2003: 536).

Page 54: "[We work] with our local partners to give them skills they need to interact with a global marketplace while not changing them in any fundamental way . . . we hope to enable [villagers] to . . . compete with larger, non-local tourism enterprises" (Bullock 2003: 571).

Page 55: The corporate Shui On Group is partnering with the government to raise "the sophistication of tourism,...[and] leisure facilities, enhancing the ethnic experience, and developing ecotourism" (Shui On Group 2007: 1).

Chapter 4. Old Mountains, Young Parks

Page 70: Each group also brings its own agenda—there are biologists, community experts, and donors, each holding a definition of "success" and each learning how to operate in the institutional ambiguity and messiness that is today's China (Ho and Edmonds 2007: 332).

Chapter 6. Into the Great Green Triangle

Page 95: For the bank, it is a visionary project with two mandates: to "restore ecological connectivity and integrity in a selected set of important biodiversity areas" while "improving livelihoods of peoples living in and around the biodiversity conservation corridors" (Asian Development Bank 2008c: 2).

Today, Chinese biologist Li Hongmei and her colleagues describe the reserves as "virtual islands" in a sea of rubber with "little or no appropriate habitat connecting them" (H. Li et al. 2007: 1743).

Page 105: Another anonymous source was quoted in the *Asian Times* saying that "Nam Ha will be gone in ten years" (McCartan 2007: 4).

Page 107: Five of the six GMS countries have national biodiversity action plans, but they are "paper thick, action limited" (UNEP 2007: 7).

Chapter 7. The Dragon Meets the Angry River

Page 111: With roots in regional development stretching back before the Vietnam War, the MRC's mandate is "to cooperate . . . in sustainable development of the Mekong River basin . . . in a manner to optimize . . . benefits . . . and to minimize harmful effects" (MRC 1995, 6).

Page 112: In 2007, the UN Environmental Programme published an environmental outlook for the Greater Mekong: biodiversity "faces many serious threats" (UNEP 2007: 7); "there is evidence to justify" fisheries concerns (7); food insecurity is resulting from "concentration of the benefits of economic growth" (80); and, as far as dams, "much depends on how they are managed" (75).

Baran and his team (2007) also discovered that, more often than not, "the resources of the poor are not included in impact assessments" (18). Overall, the researchers noted a "general disinterest in accuracy" (21).

Page 118: The Ministry of Water Resources countered that "comprehensive environmental reports were being prepared" (A. Wang 2007).

Page 121: On a 2006 site visit to check on allegations of threats to Three Parallel Rivers, UN inspectors discovered proposals for dams, mines, and tourism development that would "result in a 20% reduction in area of the original heritage site," directly affecting "the integrity and authenticity" of the World Heritage Site (Zhang 2006: 1).

As for boundary reductions, none were "yet approved," "all questions are under examination," environmental reviews were in process, and the United Nations would receive results in due time as required by World Heritage agreements (Management Bureau of the Three Parallel Rivers National Park, Yunnan 2007: 6-9).

Chapter 8. China 2020

Page 123: Meeting with a Taiwanese political leader in 2006, President Hu Jintao declared, "Frankly speaking, we do not want to pursue excessively rapid economic growth. What we are seeking is efficiency and quality of development, the change in the economic growth mode, resources conservation, environmental protection and improvement of people's livelihood" (Xinhua News Agency 2006).

Page 124: Development and implementation of renewable energy—in Kunming and every other city in the PRC—will be critical if China is to "build a well-off society in an all-round way" (Development Research Center 2004: 3).

Page 126: This will be a world in which, as a recent *New York Times* article said, "America is not the engine of globalization anymore . . . it might be China, it might be Europe—but it's not the U.S." (Bradsher and Peters 2007: C2).

Page 130: Farming has been part of the Middle Kingdom's cultural identity for millennia; twenty-five hundred years ago, the definition of an incompetent ruler was one who allowed "farmland [to lie] uncultivated," proving that food security was an issue even for Chinese emperors (Elvin 2004: 103).

Since the 1980s, when China prioritized economic growth over pollution control, 40 percent of all surface water in the country has become so filthy it "is of no practical or functional use" (Z. Li 2006: 356).

Page 138: "No one really knew what was driving the economy, which is why the predictions were so wrong," said Yang Fuiqiang, one of the PRC energy planners who worked on the report (quoted in Kahn and Yardley 2007: 4).

Page 140: For plants and animals, the IPCC states that "up to 50% of Asia's total biodiversity is at risk due to climate change" (IPCC 2007: 485).

Page 142: "You are talking about hundreds of millions of additional people looking for food," said David Battisti, coauthor of an influential 2009 study of climate-change impacts on agriculture, "because they won't be able to find it where they find it now" (quoted in Stricherz 2009: 1).

Craig Johnstone, the deputy commissioner with the UN High Commissioner for Refugees, said recently that because there are a potential 250 million to 1 billion people that may lose their homes by 2050, the world must prepare for a "global-scale emergency" (quoted in Morris 2008: 2).

At a spring 2008 summit in Brussels, EU officials warned that the international "multi-lateral system is at risk ... climate change impacts will fuel the politics of resentment between those most responsible for climate change and those most affected by it" (Solana and Ferrero-Waldner 2008: 3).

Page 143: "Our country's development path cannot repeat the unconstrained emissions of developed countries' energy use," states the 2008 China energy report (quoted in Buckley 2008: 2).

Chapter 9. Conservation with Chinese Characteristics

Page 146: At the village level, virtually every study concludes that successful community-based conservation "requires collaboration, transparency, and accountability so that a learning environment can be created" (Berkes 2004: 624).

Page 147: "Protecting Yunnan's biodiversity is not only the responsibility of the government ... it's our responsibility to the nation and the world": Yunnan provincial governor Qin Guangrong spoke these words with authority in February 2008 as he announced a bold new program to protect biodiversity in northwest Yunnan (Jiao 2008: 2).

Page 149: In May 2009, Premier Wen Jiabao once again extended the Nujiang dams moratorium—"for a while" (J. Shi 2009).

Page 152: Twenty-six hundred years ago, Old Master Lao looked inward and remarked, "Knowing others is wisdom; knowing the self is enlightenment" (Feng and English 1972).

Confucius also illuminated abiding links between humans and *tian* (heaven): "when personal lives are cultivated, states are governed; only when states are governed is there peace all under Heaven" (Tu 2001: 4).

Page 153: In 1793, after expelling the British trade envoy Lord MacCartney from his kingdom, Emperor Qianlong sent a letter to King George III: "our celestial empire possesses all things in prolific abundance and lacks no product within its borders" (quoted in Marks 2002: 114).

Page 156: This brand of politics could spark multilateral collaboration to reduce CO_2 emissions; after all, even conservative Chinese policy analysts can see that "a Harmonious Society cannot be built in just one country" (Lau 2006: 3).

Bibliography

Acheson, J. 2006. Institutional failure in resource management. Annual Review of Anthropology 35:117–134.

Adam, D. 2008. Aviation and shipping cannot trade away emissions, scientist warns. Guardian. Available from http://www.guardian.co.uk/environment/2008/sep/24/carbonemissions.emissionstrading (accessed September 2008).

Adams, B., and G. Luchsinger. 2009. Climate justice for a changing planet: a primer for policymakers and NGOs. UN Non-Governmental Liason Service, Geneva, Switzerland.

Adler, J., et al. 1998. Confucianism and ecology: the interrelation of heaven, earth, and humans. Harvard University Press, Cambridge, Massachusetts.

Agrawal, A. 1999. Enchantment and disenchantment: the role of community in natural resource conservation. World Development 27:629–649.

———. 2005. Environmentality. Duke University Press, Durham, North Carolina.

Ahn, S., and M. Jones. 2008. Northeast Asia's Kovykta conundrum: a decade of promise and peril. Asia Policy 5:105–140.

Alton, C., D. Bluhm, and S. Sananikone. 2005. Para rubber study *Hevea brasiliensis* Lao PDR. GTZ Rural Development in Mountainous Areas Program. Lao-German Technical Cooperation, Luang Namtha, Lao PDR.

Anderlini, J. 2008. China eyes overseas land in food push. Financial Times. Available from http://www.ft.com/cms/s/0/cb8a989a-1d2a-11dd-82ae-000077b07658.html?nclick_check=1 (accessed July 2008).

Anderson, K., and A. Bows. 2008. Reframing the climate change challenge in light of post-2000 emission trends. Philosophical Transactions of the Royal Society A: Mathematical, Physical, and Engineering Science 366(1882): 3863–3882.

Asia Society. 2009. Asia's next challenge: securing the region's water future. Asia Society, New York.

Asia Society/Pew Center on Global Climate Change. 2009. A roadmap for U. S.-China cooperation on energy and climate change. Asia Society, New York.

Asian Development Bank. 2005. Xishuangbanna biodiversity conservation corridors, Peoples Republic of China, pilot project profile (2005–2008). Asian Development Bank Core Environment Program, Greater Mekong Subregion, Bangkok, Thailand. Available from www.adb.org/Documents/Reports/GMS-BCI/annex3-prc.pdf (accessed October 2007).

———. 2007. Biodiversity conservation corridors initiative status report 2007. Asian Development Bank Core Environment Program, Greater Mekong Subregion, Bangkok, Thailand.

———. 2008a. Biodiversity conservation corridors initiative. Pilot site implementation status report 2007. Asian Development Bank Core Environment Program, Greater Mekong Subregion, Bangkok, Thailand. Available from http://www.gms-eoc.org/Publication/Publication.aspx (accessed March 2008).

———. 2008b. Emerging Asian regionalism. Asian Development Bank, Manila, Philippines.

———. 2008c. Managing Asian cities. Asian Development Bank, Manila, Philippines.

Aufhammer, M., and R. Carson. 2008. Forecasting the path of China's CO_2 emissions using province-level information. Journal of Environmental Economics and Management 55(3):229–247.

Bagla, P. 2009. No sign yet of Himalayan meltdown, Indian report finds. Science 326:924–925.

Baran, E., T. Jantunen, and C. Chong. 2007. Values of inland fisheries in the Mekong River basin. World Fish Center, Phnom Penh, Cambodia.

Barma, N., E. Ratner, and S. Weber. 2007. A world without the west. National Interest 90:23–31.

Barrett, C., et al. 2001. Conserving tropical biodiversity amid weak institutions. BioScience 51:497–502.

Bates, B., et al., eds., 2008. Climate change and water. Technical paper. Intergovernmental Panel on Climate Change, Geneva, Switzerland.

Batson, A. 2009. China's farmers raise rents. Wall Street Journal, September 17, A7.

Battisti, D., and R. Naylor. 2009. Historical warnings of future food insecurity with unprecedented seasonal heat. Science 323: 240–244.

Beddor, C., et al. 2009. Securing America's future. Center for American Progress, Washington, D.C.

Beier, P., D. Majka, and W. Spencer. 2008. Forks in the road: choices in procedures for designing wildland linkages. Conservation Biology 22:836–851.

Bell, D. 2008. China's new Confucianism. Princeton University Press, Princeton, New Jersey.

Bergsten, C., et al. 2006. China: the balance sheet. Public Affairs, New York.

Bergsten, C., et al. 2008. China's rise: challenges and opportunities. Peterson Institute for International Economics, Center for Strategic and International Studies, Washington, D.C.

Berkes, F. 2004. Rethinking community-based conservation. Conservation Biology 18:621–630.

———. 2009. Community conserved areas: policy issues in historic and contemporary context. Conservation Letters 2:19–24.

Bezlova, A. 2008. China quake shakes dam ambitions. Imaging Our Mekong. Quezon City, Philippines. Available from http://www.news-mekong.org/node/767/print (accessed July 2008).

Bhattacharyay, B., and P. De. 2005. Promotion of trade and investments between China and India: the case of Southwest China and East and Northeast India. CESifo working paper no. 1508. Asian Development Bank, Manila, Philippines.

Biel, S., and C. Muffett. 2009. America's share of the climate crisis. Greenpeace USA, Washington, D.C.

Biello, D. 2007. Global warming conservative climate may understate the climate change problem. Scientific American Online. Available from http://www.sciam.com/article.cfm?chanID=sa006&articleID=5B9E73AD-E7F2-99DF-3F (accessed March 2007).

Biermann, F., and I. Boas. 2008. Protecting climate refugees: the case for a global protocol. Environment 50:8–16.

Blakie, P., and J. Muldavin. 2004. Upstream, downstream, China, India: the politics of environment in the Himalayan region. Annals of the Association of American Geographers 94:520–548.

Blas, J. 2008. UN warns of food "neo-colonialism." Financial Times, August 19. Available from http://www.ft.com/cms/s/0/3d3ede92-6e02-11dd-65df-0000779fd18c.html (accessed August 2008).

Blum, S. 2001. Portraits of "primitives": ordering human kinds in the Chinese nation. Rowman and Littlefield, Lanham, Maryland.

Bosshard, P. 2008. New financiers and the environment. International Rivers, Berkeley, California.

Bradshaw, C., et al. 2009. Tropical turmoil: a biodiversity tragedy in progress. Frontiers in Ecology and Environment 7:79–87.

Bradsher, K. 2009a. China's route forward. New York Times, January 23, B1.

———. 2009b. China far outpaces U.S. in building cleaner coal-fired plants. New York Times, May 11, A1, A3.

Bradsher, K., and J. Peters. 2007. Struggles of U.S. economy are seen as a test of Asia's resilience. New York Times, August 17, C1, C2.

Brahic, C., and Reuters. 2008. China warns of huge rise in emissions. New Scientist. Available from http://www.newscientist.com/article/dn15011-china-warns-of-huge-rise-in-emissions.html (accessed November 2008).

Brainard, L., et al. 2009. Climate change and global poverty. Brookings Institution, Washington, D.C.

Brechin, S. R., et al. 2002. Beyond the square wheel: toward a more comprehensive understanding of biodiversity conservation as social and political process. Society and Natural Resources 15:41–64.

Brewer, N. 2007. Made by China: damming the world's rivers. International Rivers, Berkeley, California. Available from http://internationalrivers.org (accessed December 2007).

———. 2008. The new great walls. A guide to China's overseas dam industry. International Rivers, Berkeley, California.

Brooks, I., and H. Liu. 2006. River basin commissions as a mechanism for mitigating and resolving conflicts. China Environment Series, Woodrow Wilson Center, Washington, D.C.

Brown, P., and Y. Xu. In press. Hydropower development and resettlement policy on China's Nu River. Journal of Contemporary China.

Buckley, C. 2008. China report warns of greenhouse gas leap. Reuters News Online, October 22. Available from http://www.reuters.com/article/environmentNews/idUSTRE49LOZ920081022 (accessed October 2008).

———. 2009. China think-tank charts costs of low-carbon growth. Reuters, London. Available from http://www.alertnet.org/thenews/newdessk/PEK276833.htm (accessed September 2009).

Buckley, L. 2006. Rethinking conservation: ecotourism offers hope for Chinese ecosystems and the people who live in them. China Watch. Worldwatch Institute, Washington, D.C. Available from http://www.worldwatch.org/node/4501 (accessed September 2006).

———. 2007. Can corporations help Chinese nonprofits overcome funding barriers? China Watch. Worldwatch Institute, Washington, D.C. Available from http://www.worldwatch.org/node/5356 (accessed September 2007).

Bullock, G. 2003. Creating positive synergies in mountain-based ecotourism development: case studies from the Yunnan Great Rivers Project. Pages 567–576 in J. Xu and S. Mikesell, eds. Landscapes of diversity: indigenous knowledge, sustainable livelihoods, and resource governance in montane mainland southeast Asia. Proceedings of the III Symposium on MMSEA, Lijiang, China. Science and Technology Press, Kunming, China.

Buntaine, M., et al. 2006. Human-use and conservation planning in alpine areas of northwestern Yunnan, China. Environment, Development, and Sustainability. DOI: 10.1007/s10668-006-9025-8.

Bush, S. 2008. Contextualizing fisheries policy in the lower Mekong Basin. Journal of Southeast Asian Studies 39:329–353.

Bustelo, P. 2005. China and the geopolitics of oil in the Asian Pacific Region. Working paper 38/2005. Real Instituto Elcano, Madrid, Spain.

Butler, R. 2009. Laos emerges as key source in Asia's illicit wildlife trade. Yale Environment 360, February 26. Available from http://e360.yale.edu/content/feature.msp?id=2126 (accessed December 2009).

Byg, A., and J. Salick. 2009. Local perspectives on a global phenomenan-Climate change in Eastern Tibetan villages. Global Environmental Change 19:156–166.

Canberra Times. 2009. China to increase coal output by 30pc. Canberra Times, September 9. Available from http://www.canberratimes.com.au/news/local/news/business/china-to-increase-coal-output- (Accessed January 2009).

Chan, K. 2007. Misconceptions and comparatives in the study of China's cities: definition, statistics, and implications. Eurasian Geography and Economies 48:383–412.

Chan, W. 1963. A sourcebook in Chinese philosophy. Princeton University Press, Princeton, New Jersey.

Chandler, W. 2008. Breaking the suicide pact: U.S.-China cooperation on climate change. Policy Brief 57. Carnegie Endowment for International Peace, New York.

Chang, L. 2008. Gilded age, gilded cage. National Geographic 213(5):77–85, 93–95.

Chatterjee, R. 2007. Outsourcing U.S. greenhouse gas emissions. Environmental Science and Technology Online News, June 13. Available from http://pubs.acs.org/subscribe/journals/esthag-w/2007/june/policy/rc_greenhouse.html (accessed October 2007).

Chazdon, R. 2008. Beyond deforestation: restoring forests and ecosystem services on degraded lands. Science 320:1458–1460.

Chen, X. et al. 2008. Carbon sequestration potential of the stands under the

Grain for Green Program in Yunnan Province, China. Forest Ecology and Management 258:199–206.

Cheung, R., and A. Kang. 2008. China's booming energy efficiency industry. New Ventures, World Resources Institute, Washington, D.C. Available from http://www.wri.org (accessed August 2008).

China Briefing News. 2008a. As ASEAN develops, Kunming becomes vital trade link. China Briefing, Beijing. Available from http://www.china-briefing.com/news/2008/10/03/as-asean-develops-kunming-becomes-vital-trade-link (accessed October 2008).

———. 2008b. Trade between China, ASEAN hits $202.6 bln, three years ahead of schedule. China Briefing, Beijing. Available from http://www.chinaview.cn (accessed July 2008).

China Daily. 2009. Low-carbon industrialization 'possible but hard'. China Daily, Beijing. September 16. Available from http://www.chinadaily.com.cn/china/2009-09/16/content_8700435.htm (accessed September 2009).

China Statistical Yearbook. 2006. China Statistical Publishing House, Beijing.

Chow, K., and I. Kramer. 1990. All the tea in China. China Books and Periodicals, San Francisco.

CIA (Central Intelligence Agency). 2009. Country comparison: GDP—per capita (PPP). In The world factbook. Available from https://www.cia.gov/library/publications/the-world-factbook (accessed August 2009).

Clake, J. 2007. Regional economic integration and the poor. Mekong Brief Number 8. Australian Mekong Resource Centre, University of Sydney, NSW, Australia.

Climate Progress. 2008a. Stabilize at 350 ppm or risk ice-free planet, warn NASA, Yale, Sheffield, Versailles, Boston et al. Climate Progress, November 9. Available from http://www.climateprogress.org/2008/11/09/stabilize-at-350-ppm-or-risk-ice-free-planet-warn- (accessed November 2008).

———. 2008b. If there's no U.S. climate bill in 2009, would U.N. climate talks collapse in Copenhagen? Climate Progress, December 2. Available from http://www.climateprogress.org/2008/12/02/would-no-us-climate-bill-in-2009-mean-a-collapse- (accessed December 2008).

———. 2008c. Hadley Centre: "catastrophic" 5–7 C warming by 2100 on current emission path. Climate Progress, December 21. Available from http://www.climateprogress.org/2008/12/21/hadley-study-warns-of-catastrophic- (accessed January 2009).

———. 2009a. AAAS: Climate change is coming much harder, much faster than predicted. Climate Progress, February 15. Available from http://climateprogress.org/2009/02/15/aaas-climate-change-is-coming-much-harder- (accessed March 2009).

———. 2009b. MIT joins climate realists, doubles its projection of global warming by 2100 to 5.1 C. Climate Progress, February 23. Available from http://climateprogress.org/2009/02/23/mit-doubles-global-warming-projections (accessed March 2009).

———. 2009c. UK Met Office: catastrophic climate change, 13–18 F over most of U.S. and 27 F in the Arctic, could happen in 50 yrs., . . . Climate Progress, September 28. Available from http://climateprogress.org/2009/09/28/uk-met-office-catastrophic- (accessed September 2009).

———. 2009d. Boxer, Kerry set to introduce climate bill in Senate; China leads way for solar energy. Climate Progress, September 29. Available from http://climateprogress.org/2009/09/29/energy-and-global-warming-news-for-september-29- (accessed September 2009).

Connor, S. 2008. Arctic thaw threatens Siberian permafrost. Independent. Available from http://www.independent.co.uk/environment/climate-change/arctic-thaw-threatens-siberian-permafrost-846951.html (accessed November 2008).

Cooley, A. 2009. Behind the Central Asian curtain: the limits of Russia's resurgence. Current History 108:325–332.

Critical Ecosystem Partnership Fund. 2005. The mountains of southwest China hotspot briefing book. Presented at Improving Linkages Between CEPF and the World Bank Operations, Asia Forum, June 23–25 Medan, Indonesia. Available from author.

Crooks, E. 2008. Energy: centre of power is on the move. Financial Times, January 23. Available from http://www.uofaweb.ualberta.ca/chinainstitute/nav03.cfm?nav03=72393&nav02=57580& (accessed July 2008).

Cruz, R., et al. 2007. Asia: climate change 2007; impacts, adaptation and vulnerability. Pages 469–506 in M. L. Parry et al., eds. Contribution of Working Group II to the Fourth Assessment Report of the IPCC. Cambridge University Press, Cambridge, UK.

Cui, X. 2009. Extra 2000 cars on road every day. China Daily, Beijing, September 18. Available from http://www.chinadaily.com.cn/metro/2009-09/18/content_8707251.htm (accessed September 2009).

Cui, X., and H.-F. Graf. 2009. Recent land cover changes on the Tibetan Plateau: a review. Climatic Change 94:47–61.

Cyranoski, D. 2008. Visions of China. Nature 454:384–387.

Development Research Center. 2004. National energy policy strategy and policy report (NESP). China State Council, Beijing. Available from http://www.efchina.org/documents/DraftNatlEPlano31.pdf (accessed February 2005).

Diamond, J. 2008. What's your consumption factor? New York Times, January 2. Available from http://www.nytimes.com/2008/01/02/opinion/02diamond.html?ei=5070&en=6e301caad83f (accessed January 2008).

Dinaburg, J. 2008. Making the medicine mountains: the politics of Tibetan doctors and medicinal plant management in the Meilixueshan Conservation Area, PRC. MA thesis, Prescott College, Prescott, Arizona.

Dinerstein, E., et al. 2007. The fate of wild tigers. BioScience 57:508–514.

Dominguez, J. 2006. China's relations with Latin America: shared gains, asymmetric hopes. China working paper. Inter-American Dialogue, Washington, D.C.

Donald, S., and R. Benewick. 2005. The state of China atlas. University of California Press, Berkeley.

Donaldson, J. A.. 2007. Tourism, development, and poverty reduction in Guizhou and Yunnan. China Quarterly 190:333–351.

Dore, J., and X. Yu. 2004. Yunnan hydropower expansion: update on China's energy industry reforms and the Nu, Lancang, and Jinsha hydropower dams. Chiang Mai University's Unit for Social and Environmental Research, Chiang Mai, Thailand and Green Watershed, Kunming, China.

Dore, J., X. Yu, and L. Yuk-sing. 2007. Energy: China's energy industry reforms and Yunnan hydropower expansion. Pages 55–92 in L. Lebel et al., eds. Democratising water governance in the Mekong Region. Silkworm and Mekong Press, Bangkok, Thailand.

Dudgeon, D. 2005. River rehabilitation for conservation of fish biodiversity in monsoonal Asia. Ecology and Society 10(2):15. Available from http://www.ecologyandsociety.org/vol10/iss2/art15 (accessed October 2007).

Eccleston, P. 2008. Illicit trade in big cat skins continues in China. World Conservation Society. Available from http://www.chinabiodiversity.com/read.php?tid=6697 (accessed September 2008).

Economist. 2008a. Rushing on by road, rail and air. Economist, February 14. Available from http://www.economist.com/world/asia/displaystory.cfm?story_id=10697210 (accessed January 2009)

———. 2008b. A new itinerary. Emerging economies as transforming the travel industry. Economist, May 15. Available from http://www.economist.com/PrinterFriendly.cfm?story_id=11374574 (accessed July 2008).

————. 2008c. Melting Asia. Economist, June 5. Available from http://www.economist.com/PrinterFriendly.cfm?story.id=11488548 (accessed July 2008).

————. 2008d. The home team: cars in emerging markets. Economist, November 13. Available from http://www.economist.com/specialreports/displaystory.cfm?story_id=12544893 (accessed November 2008).

Economy, E. 2004. The river runs black. Cornell University Press, Ithaca, New York.

————. 2007. The great leap backward? The cost of China's environmental crisis. Foreign Policy 86(5):38–59.

Ediger, L., and H. Chen. 2006. Upland China in transition. Mountain Research and Development 26:220–226.

EIA (Energy Information Administration). 2008. International energy outlook. Energy Information Administration, U.S. Department of Energy, Washington, D.C.

Elvin, M. 2004. The retreat of the elephants: an environmental history of China. Yale University Press, New Haven, Connecticut.

Energy Foundation. 2008. Fact sheet: China emerging as new leader in clean energy policies. China Sustainable Energy Program, Energy Foundation, San Francisco. Available from http://www.efchina.org/FNewsroom.do?act=detail&newsTypeId=1&id=107 (accessed July 2008).

Engdahl, F. W. 2006. U.S. outflanked in Eurasian energy politics. Asia Times Online, June 10. Available from http://www.atimes.com/atimes/Global_Economy/HF10D;01.html (accessed June 2006).

EU-China Biodiversity Programme. 2009. Annual report for 2008. EU-China Biodiversity Programme, Beijing.

Fairclough, G., and S. Oster. 2006. As China's car market booms, lenders clash over heavy toll. Wall Street Journal, June 13.

Fan, C. 2008. Migration, *hukuo*, and the Chinese city. Pages 65–90 in S. Yusef and K. Nabeshima, eds. China urbaniz: consequences, strategies, and policies. World Bank Publications, Washington, D.C.

Farrell, D., et al. 2006. The value of China's emerging middle class. McKinsey Global Instititute, New York.

Fazl-e-Haider, S. 2009. China calls halt to Gwadar refinery. Asia Times, August 14. Available from http://www.atimes.com/atimes/South_Asia/KH14Df02.html (accessed December 2009).

Feng, G., and J. English, trans. 1972. Tao Te Ching by Lao-Tsu. Vintage Books, New York.

Fenn, J. 2009. China grapples with a burning question. Science 325:1646.

Fernandez, J. 2007. Resource consumption of new urban construction in China. Journal of Industrial Ecology 11:99–115.

Fiskesjo, M. 2006. Rescuing the empire: Chinese nation-building in the twentieth century. European Journal of East Asian Studies 5:15–44.

Fitzgerald, C. 1972. The southern expansion of the Chinese people. Australian National University Press, Canberra.

Flavin, C., and C. Gardner. 2006. China, India, and the new world order. Pages 3–23 in L. Starke, ed. State of the world 2006. W. W. Norton, New York.

Fortey, R. 2004. Earth. Knopf, New York.

Fox, D. 2007. Back to the no-analog future? Science 316:823–824.

Fravel, M. 2008. Strong borders, secure nation. Princeton University Press, Princeton, New Jersey.

Frazier, M. 2006. Pensions, public opinion, and the graying of China. Asia Policy 1:43–68.

French, H. 2008. Despite flaws, rights in China have expanded. New York Times, August 2, A1, A6.

Friedman, L. 2009. The spectre of climate migration. China Dialogue, Beijing. Available from http://www.chinadialogue.cn/article/show/single/en/2832-The-spectre-of-climate-migration (accessed March 2009).

Friends of Nature. 2008. A new frontier for public participation. China Dialogue, Beijing. Available from http://www.chinadialogue.cn/article/show/single/en/1964-A-new-frontier-for-public- (accessed May 2008).

Fu, J. 2008. Government to fund rural growth. China Daily, Beijing, September 9, p. 13.

Fu, Y., et al. 2006. Household differentiation and on-farm conservation of biodiversity by indigenous households in Xishuangbanna, China. Biodiversity and Conservation 15:2687–2703.

Garver, J. 2006. Development of China's overland transportation links with Central, South-west and South Asia. China Quarterly 185:1–22.

Girardot, N., Miller, J., and X. Liu. 2001. Daoism and ecology. Harvard University Press, Cambridge, Massachusetts.

Global Carbon Project. 2008. Carbon budget and trends 2007. Available from http://www.globalcarbonproject.org/carbontrends/index_new_htm (accessed October 2008).

Goh, E. 2004. China in the Mekong River basin: the regional security implications of resource development in the Lancang Jiang. Working paper 69. Institute of Defense and Strategic Studies, Singapore.

Goodman, D. 2004. The campaign to "open up the West": national, provincial-level and local perspectives. China Quarterly 178:317–334.

Goodman, J. 2000. The exploration of Yunnan. Yunnan People's Publishing House, Kunming, China.

Graham-Harrison, E. 2008. China aims for fast zero emission power by 2015. Reuters, April 24. Available from http://www.planetark.com/dailynewsstory.cfm/newsaid/48117/story.htm (accessed April 2008).

Greater Mekong Subregion Economic Cooperation Program. 2009. Joint ministerial statement. Presented at 15th Ministerial Meeting, Cha-am, Petchburi Province, Thailand, June 19. Available from http://www.adb.org/GMS (accessed August 2009).

Grueter, C., et al. 2008. Ranging of snub-nosed monkeys (*Rhinopithecus bieti*) at the Samage Forest, China. I. Characteristics of range use. International Journal of Primatology 29:1121–1145.

Grumbine, R. 2007. China's emergence and prospects for global sustainability. BioScience 57:249–255.

Grumbine, R., and J. Xu. 2009. Creating a conservation with Chinese characteristics. Paper presented at the International Society for Conservation Biology meeting, July 13, Beijing, China.

Guttman, H. 2006. River flows and development in the Mekong River basin. Mekong Update and Dialogue 9:2–4.

Haider, Z. 2005. Baluchis, Beijing, and Pakistan's Gwador port. Georgetown Journal of International Affairs (Winter/Spring):95–103.

Han, N., and Z. Ren. 2001. Ecotourism in China's nature reserves: opportunities and challenges. Journal of Sustainable Tourism 9:228–247.

Hansen, J., et al. 2008. Target atmospheric CO_2: where should humanity aim? Open Atmospheric Science Journal 2:217–231.

Hanser, A. 2005. Made in the P.R.C.: China's consumer revolution. Current History 104:272–277.

Hanssen, C. 2007. Lao land concessions, development for the people? Paper presented at the International Conference on Poverty Reduction and Forest: Tenure, Market, and Policy Reforms, September, Regional Community Forestry Training Center for Asia and the Pacific, Bangkok, Thailand.

Hare, W. 2009. A safe landing for the climate. Pages 13–29 in L. Starke et al., eds. 2009 state of the world: into a warming world. W. W. Norton, New York.

Harkness, J. 1998. Recent trends in forestry and conservation of biodiversity in China. China Quarterly 156:911–934.

Harman, D. 2008. China's arable land acreage falls in 2007. Resource Investor, China. Available from http://www.resourceinvestor.com/pebbel.asp?relid=42019 (accessed February 2009).

Harney, A. 2008. The China price. Penguin Press, New York.

Harris, P. 2004. "Getting rich is glorious": environmental values in the People's Republic of China. Environmental Values 13:145–165.

Harris, R. 2008. Wildlife conservation in China. M. E. Sharpe, Armonk, New York.

Harvey, D. 2005. A brief history of neoliberalism. Oxford University Press, New York.

Haw, S. 2007. Beijing—a concise history. Routledge, London.

Hedemark, M., and U. Vongsak. 2003. Wildlife survey of the Nam Ha NPA. Wildlife Conservation Society Lao Program, Vientiene, Lao PDR.

Helmer, J. 2008. China stumbles in forging Russia gas deals. Asia Times Online, Hong Kong. Available from http://www.atimes.com (accessed June 2008).

Hillman, B. 2003. Paradise under construction: minorities, myths and modernity in Northwest Yunnan. Asian Ethnicity 4:175–188.

Hilton, I. 2008. No more time for sound bites. China Dialogue, Beijing. Available from http://www.chinadialogue.cn/article/show/single/cn/2261-no-more-time-for-sound-bites (accessed August 2008).

———. 2009. Building regional cooperation. China Dialogue, Beijing. Available from http://www.chinadialogue.net/article/summary/3229-Building-regional-cooperation (accessed August 2009).

Hilty, J., W. Lidicker Jr., and A. Merenlender. 2006. Corridor ecology. Island Press, Washington, D.C.

Hinton, D., trans. 1993. Selected poems of T'ao Ch'ien. Copper Canyon Press, Port Townsend, Washington.

———. 2005. Mountain home: the wilderness poetry of ancient China. New Directions, New York.

Ho, M., and C. Nielsen. 2007. Cleaning the air: the health and economic damage of air pollution in China. MIT Press, Cambridge, Massachusetts.

Ho, P. 2001. Who owns China's land? Policies, property rights, and deliberate institutional ambiguity. China Quarterly 166:394–421.

Ho, P., and R. Edmonds. 2007. Perspectives of time and change. China Information 21:331–344.

Hoffman, J. 2008. The frugal teenager, ready or not. New York Times, October 12, ST 1, ST 9.

Holz, C. 2005. China's economic growth 1978–2025: what we know today about China's economic growth tomorrow. Paper presented at the Center on China's Transnational Relations, Hong Kong University of Science and Technology, September 30, Hong Kong, China.

———. 2007. Have China scholars all been bought? Far Eastern Economic Review 170:36–40.

Honey, M. 2008. Ecotourism and sustainable development. Island Press, Washington, D C.

Hu, H. 2008. Biodiversity conservation corridor-Xishuangbanna. Presentation at the Biodiversity Corridor Initiative Exchange Meeting for Implementing Agencies, Environmental Operations Center, Greater Mekong Subregion, Asian Development Bank, September 14–16, Bangkok, Thailand.

Huber, T. 1997. Green Tibetans: a brief social history. Pages 103–119 in F. Korom, ed. Tibetan culture in the diaspora. Verlag der Osterreichischen Aka demie der Wissenschalfen, Wein, Germany.

Hudson, V., and A. den Boer. 2004. Bare branches: the security implications of Asia's surplus male population. MIT Press, Cambridge, Massachusetts.

Hulme, M. 2009. Why we disagree about climate change. Cambridge University Press, New York.

Hung, W. 1952. Tu Fu: China's greatest poet. Harvard University Press, Cambridge, Massachusetts.

IEA (International Energy Agency). 2008. World energy outlook 2008. International Energy Agency, Paris.

———. 2009. World energy outlook 2009. International Energy Agency, Paris.

Igoe, J., and S. Sullivan. 2008. Problematizing neoliberal biodiversity conservation: displaced and disobedient knowledge. Executive summary of a workshop held at American University, May 16–19, Washington, D.C. Available from author.

Intellasia. 2008. China and Vietnam square off in Laos. Intellasia News Online, Hanoi, Vietnam. Available from http://www.intellasia.net/news/articles/regional/11249238.shtml (accessed September 2008).

IPCC (Intergovernmental Panel on Climate Change). 2007. Climate change 2007: the physical science basis. Cambridge University Press, New York.

IUCN (International Union for the Conservation of Nature). 2003. A new era. World Conservation Bulletin 2:2.

———. 2008. *Panthera tigris*: assessment information. IUCN Red List of Threatened Species 2008. IUCN, Gland, Switzerland. Available from http://www.iucnredlist.org/details/15955 (accessed October 2008).

Jackson, R., and N. Howe. 2004. The graying of the middle kingdom: the demographics and economies of retirement policy in China. Center for Strategic and International Studies, Washington, D.C.

Jacques, M. 2009. When China rules the world. Penguin, New York.

Jagerskog A., and M. Zeitoun. 2009. Getting transboundary water right: theory and practice for effective cooperation. Report no. 25. Stockholm International Water Institute, Stockholm.

James, A. 1999. Institutional constraints of protected area funding. Parks 9:15–25.

Jiang, Z. 2005. On considering an upper limit to the area of China's nature reserves. Acta Ecologica Sinica 25:14–21. In Chinese.

Jiao, X. 2008. Yunnan invests in fragile northwest. China Daily, Beijing, March 10. Available from http://www.chinadaily.com.cn/china/2008npc/2008-03/10/content_6521611.htm (accessed April 2008).

Jim, C. and S. Xu. 2003. Getting out of the woods: quandaries of protected area management in China. Mountain Research and Development 23:222–226.

Jinnah, S., et al. 2009. Tripping points: barriers and bargaining chips on the road to Copenhagen. Environmental Research Letters 4: 1-6.

Johnson, A., et al. 2006. Effects of human-carnivore conflict in tiger (*Panthera tigris*) and prey populations in Lao PDR. Animal Conservation 9:421–430.

Kahn, J., and J. Yardley. 2007. As China roars, population reaches deadly extremes. New York Times, August 26, pp. 1, 6–7.

Kandiyoti, R. 2007. China's pipeline politics. China Dialogue, Beijing. Available from http://www.chinadialogue.net/article/show/single/en/880-China's-pipeline-politics (accessed April 2007).

Kang, D. 2007. China rising: peace, power, and order in East Asia. Columbia University Press, New York.

Kaplan, R. 2009. Pakistan's fatal shore. Atlantic 303:70–76.

Kennedy, J. 2007. The implementation of village elections and tax-for-fee reform in rural Northwest China. Pages 48–74 in E. Perry and M. Goldman, eds. Grassroots political reform in contemporary China. Harvard University Press, Cambridge, Massachusetts.

Kennedy, M., et al. 2008. Snowball Earth termination by destabilization of equatorial permafrost methane clathrate. Nature 453:642–645.

Khanna, P. 2008. The second world: empires and influence on the new global order. Random House, New York.

Klein, N. 2008. China's all-seeing eye. Rolling Stone 1053:59–66.

Koser, K. 2009. Why migration matters. Current History 108:147–153.

Krech, S. 2005. Reflections on conservation, sustainability, and environmentalism in indigenous North America. American Anthropologist 107:78–86.

Kuchins, A. 2007. Russia and China: the ambivalent embrace. Current History 106:321–327.

Kurlantzick, J. 2008. Asia's democracy backlash. Current History 107:375–380.

Kylychbekova, M. 2007. UNESCO visit to Altai manipulated to silence environmentalism. Pacific Environment Russian Program, San Francisco. Available from http://pacificenvironment.org (accessed July 2008).

LaFraniere, S. 2009. Scientists point to possible link between dam and China quake. New York Times, February 6, A1, A7.

Lamont, J. 2009. New Delhi and Beijing work to save glaciers of the Himalayas. Financial Times. Available from http://www.ft.com/cms/s/0/55909f74-7fc4-11de-85dc-OO144feabdcO.htm (accessed August 2009).

Lampton, D. 2008. The three faces of Chinese power. University of California Press, Berkeley.

Lapham, N., and R. Livermore. 2003. Striking a balance: ensuring conservation's place on the international biodiversity assistance agenda. Conservation International, Washington, D.C.

Larson, A., and F. Soto. 2008. Decentralization of natural resources governance regimes. Annual Review of Environment and Resources 33:213–239.

Larson, C. 2008. The Middle Kingdom's dilemma (part one). China Dialogue, Beijing. Available from http://www.chinadialogue.net/homepage/show/single/en/1808-The-Middle-Kingdom- (accessed March 2008).

———. 2009. China's green leap forward? Christian Science Monitor, April 12, p. 36.

Lau, N. 2006. Harmonious society will impact the world. China Daily, Beijing, October 20. Available from http://www.chinadaily.com.cn/opinion/2006-10-20/content_712596.htm (accessed October 2006).

Law, W., and J. Salick. 2007. Comparing conservation priorities for useful plants among botanists and Tibetan doctors. Biodiversity and Conservation 16:1757–1759.

Lawrence, D., et al. 2008. Accelerated Arctic land warming and permafrost degradation during rapid sea ice loss. Geophysical Research Letters 35, L11506. DOI: 10.1029/2008/GL033985.

Lawrence, S. 2008. Power surge: the impacts of rapid dam development in Laos. International Rivers, Berkeley, California.

Layne, C. 2008. China's challenge to U.S. hegemony. Current History 13:13–18.

Leichenko, R., and K. O'Brien. 2008. Environmental change and globalization. Oxford University Press, New York.

Leonard, M. 2008. What does China think? Public Affairs, New York.

Leverett, F., and J. Bader. 2005–2006. Managing China-U.S. energy competition in the Middle East. Washington Quarterly 29:187–201.

Levine, M., and N. Aden. 2008. Global carbon emissions in the coming decades: the case of China. Annual Review of Environment and Resources 33:12.1–12.20.

Lewis, J. 2007–2008. China's strategic priorities in international climate change negotiations. Washington Quarterly 31:155–174.

———. 2008. The exigent city. New York Times Magazine, June 8.

Li, B. 2003. Obstructions to local governance in natural resources management—a case study in Jisha village, northwest Yunnan. Pages 277–285 in J. Xu and S. Mikesell, eds. Landscapes of diversity: indigenous knowledge, sustainable livelihoods and resource governance in Montane Mainland Southeast Asia. Proceedings of the III Symposium on MMSEA. Yunnan Science and Technology Press, Kunming, China.

Li, D., et al. 2008. Ranging of snub-nosed monkeys (*Rhinopithecus bieti*) at the Samage Forest, China. II. Use of land cover types and altitudinal zones. International Journal of Primatology 29:1147–1173.

Li, H., et al. 2007. Demand for rubber is causing the loss of high diversity rain forest in Southwest China. Biodiversity Conservation 16:1731–1745.

Li, H., et al. 2008. Past, present, and future land use in Xishuangbanna, China and the implications for carbon dynamics. Forest Ecology and Management 255:16–24.

Li, M. 2008. Climate change, limits to growth, and the imperative of socialism. Monthly Review, July–August.

Li, S., and D. He. 2008. Water level responses to hydropower development in the upper Mekong River. Ambio 37:164–169.

Li, W., and N. Han. 2001. Ecotourism management in China's nature reserves. Ambio 30:62–63.

Li, Y. 2007. The Gwadar port issue in Sino-U.S. relations. Contemporary International Relations 17:105–112.

Li, Z. 2006a. China to become second largest tourism economy within the decade. China Watch. Worldwatch Institute, Washington, D.C.

Available from http://www.worldwatch.org/features/chinawatch/stories/20060502-1 (accessed May 2006).

———. 2006b. Rapid growth of China's cities challenges urban planners, migrant families. China Watch. Worldwatch Institute, Washington, D.C. Available from http://www.worldwatch.org/node/4148 (accessed June 2006).

Li, Z., et al. 2008. Wildlife trade, consumption, and conservation awareness in southwest China. Biodiversity Conservation 17:1493–1516.

Lieberthal, K., and D. Sandalow. 2009. Overcoming obstacles to U.S.-China cooperation on climate change. Brookings Institution, Washington, D.C.

Lin, E., et al. 2008. Climate change and food security in China. Greepeace China, Beijing.

Lindberg, K., et al. 2003. Ecotourism in China's nature reserves. Pages 103–125 in A. Lew et al., eds. Tourism in China. Haworth Hospitality Press, New York.

Litzinger, R. 2007. In search of the grassroots: hydropower politics in Northwest Yunnan. Pages 282–299 in E. Perry and M. Goldman, eds. Grassroots political reform in contemporary China. Harvard University Press, Cambridge, Massachusetts.

Liu, D., et al. 2009. Constructed wetlands in China: recent development and future challenges. Frontiers in Ecology and Environment 7:261–268.

Liu, H., et al. 2002. Practice of conserving plant diversity through traditional beliefs: a case study in Xishuangbanna, southwest China. Biodiversity and Conservation 11:705–713.

Liu, J. 2007. Nu River lessons. China Dialogue, Beijing. Available from http://www.chinadialogue.net/article/show/single/en/885-Nu-River-lessons (accessed April 2007).

Liu, J., and J. Diamond. 2008. Revolutionizing China's environmental protection. Science 319:37–38.

Liu, J., et al. 2008. Ecological and socioeconomic effects of China's policies for ecosystem services. Proceedings of the National Academy of Sciences (USA) 105:9477–9482.

Liu, T. 2005. Chinese tea. Chinese Intercontinental Press, Beijing.

Liu, W., et al. 2006. Environmental and socioeconomic impacts of increasing rubber plantations in Menglun Township, Southwest China. Mountain Research and Development 26:245–253.

Lobell, D., et al. 2008. Prioritizing climate change adaptation needs for food security in 2030. Science 319:607–610.

Locke, H., and P. Dearden. 2005. Rethinking protected area categories and the new paradigm. Environmental Conservation 32:1–10.

Lu, X., Wang, J. J., and C. Grundy-Warr. 2008. Are the Chinese dams to be blamed for the lower water levels in the Lower Mekong? Pages 7–9 in M. Kummi et al., eds. Modern myths of the Mekong—summaries. Water and Development Publications, Helsinki University of Technology, Helsinki.

Lu, Y. 2005. Environmental civil society and governance in China. Briefing paper ASP BP 05/04. The China Project, Asia Programme, Chatham House. Available from http://www.chathamhouse.org/uk/index.php?id=272 (accessed August 2006).

Lum, T. 2006. Social unrest in China. Congressional Research Service, Library of Congress, Washington, D.C.

Lynch, D. 2006. Rising China and Asian democratization. Stanford University Press, Stanford, California.

Ma, C., et al. 2006. Plant diversity and priority conservation areas of Northwestern Yunnan, China. Biodiversity and Conservation 16:757–774.

Ma, J. 2008. Your right to know: a historic moment. China Dialogue, Beijing. Available from http://www.chinadialogue.cn/article/show/single/en/1962-Your-right-to-know-a-historic- (accessed May 2008).

Maass, P. 2009. Crude world. Alfred Knopf, New York.

MacKinnon, J., and P. Moore. 2006. China's protected areas: why is there a problem? Lessons from international best practices regulatory and management issues. IUCN (International Union for the Conservation of Nature), Gland, Switzerland.

MacKinnon, J., and H. Wang. 2008. The green gold of China. EU-China Biodiversity Programme, Beijing.

Magee, D. 2006. Powershed politics: Yunnan hydropower under Great Western Development. China Quarterly 185:23–41.

Mahbubani, K. 2008. The new Asian hemisphere. Public Affairs, New York.

Management Bureau of the Three Parallel Rivers National Park, Yunnan. 2007. Protection Report, Three Parallel Rivers of Yunnan protected areas, China. January 19. Management Bureau of the Three Parallel Rivers National Park, Yunnan.

Manalo, I. 2009. In China's Lijiang, heritage tourism sells. Philippine Daily Inquirer, August 28.

Maneeratana, B., and P. Hoare. 2007. When shifting cultivators migrate to the cities, how can the forest be rehabilitated? Pages 137–141 in M. Cairns, ed. Voices from the forest: Integrating indigenous knowledge into sustainable upland farming. Resources for the Future, Washington, D.C.

Manivong, V., and R. Cramb. 2008. Economies of smallholder rubber expansion in northern Laos. Agroforestry Systems 74:113–125.

Marks, R. 2002. The origins of the world. Rowman and Littlefield, Lanham, Maryland.

Martens, S. 2006. Public participation with Chinese characteristics: citizen consumers in China's environmental movement. Environmental Politics 15:211–230.

Martin, D. N.d. Altai gas pipeline: a stake through the heart of a sacred culture. Pacific Environment Russian Program, San Francisco. Available from http://www.pacificenvironment.org (accessed July 2008).

Mascarelli, A. 2009. A sleeping giant? Nature Reports Climate Change, March 5. DOI: 1038/climate.2009.24.

MaximsNews Network. 2008. Economic growth spurs changes along the Mekong River basin. Available from http://www.maximsnews.com/news20080314mrcforum10803140801.htm (accessed June 2008).

McBeath, J., and J. McBeath. 2006. Biodiversity conservation in China: policies and practices. Journal of International Wildlife Law and Policy 9:293–317.

McCartan, B. 2007. China rubber demand stretches Laos. AsiaTimes Online. Available from http://www.atimes.com/atimes/China_Business/IL19C601.html (accessed September 2008).

———. 2008. China farms abroad. Asia Sentinel, Hong Kong. Available from http://www.asiasentinel.com/index.php?option=com_content&task=view&id=1361&Itemid=32 (accessed September 2008).

McDonald, K. 2007. Damming China's grand canyon: pluralization without democratization in the Nu River Valley. PhD dissertation, Environment, Science, Policy, and Management, University of California, Berkeley. Available from author.

McElwee, C. 2008. The environmental impact assessment in China: the first step toward compliant operations. International Environmental Law Committee Newsletter 10(4): 1–10

McEvedy, C., and R. Jones. 1978. Atlas of world population history. Viking Penguin, New York.

McKhann, C. F. 2001. The good, the bad and the ugly: observations on tourism development in Lijiang, China. Pages 147–166 in C. Tam, et al., eds. Tourism, anthropology and China. White Lotus Press, Bangkok, Thailand.

McKie, R. 2009. Arctic seas turn to acid, putting vital food chain at risk. Guardian. Available from http://www.guardian.co.uk/world/2009/oct/04/arctic-seas-turn-to-acid (accessed October 2009).

McMillion, C. 2007. China's soaring financial, industrial, and technological power. MBG Information Services, Washington, D.C.

McNeely, J., et al. 2009. Conservation biology in Asia: the major policy challenges. Conservation Biology 23:805–810.

Medeiros, E. 2009. Is Beijing ready for global leadership? Current History 198:250–256.

Mehtonen, K. 2008. Do the downstream countries oppose the upstream dams? Pages 38–39 in M. Kummi et al., eds.. Modern myths of the Mekong: summaries. Water and Development Publications, Helsinki University of Technology, Helsinki.

Meinshausen, M., et al. 2009. Greenhouse gas emission targets for limiting global warming to 2 C. Nature 458:1158–1162.

Melick, D., et al. 2007. Seeing the wood for the trees: how conservation policies can place greater pressure on village forests in southwest China. Biodiversity Conservation 16:1959–1971.

Menniken, T. 2007. Lessons from the Mekong: China's performance in international resource politics. Contemporary Southeast Asia 29:1–24.

Menon, R., and A. Motyl. 2007. The myth of Russian resurgence. American Interest Online. Available from http://www.the-american-interest.com/ai2/article.cfm?Id=258&MId=8 (accessed April 2008).

Menzies, N. 2007. Our forest, your ecosystem, their timber: communities, conservation, and the state in community-based forest management. Columbia University Press, New York.

MEP (Ministry of Environmental Protection). 2009. The state of the environment of China in 2008. Available from http://english.mep.gov.cn/News_service/news_release/200906/t20090618_152932.htm (accessed September 2009).

Mertha, A. 2008. China's water warriors: citizen action and policy change. Cornell University Press, Ithaca, New York.

Meyer, L., et al. 2009. News in climate science and exploring boundaries: a policy brief on developments since the IPCC AR4 report in 2007. Netherlands Environmental Assessment Agency, Bilthoven.

Meyerson, F., L. Merino, and J. Durand. 2007. Migration and environment in the context of globalization. Frontiers in Ecology and Environment 5:182–190.

Michaud, A. 2006. Historical dictionary of the people of the Southeast Asian massif. Scarecrow Press, Lanham, Maryland.

Middleton, C. 2007. China's charm offensive in Southeast Asia bodes ill for Mekong Basin. International Rivers, Berkeley, California. Available from http://www.internationalrivers.org/en/node/1890 (accessed June 2008).

———. 2008a. New report urges better energy planning in Cambodia before hydropower dams are developed. International Rivers, Berkeley, California. Available from http://www.internationalrivers.org/en/way-forward/world-commission-dams/new-report-(accessed June 2008).

———. 2008b. Perspective from the Mekong Region: new financiers and familiar problems. Pages 12–15 in P. Bosshard, ed. New financiers and the environment. International Rivers, Berkeley, California.

Ministry of Water Resources, PRC. 2009. China to input 468.9 bln yuan for western development. Available from http://www.mwr.gov.cn/dlzz/2009english/news/20091016080651f7ff4c.aspex (accessed October 2009).

MIT (Massachusetts Institute of Technology). 2007. The future of coal. MIT, Boston, Massachusetts.

Mittermeier, R., et al. 2004. Hotspots revisited: Earth's biologically richest and most endangered ecoregions. CEMEX, Mexico City.

Molle, F., et al. 2009. Contested waterscapes in the Mekong Region: hydropower, livelihoods, and governance. Earthscan, London.

Mooney, P. 2006. The long road ahead for China's universities. Chronicle of Higher Education 52(37):A42–46.

Morell, V. 2007. Can the wild tiger survive? Science 317:1312–1314.

Morris, N. 2008. Climate change could force 1 billion from their homes by 2050. Independent. Available from http://www.independent.co.uk/environment/climate-change/climate-change-could-force-1-billion-from-their-homes-by-2050-817223.html (accessed April 2008).

Morton, K. 2008. China and environmental security in the age of consequences. Asia-Pacific Review 15:52–67.

Mosolova, T. 2008. Russia pipeline to China 75 pct built. Reuters News, New York. Available from http://www.uofaweb.ualberta.ca/chinainstitute/nav03.cfm?nav03=79391&nav02=74693& (accessed July 2008).

Mouawad, J. 2008. As oil giants lose influence, supply drops. New York Times, August 19, A1, A8.

Mozur, P. 2008. Preserving China's reserves. Far Eastern Economic Review 171:77–79.

MRC (Mekong River Commission). 1995. Agreement on the cooperation for the sustainable development of the Mekong River basin. MRC, Phnom Penh, Cambodia. Available from http://www.mrcmekong.org/agreement_95/agreement_95.htm (accessed July 2007).

————. 2002. Annual report 2001. MRC, Phnom Penh, Cambodia. Available from http://www.mrcmekong.org/annual_report/annual_report. htm (accessed June 2008).

————. 2006. IBFM puts triple bottom line assessment into practice. MRC Annual Report 2006. MRC, Phnom Penh, Cambodia.

————. 2007. Consumption and yield of fish and other aquatic animals from the lower Mekong Basin. Technical paper 16. MRC, Phnom Penh, Cambodia.

Mufson, S., and B. Harden. 2008. Coal can't fill world's burning appetite. Washington Post, March 20, A01.

Mukherjee, K. 2008. India focuses on renewables in new climate plan. Reuters. Available from http://www.alertnet.org/thenews/newsdesk/ BOM258316.htm (accessed July 2008).

Myers, N., and J. Kent. 2003. The new consumers: the influence of affluence on the environment. Proceedings of the National Academy of Sciences (USA) 100:4963–4968.

Nation. 2007. Chinese investors invade Laos. Nation, Bangkok, Thailand, October 17. Available from http://www.nationmultimedia.com/2007/ 10/08/regional/regional_30051701.php (accessed September 2008).

The Nature Conservancy and Yunnan Provincial Government. 2001. Northwest Yunnan conservation and development action plan. Kunming, China.

Naumann, K., et al. 2007. Towards a grand strategy for an uncertain world: renewing transatlantic partnership. Noaber Foundation, Lunteren, Germany. Available from http://www.ssronline.org/edocs/ 3eproefGrandStrat_b.pdf (accessed May 2008).

Needham, J., and W. Ling. 1954. Science and civilization in China. Volume 1. Cambridge University Press, Cambridge, Great Britain.

New York Times. 2008. Man-made hunger. New York Times, July 6, p. 9.

Noreng, O. 2004. Oil, the euro, and the dollar. Journal of Energy and Development 30:53–80.

Nowak, R. 2007. Hope I get rich before I get old. New Scientist 196(2629): 62–63.

NSIDC (National Snow and Ice Data Center). 2008. Arctic sea ice down to second-lowest extent; likely record-low volume. NSIDC, Cooperative Institute for Research in Environmental Sciences, University of Colorado, Boulder. Available from http://nsidc.org/news/press/20081002_ seaice_pressrelease.html (accessed November 2008).

Nyaupane, G., Morais, D., and L. Dowler. 2006. The role of community involvement and number/type of visitors on tourism impacts: a controlled comparison of Annapurna, Nepal and Northwest Yunnan, China. Tourism Management 27:1373–1385.

Oakes, T. 1997. Ethnic tourism in rural Guizhou: sense of place and the commerce of authenticity. Pages 35–70 in M. Picard and R. Wood, eds. Tourism, ethnicity, and the state in Asian and Pacific societies. University of Hawaii Press, Honolulu.

O'Brien, K., and L. Li. 2005. Popular contention and its impact in rural China. Comparative Political Studies 38:235–259.

O'Connor, M. 2000. When I find you again it will be in mountains. Selected poems of Chia Tao. Wisdom Publications, Boston.

Oehlers, A. 2006. A critique of ADB policies towards the Greater Mekong Sub-region. Journal of Contemporary Asia 36:464–479.

Oi, J., and A. Walden, eds. 1999. Property rights and economic reform in China. Stanford University Press, Stanford, California.

Oppenheimer, A. 2008. China-India trade and Latin America. SignOn San Diego, January 18. Available from http://www.signonsandiego.com/uniontrib/20080118/news_1z1e18oppenhe.html (accessed July 2008).

Osnos, E. 2008. Angry youth. New Yorker, July 28, pp. 27–34.

Oster, S. 2008. U.S. asks China to join global energy group. Wall Street Journal, May 21. Available from http://www.uofaweb.ualberta.ca/chinainstitute/nav03.cfm?nav03=78363&nav02=57578& (accessed July 2008).

Overholt, W. 2008. Asia, America, and the transformation of geopolitics. Cambridge University Press, New York.

Pan, E. 2006. Sino-Russian energy ties. 2006. Council on Foreign Relations, New York. Available from http://www.cfr.org/publications/10363/sinorussian-energy-ties.html (accessed April 2006).

Parenti, C. 2008. Class struggle in the new China. Nation 287(5):11–16.

Parry, M., et al. 2004. Effects of climate change on global food production under SRES emissions and socio-economic scenarios. Global Environmental Change 14:53–67.

Parry, M., et al. 2009. Overshoot, adapt, and recover. Nature 458:1102–1103.

PATF (Protected Area Task Force). 2004. Report to the China Council for International Cooperation on Environment and Development (CCICED): Evaluation on and policy recommendations to the protected area system of China. State Environmental Protection Administration, Beijing.

Pech, S., and K. Sunada. 2008. Population growth and natural resource pressures in the Mekong River basin. Ambio 37:219–224.

Pei, M., and J. Anderson. 2009. The color of China. National Interest

Online. Available from http://www.nationalinterest.org/PrinterFriendly. aspx?id=20952 (accessed March 2009).

Pei, S. 1991. Managing for biological diversity conservation in temple yards and holy hills: the traditional practices of the Xishuangbanna Dai community, southwest China. Pages 118–132 in L. Hamilton, ed. Ethics, religion and biodiversity. White Horse Press, Cambridge, UK.

People's Daily Online. 2008. China-ASEAN trade prospects promising. People's Daily Online, Beijing. Available from http://english.peopledaily. com.cn/90001/90780/91344/6458369.html (accessed October 2008).

Perng, J. 2007. Eco-tourism: snapshots from four villages. China Development Brief, Beijing. Available from http://www.chinadevelopmentbrief. com/node/1218/print (accessed January 2008).

Pffefer, W., J. Harper, and S. O'Neel. 2008. Kinematic constraints on glacier contributions to 21st-century sea-level rise. Science 321:1340–1343.

Phillips, A. 2003. A modern paradigm. World Conservation Bulletin 2:6–7.

Phillips, L., and S. Ilcan. 2004. Capacity-building: the neoliberal governance of development. Canadian Journal of Development Studies 25:393–409.

Plummer, J., and J. Taylor, eds. 2004. Community participation in China. Issues and processes for capacity building. Earthscan, London.

Pomerance, K. 2009. The great Himalayan watershed. New Left Review. Available from http://www.newleftreview.org/?page=article&view=2788 (accessed July 2009).

Porter, B. 1993. Road to heaven: encounters with Chinese hermits. Mercury House, San Francisco.

———. 1996. Lao-tzu's Taoteching. Mercury House, San Francisco.

Pozen, R. 2006. China goes from red to gray. Fortune Online, June 13. Available from http://money.cnn.com/2006/06-12/magazine/fortune/ china_fortune/index.htm (accessed August 2006).

PRO (Policy Research Office of the People's Government of Yunnan Province) et al. 2006. The Three Parallel Rivers. Yunnan Peoples' Publishing House, Kunming, China.

PRO/TNC (Policy Research Office of Yunnan Provincial Government and The Nature Conservancy). 2009. Yunnan national parks: from theory to practice. PRO of the Yunnan Provincial Government, Kunming, China.

Qie, J. 2009. One year of open information. China Dialogue, Beijing. Available from http://www.chinadialogue.cn/article/show/single/en/3015- One -year-of-open-information- (accessed May 2009).

Qiu, J. 2009. Where the rubber meets the garden. Nature 457:246–247.

Qiu, X., trans. 2005. Poems of Tang and Song Dynasties. East China Normal University Press, Shezhi, China.

Quenemoen, M. 2004. In search of "Dai identity" in Xishuangbanna, China. Pages 194–237 in S. Mitchell, ed. Ethnic minority issues in Yunnan. Yunnan Fine Arts Publishing House, Kunming, China.

Rahmstorf, S. 2007. A semi-empirical approach to sea level rise. Science 315:368–370.

Redford, K., et al. 2008. What is the role for conservation organizations in poverty alleviation in the world's wild places? Oryx 42(3):1–14.

Reuters. 2009. China's rise in the global auto market. China Daily, Beijing, July 20–26, p. 12.

Ripple, W., and R. Beschta. 2009. Large predators and trophic cascades in terrestrial ecosystems of the western United States. Biological Conservation 142: 2401–2414.

Rogelj, J., et al. 2009. Half way to Copenhagen, no way to 2 C. Nature Reports Climate Change, June 11. DOI: 10.1038/climate.2009.57.

Romero, S., and A. Barrionuevo. 2009. Deals help China expand its sway in Latin America. New York Times, April 16, A1, A8.

Roque, J. 2007. China lays its stake on Central Asia. China Briefing News, Beijing. Available from http://www.china-briefing.com/ news/2007/12/18/China-lays-its-stake (accessed July 2008).

Rosen, S. 2009. Contemporary Chinese youth and the state. Journal of Asian Studies 68:359–369.

Rosenthal, E. 2007. U.N. report describes the risks of inaction on climate change. New York Times, November 17. Available from http:// www.nytimes.com/2007/11/17/science/earth/17cnd-climate.html?_ r=4&hp=&adxn (accessed November 2008).

Rowcroft, P. 2008. Frontiers of change: the reasons behind land-use change in the Mekong Basin. Ambio 37:213–218.

Ruch, J. 2006. They have buried Talu: ethnic theme parks and Chinese utopia. http://obscurearchives.stupidquestion.net/ethnicthemeparks. html (accessed January 2008).

Salick, J., et al. 2005. Tibetan land use and change near Khawa Karpo, eastern Himalayas. Economic Botany 59:312–325.

Salick, J., et al. 2006. Tibetan sacred sites conserve old-growth trees in the eastern Himalayas. Biodiversity and Conservation 16:693–706.

Sanderson, S. 2005. Poverty and conservation: the new century's "peasant question?" World Development 33:323–332.

Schellnhuber, H., et al. 2007. Climate change as a security risk. Earthscan, London.

Schiermeier, Q. 2007. What we don't know about climate change. Nature 445:580–581.

Schoenhals, M. 2004. Cultural revolution on the border: Yunnan's "political frontier defense" (1969–1971). Copenhagen Journal of Asian Studies 19:27–54.

Scott, J. 2009. The art of not being governed. Yale University Press, New Haven, Connecticutt.

Seligsohn, D., et al. 2009. China, the United States, and the climate change challenge. World Resources Institute, Washington, D.C.

SFA (State Forestry Administration) et al. 2008. China Protected Areas Leadership Alliance Project. East-West Center, Honolulu.

Shakhova, N., et al. 2008. Anomalies of methane in the atmosphere over the east Siberian shelf: is there any sign of methane leakage from shallow shelf hydrates? Geophysical Research Abstracts 10: EGU2008-A-01526.

Shambaugh, D., ed. 2006. Power shift: China and Asia's new dynamic. University of California Press, Berkeley.

Shao, M., et al. 2006. City clusters in China: air and surface water pollution. Frontiers in Ecology and Environment 4:353–361.

Shapiro, J. 2001. Mao's war against nature. Cambridge University Press, New York.

Sharma, S. 2006. Asia's challenged giants. Current History 105:170–175.

Shen, R. 2008. Rubber trees for tyre industry shrink China rain forests. Reuters News Service, New York. Available from http://www.planetark.org/dailynewsstory.cfm/newsid/47833/story.htm (accessed June 2008).

Shi, J. 2009. Wen calls halt to Yunnan dam plan. Premier orders further environmental checks. South China Morning Post, May 21. Available from http://mouthtosource.net/rivers/blog/2009/05/21/chinas-premier-orders-halt-to-a-dam- (accessed May 2009).

Shi, W. 2008. Rubber boom in Luang Namtha: a transnational perspective. GTZ Rural Development in Mountainous Areas Program. Lao-German Technical Cooperation, Luang Namtha, Lao PDR.

Shi, Y., et al. 1999. Uplift of the Qinghai-Xizang (Tibetan) Plateau and east Asia environmental change during the late Cenozoic. Acta Geography Sinica 54(1):10–21. In Chinese with English abstract.

Shirk, S. 2007. China: fragile superpower. Oxford University Press, New York.

Shui On Group. 2007. Shui On Group forms strategic partnership with Yunnan Provincial Government. Press release, September 23. Available from http://www.shuionland.com (accessed January 2008).

Shuster, E. 2008. Tracking new coal-fired power plants. National Energy Technology Laboratory, U.S. Department of Energy, Washington, D.C.

Sicroff, S., E. Alos, and R. Shrestha. 2003. Independent backpacker tourism: key to sustainable development in remote mountain destination. Pages 527–543 in J. Xu and S. Mikesell, eds. Landscapes of diversity: indigenous knowledge, sustainable livelihoods, and resource governance in montane mainland southeast Asia. Proceedings of the III Symposium on MMSEA, Lijiang, China. Science and Technology Press, Kunming, China.

Siddiqi, T. 2007. Viable and environment-friendly sources for meeting South Asia's growing energy needs. Asia Pacific Issues No. 83. East-West Center, Honolulu.

Simpson, P. 2009. Yunnan: the economy. South China Morning Post, June 9, p. 7.

Smith, A., and Y. Xie, eds. 2008. A guide to the mammals of China. Princeton University Press, Princeton, New Jersey.

Snyder, G. 2003. Empty mountain. Distant hills. Pages 203–208 in E. Weinberger, ed. The New Directions anthology of classical Chinese poetry. New Directions, New York.

Sofield, T. H., and F. M. Li. 1998. China: tourism development and cultural policies. Annals of Tourism Research 25:362–392.

Solana, J., and B. Ferrero-Waldner. 2008. Climate change and international security. Paper from the High Representative and the European Commission to the European Business Council. Brussels, Belgium.

Solomon, S., et al. 2009. Irreversible climate change due to carbon dioxide emissions. Proceedings of the National Academy of Sciences (USA) 106:1704–1709.

Soule, M., et al. 2005. Strongly interacting species: conservation policy, management, and ethics. BioScience 55:168–176.

Stal, M., and K. Warner. 2009. The way forward: researching the environment and migration nexus. United Nations University—Institute for Environment and Human Security, Bonn, Germany.

Stein, B., L. Kutner, and J. Adams. 2000. Precious heritage: the status of biodiversity in the United States. Oxford University Press, New York.

Stone, R. 2008. Beijing's marathon run to clean foul air nears finish line. Science 321:636–637.

———. 2009. Nursing China's ailing forests back to health. Science 325:556–558.

Stone, R., and H. Jia. 2006. Going against the flow. Science 313:1034–1037.

Storey, I. 2009. China a major player in S-E Asia pipeline politics. Viewpoints. Institute of Southeast Asian Studies, Singapore.

Stricherz, V. 2009. Half of world's population could face climate-induced food crisis by 2100. University of Washington News, Seattle. Available from http://www.uwnews.org/article.asp?articleID=46272 (accessed April 2009).

Studley, J. 2007. Hearing a different drummer: a new paradigm for the "keepers of the forest." International Institute for Environment and Development, London.

Sturgeon, J. 2007. Pathways of "indigenous knowledge" in Yunnan, China. Alternatives 32:129–153.

Sun, S. 2006. Bright, prosperous future beckons. China Daily, Beijing. Available from http://www.chinadaily.com/cn/china/2006-11/06/context_725754.htm (accessed November 2006).

Sunchindah, A. 2005. Water diplomacy in the Lancang–Mekong River basin: prospects and challenges. Paper presented at the Workshop on the Growing Integration of the Greater Mekong Sub-regional ASEAN States in the Asian Region, September 20–21, Yangon, Myanmar.

Swope, L., M. B. Swain, F. Yang, and J. D. Ives. 1997. Uncommon property rights in southwest China. Pages 43–59 in B. R. Johnson, ed. Life and death matters: human rights and the environment at the end of the millenium. Atlamina Press, Walnut Creek, California.

Tan, C. 2008. What happened at Poznan? China Dialogue, Beijing, December 22. Available from http://www.chinadialogue.cn/article/show/single/en/2646-what-happened-at-poznan- (accessed December 2008).

Tan, M., et al. 2005. Urban land expansion and arable land loss in China—a case study of Beijing-Tianjin-Hebei region. Land Use Policy 22:187–196.

Tang, C., et al. 2007. Man-made versus natural forests in mid-Yunnan, southwestern China. Mountain Research and Development 27:242–249.

Tang, H. 2008. NGOs and the government: a new basis for cooperation. China Dialogue, Beijing. Available from http://www.chinadialogue.cn/article/show/single/en/2049-NGOs-and-government-a-new- (accessed June 2008).

Terhune, L. 2008. World Bank focuses on plight of tiger. U.S. Department of State News. Available from http://www.america.gov/st/env-english/2008/June/20080613150723mlenuhreto.8161585.h (accessed June 2008).

Tian, Q. 2004. China develops its West: motivation, strategy, and prospect. Journal of Contemporary China 13:611–636.

Tollefson, J. 2008. Stoking the fire. Nature 454:388–392.

Tomberg, I. 2006. Future oil and gas development in Siberia and the Russian Far East. RIA Novosti, Moscow. Available from http://www.pacificenvironment.org/article.php?id=188 (accessed October 2006).

Traub, J. 2009. Shaking up the boardroom at World Government, Inc. New York Times, January 4.

Tu, W. 2001. The ecological turn in new Confucian humanism: implications for China and the world. Daedalus 130:243–265.

Tucker, M., and D. Williams. 1997. Buddhism and ecology. Harvard University Press, Cambridge, Massachusetts.

UNDESA (UN Department of Economic and Social Affairs/Population Division). 2008. World Urbanization prospects: the 2007 revision. Available from http://www.un.org/esa/population/publications/wup2007/2007WUP_Highlights_web.pdf (accessed October 2008).

UNEP (UN Environment Programme). 2007. Greater Mekong environmental outlook. UNEP, Bangkok, Thailand.

———. 2008. Global glacial changes: facts and figures. UNEP and World Glacier Monitoring Service, Zurich.

UNESCO. 2009. Climate change and water: a world water assessment programme special report. UN Programme Office for Global Water Assessment, Perugia, Italy.

U.S. Census Bureau. 2008a. Country scenarios. U.S. Census Bureau, Washington, D.C. Available from http://www.census.gov/ipc/wnw/idb/country/vmportal.html (accessed June 2008).

———. 2008b. Trade in goods (imports, exports, and trade balance) with China. U.S. Census Bureau, Foreign Trade Division, Data Dissemination Branch, Washington, D.C.

U.S. DOE (Department of Energy). 2008. U.S. energy sources. U.S. DOE, Washington, D.C. Available from http://www.doe.gov/energysources/hydropower.htm (accessed July 2008).

Valdez, V. 2009. China's de-socialized medicine. Foreign Policy. Available from http://www.foreignpolicy.com/story/cms.php?story_id=4999&print=1 (accessed September 2009).

Van Rijsoort, J., and J. Zhang. 2005. Participatory resource management as a means for promoting social change in Yunnan, China. Biodiversity and Conservation 14:2543–2573.

Van Rooij, B. 2006. Implementation of Chinese environmental law: regular enforcement and political campaigns. Development and Change 37: 57–74.

Vidal, J. 2009. Rich nations failing to meet climate aid pledges. Guardian. Available from http://www.guardian.co.uk/environment/200/feb/20/climate-funds-deveoping-nations (accessed February 2009).

VietNamNet Bridge. 2008. Prime minister visits China to boost ties. Vietnam Post and Telecommunications Corporation Online News Service. Available at http://english.vietnamnet.vn/politics/2008/10/809406 (accessed October 2008).

Vina, A., et al. 2007. Temporal changes in giant panda habitat connectivity across boundaries of Wolong Nature Reserve, China. Ecological Applications 17:1019–1030.

Von Braun, J., and R. Meinzen-Dick. 2009. "Land grabbing" by foreign investors in developing countries. Policy brief no. 13. International Food Policy Research Institute, Washington, D.C.

Wang, A. 2007. Environmental protection in China: the role of law. China Dialogue, Beijing. Available from http://www.chinadialogue.net/article/show/single/en/745-Environmental-protection-in-China (accessed April 2007).

Wang, D. 2000. Heavy price to pay: a study on the relationship between social and environmental development in the Nujiang Canyon region. Pages 23–33 in J. Xu and A. Wilkes, eds. Proceedings of the culture and Biodiversity Conference 2000. Yunnan Science and Technology Press, Kunming, China.

Wang, F. 2003. Organizing through division and exclusion; China's hukuo system. Stanford University Press, Stanford, California.

Wang, J. 2009. Poor areas to get free legal aid. China Daily, Beijing, July 31, p. 5.

Wang, J., et al. 2008. Can China continue feeding itself? Policy research working paper 4470. World Bank, Washington, D.C.

Wang, T., and J. Watson. 2007. Who owns China's carbon emissions? Tyndall Briefing Note No. 23, October. Tyndall Centre for Climate Change Research, London.

Wang, Y. 2007. A yellow card for Three Parallel Rivers. China Dialogue, Beijing. Available from http://www.chinadialogue.net/article/show/single/en/1200-A-yellow-card-for-the-Three-Parallel-Rivers (accessed November 2007).

Wang, Z. 2009. Charity donations down, report says. China Daily, Beijing, July 31, p. 3.

Wardell, S. 2008. China's draft energy law facing yet further delay. Global Insight Daily Analysis, January 25. Available from http://www.uofaweb.ualberta.ca/chinainstitute/nav03.cfm?nav03=72431&nav02=57580& (accessed July 2008).

Watson, B., trans. 1994. Selected poems of Su Tung-p'o (Su Shih). Copper Canyon Press, Port Townsend, Washington.

Weinberger, E. 2003. The New Directions anthology of classical Chinese poetry. New Directions, New York.

Weller, R. 2006. Discovering nature: globalization and environmental culture in China and Taiwan. Cambridge University Press, New York.

Weng, M., ed. 2006. The international competitiveness of China's agricultural products. Foreign Language Press, Beijing.

West, P., and D. Brockington. 2006. An anthropological perspective on some unexpected consequences of protected areas. Conservation Biology 20:609–616.

West, P., et al. 2006. Parks and peoples: the social impact of protected areas. Annual Review of Anthropology 35:251–277.

Wheeler, D., K. Ummel, and R. Kraft. 2008. Another inconvenient truth: A CO_2-intensive South faces environmental disaster, no matter what the North does. Working paper 134. Center for Global Development, Washington, D.C.

Wiens, H. 1954. China's march toward the tropics. Shoe String, Hamden, Connecticutt.

Wilhelm, R., and C. Baynes. 1950. The I Ching. Princeton University Press, Princeton, New Jersey.

Wilkes, A. 2003. Using the sustainable livelihoods framework to understand agro-pastoralist livelihoods in NW Yunnan. Working Paper 2. Center for Biodiversity and Indigenous Knowledge, Kunming, Yunnan.

———. 2005. Ethnic minorities, environment and development in Yunnan: the institutional contexts of biocultural knowledge production in southwest China. PhD dissertation, University of Kent, Canterbury, UK.

———. 2008. Towards mainstreaming climate change in grassland management policies and practices on the Tibetan Plateau. ICRAF working paper no. 67. World Agroforestry Centre–ICRAF China, Beijing.

Williams, J., S. Jackson, and J. Kutzbach. 2007. Projected distribution of novel and disappearing climates by 2100 AD. Proceedings of the National Academy of Sciences (USA) 104:5738–5742.

Willson, A. 2006. Forest conversion and land-use change in rural northwest Yunnan, China. Mountain Research and Development 26:227–236.

Wilson, D., and R. Purushothaman. 2003. Dreaming with BRICs: the path to 2050. Global economics paper no. 99. Goldman Sachs, New York.

Winchester, S. 2008. The man who loved China. HarperCollins, New York.

Woetzel, J., et al. 2008. Preparing for China's urban billion: summary of findings. McKinsey Global Institute, Shanghai, China.

Wong, E. 2008a. China announces land policy aimed at promoting income growth in countryside. New York Times, October 13, A6.

———. 2008b. Factories shut, China workers are suffering. New York Times, November 14. Available from http://www.nytimes.com/2008/11/14/world/asia/14china.html?_r=1&hp=&oref=slogin& (accessed November 2008).

———. 2009. Even college-educated Chinese feel job pinch as economy slumps. New York Times, January 25, A4.

Wong, J., and A. Light. 2009. China begins its transition to a clean-energy economy. Center for American Progress, Washington, D.C.

Wong, S. 2007. China bets on massive water transfer to solve crisis. International Rivers, Berkeley, California. Available from http://www.internationalrivers.org/en/china/china-bets-massive-water-transfers-solve-crisis (accessed June 2008).

Wood, M. 2002. Ecotourism: principles, practices and policies for sustainability. International Ecotourism Society, Burlington, Vermont.

World Commission on Dams. 2000. Dams and development: a new framework for decision making. World Commission on Dams, Cape Town, South Africa.

World Tourism Organization. 2001. Yunnan Province tourism development plan. World Tourism Organization, Madrid.

World Wide Fund for Nature. 2008. Living planet report. World Wide Fund for Nature, New York.

———. 2009. The Greater Mekong and climate change. World Wide Fund for Nature, Vientienne, Lao PDR.

———. 2009. The Greater Mekong and climate change: biodiversity, ecosystem services, and development at risk. WWF Greater Mekong Programme, Bangkok, Thailand.

Wright, T. 2007. Disincentives for democratic change in China. Asia Pacific Issues 82:1–8. East-West Center, Honolulu.

Wu, B., et al. 2000. Trends in China's domestic tourism development at the turn of the century. International Journal of Hospitality Management 12:296–297.

Xiao, W., et al. 2003. Habitat degradation of *Rhinopithecus bieti* in Yunnan, China. International Journal of Primatology 24: 389–398.

Xie, C. 2009. Govt. taken to court over pollution. China Daily, Beijing, July 31, p. 3.

Xin, D. 2006. Roads bring farmers path to wealth. China Daily, Beijing, August 19–20, p. 3.

Xin, H. 2008. You say you want a revolution. Science 322:664–666.

Xinhua News Agency. 2005a. Chinese premier outlines priorities for western development. Available from http://www.chinaview.cn (accessed October 2005).

———. 2005b. Wen reiterates longing for harmonious society. Available from http://www.chinadaily.com.cn/english/doc/2005-03/05/content_422077.htm (accessed October 2006).

———. 2006. 10.2 p.c. GDP growth in 1st quarter: Hu Jintao. Hindu Times, New Delhi. Available from http://www.hindu.com/2006/04/17/stories/2006041705321400.htm (accessed September 2009).

———. 2007a. China exports electricity to Vietnam. Available from http://www.newsmekong.org/china_exports_electricity_to_vietnam (accessed October 2007).

———. 2007b. China's first national park unveiled in Shangri-La. Beijing. Available from http://www.china.org.cn/english/environment/214718.htm (accessed June 2007).

———. 2007c. Hu stresses scientific development. Available from http://www.chinadaily.com/cn/china/2007-06/26/content_902179.htm (accessed June 2007).

———. 2008a. Myanmar-China border trade fair to be held in Muse this year. Available from http://www.xinhuanet.com/english/2008-09/29/content_10132109.htm (accessed October 2008).

———. 2008b. Traffic slowly restoring in disaster-hit south China, thousands still stranded. Available online at http://news.xinhuanet.com/english/2008-01/30/content_7527928.htm (accessed January 2008).

———. 2009. Permafrost soil in Yangtze River area disappearing. Available form http://news.xinhuanet.com/english/200-02/13/content_10816480.htm (accessed August 2009).

Xu, D. 2000. Resources management within nature reserves in China. Economics, ecology and environment. Working paper no. 51, Department of Economics, University of Queensland, Brisbane, Australia.

Xu, H., et al. 2009. China's progress toward the significant reduction of the rate of biodiversity loss. BioScience 59:843–852.

Xu, J. 2006. The political, social, and ecological transformation of a landscape: the case of rubber in Xishuangbanna, China. Mountain Research and Development 26:254–262.

Xu, J., et al. 2005. Integrating sacred knowledge for conservation: cultures and landscapes in Southwest China. Ecology and Society 10(2):7. Available from http://www.ecologyandsociety.org/vol10/isn/art7 (accessed February 2006).

Xu, J., et al. 2009a. The melting Himalayas: effects of climate change on water resources and human livelihoods in the Greater Himalayas. Conservation Biology 23:520–530.

Xu, J., L. Lebel, and J. Sturgeon. 2009b. Functional links between biodiversity, livelihoods, and culture in a Hani swidden landscape in southwest China. Ecology and Society 14(2):20. Available from http://www.ecologyandsociety.org/vol14/iss2/art20 (accessed November 2009).

Xu, J., and A. Wilkes. 2002. State simplifications of land-use and biodiversity in the uplands of Yunnan, Eastern Himalayan region. Pages 541–550 in U. Huber et al., eds. Global change in mountain regions. Springer, Netherlands.

———. 2004. Biodiversity impact analysis in northwest Yunnan, southwest China. Biodiversity and Conservation 13:959–983.

Xu, W., et al. 2009. Conservation of giant panda habitat in South Minshan, China, after the 5/08 earthquake. Frontiers in Ecology and the Environment. DOI: 10.1890/080192.

Yan, Y. 2006. Little emperors or frail pragmatists? China's '80ers generation. Current History 105:255–262.

Yang, Y., K. Tian, J. Hao, S. Pei, and Y. Yang. 2004. Biodiversity and biodiversity conservation in Yunnan, China. Biodiversity and Conservation 13:813–826.

Yardley, J. 2004a. China's premier orders halt to a dam project threatening a lost Eden. New York Times, April 9, A6

———. 2004b. In a tidal wave, China's masses pour down from farm to city. New York Times, September 12, WK6.

Yi, S., et al. 2007. Changes in livestock migration patterns in a Tibetan-style agropastoralist system. Mountain Research and Development 27:138–145.

Yin, S. 2001. People and forests: Yunnan swidden agriculture in human-ecological perspective. Yunnan Education Publishing House, Kunming, China.

Young, N. 2007a. Full steam ahead for "charity" even as brakes are applied to NGOs. China Development Brief, Beijing. Available from http://www.chinadevelopmentbrief.com/node/1222 (accessed January 2008).

———. 2007b. How much inequality can China stand? China Development Brief, Beijing. Available from http://chinadevelopmentbrief.com (accessed December 2007).

———. 2008. Culture as ideology. China Rights Forum 3:15–21.

Young, N., and J. Yang. 2005. Yunnan: a provincial profile and situation analysis. China Development Brief, Beijing. Available from http://www.chinadevelopmentbrief.com (accessed December 2007).

Yunnan Province Department of Commerce. 2006. Tourism industry in Yunnan. Available from http://eng.bofcom.gov.cn.bofcom_en/5190407 366637518848/20061114/83923.html (accessed February 2008).

Zackey, J. 2007. Peasant perspectives on deforestation in southwest China. Mountain Research and Development 27:153–161.

Zeng, N., et al. 2008. Climate change—the Chinese challenge. Science 319:730–731.

Zeng, Y., et al. 2001. The diversity and sustainable development of crop genetic resources in the Lancang River valley. Genetic Resources and Crop Evolution 48:297–306.

Zemp, M., et al., eds. 2008. Global glacial changes: facts and figures. World Glacier Monitoring Services, Zurich.

Zhang, J., and M. Cao. 1995. Tropical forest vegetation of Xishuangbanna southwest China and its secondary changes, with special reference to some problems in local nature conservation. Biological Conservation 73:225–238.

Zhang, K. 2006. Three Parallel Rivers region listed in the "key observation and protection program" of the world heritage list hydropower development endorses the environment. China's Youth Daily, July 17. Translated from http://www.sina.com.cn. In author's files in e-mail dated August 8, 2006.

———. 2008. Chinese experts appeal to authorities to suspend big dam prospects in Southwest China following Sichuan deathly earthquake. First Business Daily (Diyi caijing bao in Chinese). Translation available at http://www.internationalrivers.org/en/node/3141 (accessed July 2008).

Zhao, Q. 1996. Conservation of primates. Chinese Environment and Development 6:69–77.

Zhao, S., et al. 2006. Ecological consequences of rapid urban expansion: Shanghai, China. Frontiers in Ecology and Environment 4:341–346.

Zhou, W., and B. Chen. 2006. Biodiversity of Bitahai Nature Reserve in Yunnan Province, China. Biodiversity and Conservation 15:839–853.

Zhu, H. 2008. Advances in biogeography of the tropical rain forest in southern Yunnan, southwestern China. Tropical Conservation Science 1:34–42..

Zhu, H., M. Cao, and H. Hu. 2006. Geological history, flora, and vegetation of Xishuangbanna, southern Yunnan, China. Biotropica 38:310–317.

Zhu, H., et al. 2004. Tropical rain forest fragmentation and its ecological and species diversity change in southern Yunnan. Biological Conservation 13:1355–1372.

Zimou, S., E. Schuur, and F. Chapin III. 2006. Permafrost and the global carbon budget. Science 312:1612–1613.

Acknowledgments

Any author attempting to portray another people and culture faces a formidable task. The project is all the more challenging when that country is China. The PRC not only has a deeply layered history stretching back thousands of years; it has a complex present and an uncertain future. As a foreigner, I have worked hard to build a nuanced foundation for contemplating conservation and development from villages in Yunnan to the nation, the region, and the world. I am sure, nevertheless, that more than a few errors remain and that some of my conclusions will be seen as missing the mark. I trust that any discussion over this volume's contents will serve to clarify the next steps on China's path forward.

I wrote this book as a labor of love for China and out of a sense of responsibility to a sustainable future. I could not have completed it without assistance from many people. Though my intellectual debts are too numerous to mention here, I do want to acknowledge the instruction and inspiration provided by folks in and out of China who supported me: Ai Huaisen, Ainipa, Alou from Dimaluo village, Chen Hong, Seth Cook, Jenn Dinaburg, Duan Hui, Gezu, Rich Harris, Mark Hedemark, Hu Huabin, Hu Lushan, Stefan Kratz, Li Li Juan, Li Xiaolong, Long Yongcheng, Bob Moseley, Rose Niu, Julie Perng, Phoe Yong, Shen Shicai, the Skalsky family (Kevin, Lynn, Amos), David Smith, Andrew Smith, Tsering, Andy Wilkes, Wu Deyou, Yang Yuming, Lucy Yu, Zhang Zhiming, Zhou Dequn, and the Chinese tea mafia (Rob, Jake, Celestina, and Angel). I have changed the names of a few people and places in the text to protect them from any undue scrutiny by the authorities.

Tom Fleischner, Tim McNulty, Scott Slovic, Luisa Walmsley, and Xu Jianchu read portions of the manuscript and offered sage advice. I benefitted greatly from their feedback; the book would contain even more flaws without the assistance of these sharp readers.

The Kunming Institute of Botany (Chinese Academy of Sciences) and Prescott College provided institutional support during phases of this project. Fern Grumbine, my lovely mother, and several other individuals were kind enough to offer private funding for travel to China over several years. Jack Herring, undergraduate dean at Prescott College, provided a grant to attend the 2009 Society for Conservation Biology meeting in Beijing.

The staff at Island Press were extremely helpful and easy to work with. Jonathan Cobb, the book's original editor, was a staunch advocate from the beginning and got the project off the ground. Emily Davis carried the manuscript through to completion; she knows the nuts and bolts of this book better than anyone (with the possible exception of me!). Emily's sure sense of narrative flow kept me focused on the mainstream of the story. I owe a great debt to Julie Van Pelt for her sharp-eyed copyediting. Many thanks also to Chris Robinson for the fine maps. The photographs were taken by me on various trips from 2005 to 2009.

Special thanks are due to three people who inspired me throughout much of this work. Albie Miles accompanied me on my first trip to Yunnan. One couldn't ask for a more trustworthy travel companion. The fact that Albie is a deep critical thinker on global politics and economics is an added benefit. Luisa Walmsley word-processed most of the manuscript. More important, her companionship in China and her engagement with conservation and development on the ground helped me to better grasp the issues. Finally, Xu Jianchu of the Centre for Mountain Ecosystem Studies and the Kunming Institute of Botany (Chinese Academy of Sciences), and colleague extraordinaire, gave me all the things that a visitor to China most appreciates: intellectual honesty, office and living space, a sense of humor, a profound commitment to learning, great food, an inspiring vision for a more sustainable world--and a fine cup of green tea.

R. Edward Grumbine
Prescott, AZ
December 2009

It is dark. Birds in flight returning,
Travelers setting out—it never ends.
WANG WEI, Tang dynasty
(translation D. Hinton)

Index

About Island Press

Since 1984, the nonprofit Island Press has been stimulating, shaping, and communicating the ideas that are essential for solving environmental problems worldwide. With more than 800 titles in print
and some 40 new releases each year, we are the nation's leading
publisher on environmental issues. We identify innovative thinkers
and emerging trends in the environmental field. We work with world-
renowned experts and authors to develop cross-disciplinary
solutions to environmental challenges.

Island Press designs and implements coordinated book
publication campaigns in order to communicate our critical
messages in print, in person, and online using the latest technologies, programs, and the media. Our goal: to reach targeted
audiences—scientists, policymakers, environmental advocates,
the media, and concerned citizens—who can and will take action
to protect the plants and animals that enrich our world, the
ecosystems we need to survive, the water we drink, and the air
we breathe.

Island Press gratefully acknowledges the support of its work
by the Agua Fund, Inc., The Margaret A. Cargill Foundation, Betsy
and Jesse Fink Foundation, The William and Flora Hewlett
Foundation, The Kresge Foundation, The Forrest and Frances
Lattner Foundation, The Andrew W. Mellon Foundation, The Curtis
and Edith Munson Foundation, The Overbrook Foundation, The
David and Lucile Packard Foundation, The Summit Foundation,
Trust for Architectural Easements, The Winslow Foundation, and
other generous donors.

The opinions expressed in this book are those of the
author(s) and do not necessarily reflect the views of our donors.